Smart English

A2

Units 1-12

REBECCA ROBB BENNE
AND
ANNA WHITCHER

BROOKEMEAD ENGLISH
LANGUAGE TEACHING

Smart English A2

Units 1-12

Brookemead ELT, London and San Francisco

London, UK

Series editor: Duncan Prowse

Consultant: Mary Tomalin

Designer: Gregor Arthur at Starfish DEPM Ltd

Glossary: Mary Rigby

Proofreader: John Bowdler

Audio recordings: John Green at TEFL Audio (producer), Tim Woolf (editor)

Teachers: Thanks to Johanne Skaanes-Allo (Denmark), Viv Blanchard (UK), Emilia Velcheva (Bulgaria), Paul Braddock (Spain), Andrea Krampe (Germany), Neil Kendrick (UK)

San Francisco, USA

Editor and video producer: Anna Whitcher

Illustrators: Aaron Friedland, Carrie English

Video editor: Erin Palmquist

Music: APM Music, Hollywood, California (USA)

Teacher: Thanks to Sophie Abitbol (USA)

Videos:

Unit 1: *Circus Sunrise* (Stuart Liddell, Australia), *Genetics* (Jen Speed and Erin Palmquist, USA) **Unit 2:** *A Danish school* (Jesper Quistgaard, Henriette Hørlücks School, Denmark); *New River Academy, Chile* (Jessica Droujko) **Unit 3:** *Fight for Peace* (Benjamin Holman, UK and Brazil); *Street Art* (Jim McSilver, USA) **Unit 4:** *Camp Blaze* (Reel Grrls and the San Francisco Fire Department, USA); *London Music* (Heydon Prowse, UK) **Unit 5:** *Moods* (Erin Palmquist, USA); *The Tower* (Erin Palmquist, UK) **Unit 6:** *4Real* (Erin Palmquist, USA); *Animation Camp* (Erin Palmquist, Ex'pression College, Emeryville, USA) **Unit 7:** *The World of Fashion* (Heydon Prowse, UK); *Garbage to Art* (Erin Palmquist, Recology, San Francisco, USA) **Unit 8:** *Summer Camp: Camp Echo Lake* (Camp Echo Lake, New York, USA); *Ecotourism: Sierra Gorda* (Sierra Gorda, Mexico) **Unit 9:** *Maker Faire* (Tom Bell, Maker Faire, Brighton, UK); *Phobias* (Erin Palmquist, USA) **Unit 10:** *Teen Cook* (Erin Palmquist, USA); *Fifteen* (Jamie Oliver Foundation, UK) **Unit 11:** *School Exams in the UK* (Heydon Prowse, UK); *A Future Designer* (Erin Palmquist, USA) **Unit 12:** *Duke of Edinburgh Award* (Heydon Prowse, UK); *Space Camp* (Space Camp, Alabama, USA)

Smart English A2

Student's Book (Units 1-12): ISBN **978-1-905248-50-6**

Also available:

Workbook (Units 1-12)+Workbook CD: ISBN 978-1-905248-51-3

Video Pack (Units 1-12) DVD & Worksheets: ISBN 978-1-905248-53-7

Teacher's Guide (Units 1-12)+2 Student Book CDs: ISBN 978-1-905248-59-9

Produced and published by

Brookemead English Language Teaching, London and San Francisco

www.brookemead-elt.co.uk

Acknowledgements

Cover photos: Erin Palmquist, Stuart Liddell, Anna Whitcher

Unit 1A: Carrie English (artwork people); Greg Corbett (artwork buildings). **1B:** Aaron Friedland (artwork tidy, messy, Aiko); Anna Whitcher (Josh, Aiko). **1C:** Stuart Liddell (stills from *Circus Sunrise* video) **1D:** Erin Palmquist (stills from *Genetics* video); Aaron Friedland (artwork DNA) **Student writing:** Modified by Aaron Friedland. Thanks to Susana Chaires in Sophie Abitbol's ESL class at Burlingame High School in Burlingame, California, USA

Unit 2A: Jesper Quistgaard (stills from *A Danish school* video) **2B:** Aaron Friedland (artwork Wordle); Jesper Quistgaard (stills from *A Danish school* video) **2C:** Photos from New River Academy: David Gorski (group); Taylor Cote (hammock); David Hughes (study); Joe Kowalski (red kayak) **2D:** St. Jude's, Tanzania (photos) Thanks to Kim Saville **Student writing:** Modified by Aaron Friedland. Thanks to students in Johanne Skaanes-Allo's class at Henriette Hørlücks School in Odense, Denmark

Unit 3A: Aaron Friedland (artwork café, skate, icons); mall: © Adrian Sherratt / Alamy; street: © Big Cheese Photo LLC / Alamy; online: © Scott Hortop / Alamy; library: © Corbis Premium RF / Alamy; girls: © Janine Wiedel Photolibrary / Alamy; basketball: © Janine Wiedel Photolibrary / Alamy; Anna Whitcher (pool, beach) **3B:** Aaron Friedland (artwork signals, maps, directions, place map, maze); Duncan Prowse (photo road) **3C:** Fight for Peace (photos thanks to Luke Dowdney); Carrie English (artwork street). **3D:** Tom Burke (photo graffiti head); Anna Whitcher (photos tag, message, blue trees, girl); Jim McSilver (still from *Street art* video) **Student writing**: Modified by Aaron Friedland. Thanks to students in Emilia Velcheva's EFL class in Sofia, Bulgaria

Unit 4A: engineer: © Peter Bowater / Alamy; shop assistant: © Simon Rawles / Alamy; farmer: © OJO Images Ltd / Alamy; male nurse: © Glow Wellness / Alamy; spy: © Paul Gooney / Alamy; waitress: © Jon Arnold Images Ltd / Alamy; taxi driver: © Shaun Higson colour / Alamy; cleaner: © Zoonar GmbH / Alamy; doctor: © Blend Images / Alamy; actor: © ilian stage / Alamy; police officer: © Janine Wiedel Photolibrary / Alamy; explorer: © StockShot / Alamy. **4B:** Alex Rider helicopter: © AF archive / Alamy; Alex Rider poster: © Photos 12 / Alamy; Alex Rider hanging: © AF archive / Alamy; shark: © Martin Strmiska / Alamy; Carrie English (artwork people); Aaron Friedland (artwork icons). **4C:** San Francisco Fire Department (photos of Camp Blaze thanks to Karen Kerr and Janet George); Aaron Friedland (artwork fire fighter). **4D:** Aaron Friedland (artwork icons); Heydon Prowse (stills from *London Music* video); **Student writing:** Modified by Aaron Friedland. Thanks to Emily O'Hara, United Kingdom

Unit 5A: clouds: © Stephen Dorey Creative / Alamy; ice: © Hugh Threlfall / Alamy; fog: © Linda Reinink-Smith / Alamy; lightning: © imagebroker / Alamy; sun: © imagebroker / Alamy; rain: © Ian Francis / Alamy; wind: © John Prior Images / Alamy; Anna Whitcher (photo of snow) **5B:** Aaron Friedland (artwork skeletons, faces); hailstones: © Mark Romesser / Alamy; lightning man: © Dale O'Dell / Alamy; frog: © Kevin Schafer / Alamy; fish: © Bobby Bogren / Alamy. **5C:** Tower of London: © Jonathan Pearson / Alamy; Princes in Tower: © Art Directors & TRIP / Alamy; Aaron Friedland (artwork prisoner); Duncan Prowse (photo of Traitor's Gate); Benjamin Holman (photo of Jane graffiti). **5D:** Erin Palmquist (stills from *Moods* video); Aaron Friedland (artwork Wordle); **Student writing:** Modified by Aaron Friedland. Thanks to students in Viv Blanchard's EFL class in Cambridge, United Kingdom

Unit 6A: Aaron Friedland (artwork gadgets); video gamers: © Fancy / Alamy. **6B:** Creative Commons photos (2) from LG Mobile World Cup Competition; Carrie English (artwork phone); Aaron Friedland (artwork activities); Zits cartoon: "Reproduced with the kind permission of the ZITS Partnership and King Features Syndicate". **6C:** Thanks to Alex Fraknoi of Lick-Wilmerding High School, San Francisco, California, USA for use of his photos **6D:** Thanks to Ex'pression College in Emeryville, California, USA and students: Lydia Baillergeau (artwork ball); Daniel Machua (artwork mechanical insect); Renee Busse (artwork character); Aaron Friedland (artwork insects) **Student writing:** Thanks to students in Paul Braddock's EFL class in Barcelona, Spain

The Big Read 1: beach: © BANANA PANCAKE / Alamy; waves: © MWP / Alamy; surfer: © Buzz Pictures / Alamy; sunset: © Tremorvapix / Alamy; Carrie English (artwork map); Text extract and cover, *Waves* text © Sharon Dogar 2001, Reproduced with permission of Chicken House Publishing, All Rights Reserved.

The Big Read 2: John Smith: © Walt Disney / Everett Collection / Rex Features; Sarah Hart: © Walt Disney / Everett Collection / Rex Features; Text extract from *I am Number Four* by Pittacus Lore (Penguin Books 2010). Copyright © Big Jim Industries, Inc and Neurotic Scrawl, Inc, 2010. Cover by permission of Penguin Books 2010.

Unit 7A: Carrie English (artwork money) **7B:** Carrie English (artwork clothes); Anna Whitcher (photos four fashion students) **7C:** Heydon Prowse (stills from *The World of Fashion* video); Anna Whitcher (photo stuff) **7D:** Carrie English (artwork gadgets, artwork shoes); laptop: ©RobinBeckham-Beepstock / Alamy **Student writing:** Modified by Aaron Friedland. Thanks to Ivy Zhang in Sophie Abitbol's ESL class at Burlingame High School in Burlingame, California, USA

Unit 8A: Carrie English (artwork flags); Swedish hotel: © Howard Davies / Alamy; caboose hotel © Danita Delimont / Alamy; airplane hotel (2): © Vincent Castello and Manuel Antonio of Hotel Costa Verde, Costa Rica www.costaverde.com; Latvian prison: © TNT Magazine / Alamy; tent & caravan: © Jeff Gilbert / Alamy; Aaron Friedland (artwork nature places) **8B:** Alton Towers: © Greg Balfour Evans / Alamy; Windsor Castle: © Chantelle Oliver / Alamy; Stonehenge: © Stephen Dorey ABIPP / Alamy Norfolk Broads: © Justin Kase z13z / Alamy; Brighton: © Paul Carstairs / Alamy **8C:** Camp Echo Lake photo archive (friends, tennis, lake, menu, mountain, water skiing, campfire) www.campecholake.com. Thanks to Tony Stein and Peter Shifrin; black bear: © Richard Duguay / Alamy; Aaron Friedland (artwork six embarrassing stories) **8D:** Anna Whitcher (photos of iguna & turtles) **Student writing:** Modified by Aaron Friedland. Thanks to Marie Bergmann in Sophie Abitbol's ESL class at Burlingame High School in Burlingame, California, USA

Unit 9A: Carrie English (artwork four things to make, four things to collect); Tom Bell (stills from *Maker Faire* video); Anna Whitcher (photos of collectors, Rommel & Maholy) **9B:** gymnast: © PCN Photography / Alamy; Carrie English (artwork ten sports); girls' Afghan football team (still from "Afghan Girls Can Kick", a Filmdependence film by Bahareh Hosseini) **9C:** Shaun White (three photos): © PCN Photography / Alamy **9D:** Aaron Friedland (artwork phobias Wordle, clouds, beards, clowns) **Student writing:** Modified by Aaron Friedland. Photo of Bao Chunlai: © Daniel Swee / Alamy. Thanks to Cathy Chen in Sophie Abitbol's ESL class at Burlingame High School in Burlingame, California, USA

Unit 10A: sushi: © Valentyn Volkov / Alamy; Greek salad: © City Image / Alamy; English breakfast: © Stefanie Mohr / Alamy; spaghetti Bolognese: © Zoonar GmbH / Alamy; chow mein: © mediablitzimages (uk) Limited / Alamy; hamburger: © Noam Armonn / Alamy; chilli: © Bon Appetit / Alamy; fruit salad: © joefoxphoto / Alamy **10B:** Carrie English (artwork seven foods & five animals); Zits cartoon: "Reproduced with the kind permission of the ZITS Partnership and King Features Syndicate"; Carrie English (artwork calorie food quiz) **10C:** speed eating competition & girl speed eater: © Cal Vornberger / Alamy; scoreboard: © Michael Matthews / Alamy; Carrie English (artwork worm, die, game) **10D:** water girl: © Megapress / Alamy; Carrie English (body diagram) **Student writing:** Modified by Aaron Friedland, photo by Erin Palmquist. Thanks to Liliana Santos of Lick-Wilmerding High School, San Francisco, California, USA

Unit 11A: nursery: © Imagestate Media Partners Limited – Impact Photos / Alamy; primary: © Avril O'Reilly / Alamy; secondary girl: © Janine Wiedel Photolibrary / Alamy; secondary boy: © Mike Booth / Alamy; taking exams: © Eye Ubiquitous / Alamy; stay at school: © Stockbroker / Alamy; art college: © walespix / Alamy; job interview: © Ambient Excellence / Alamy; garage: © Exotica.im 10 / Alamy; garden volunteer: © Richard Levine / Alamy; traveller: © Greg Balfour Evans / Alamy **11B:** boy at exams © Jim Wileman / Alamy; girl sleeping: © Design Pics Inc. / Alamy; Duncan Prowse (photo from Carlton le Willows Academy, Nottingham, UK); video gamers: © fStop / Alamy; video controllers: © Corbis Bridge / Alamy **11C:** Erin Palmquist (top photo of Shireen); Anna Whitcher (middle photo of Shireen, sculpture, scrapbooking; photo of Shireen & Millie); Thanks to Shireen Teheranian for her photos of her jewellery and artwork **11D:** Carrie English (artwork computer) **Student writing:** Modified by Aaron Friedland. Thanks to Tessa Heinrichsrüscher in Andrea Krampe's class at Hauptschule Ostenland in Delbrück-Ostenland

Unit 12A: soup kitchen: © Jim West / Alamy; animal shelter: © Catchlight Visual Services / Alamy; water fight: © PhotoAlto / Alamy; bowling: © PhotoStock-Israel / Alamy; barbecue: © {TWHPhotography} / Alamy; museum: © Jeff Greenberg / Alamy; garage sale: © Images-USA / Alamy; hiking: © J.R. Bale / Alamy **12B:** La Tomatina: © Ozimages / Alamy; mud festival: © Getty Images; monkey banquet: © Dan Vincent / Alamy; cheese competition: © Cotswolds Photo Library / Alamy; Ben Wheatcroft (photo of expedition); violinist: © David L. Moore – Lifestyle / Alamy; Heydon Prowse (still from *Duke of Edinburgh's Award* video); volunteer activity: © greenwales / Alamy **12C:** Space Camp & Space Academy photo archive (flight simulator, underwater simulator, moonwalk simulator) Thanks to Tim Hall and Charity Stewart; Carrie English (artwork space activities) **12D:** Carrie English (diagram and gravity) **Student writing:** Modified by Aaron Friedland. Thanks to Alena Moskalenko in Ilya Denisenko's EFL class in Russia.

The Big Read 3: Aaron Friedland (artwork lizard, scorpion, rattlesnake); lizard: © Malcolm Schuyl / Alamy; spider: © B Christopher / Alamy; Text extract from *Holes* by Louis Sachar published by Bloomsbury Publishing Ltd (Copyright © Louis Sachar, 1998); text and cover image reproduced by permission of Bloomsbury Publishing Ltd.

The Big Read 4: People mosaic: ©Bjarki Reyr / Alamy; teens at computer: © PhotoAlto sas / Alamy; Text extract from *Girl, Missing* by Sophie McKenzie published by Simon & Schuster (Copyright © Sophie McKenzie, 2006) reproduced by permission of United Agents (www.unitedagents.co.uk) on behalf of Sophie McKenzie. Cover by permission of Simon & Schuster Ltd.

Partner Exercises: Aaron Friedland (artwork) and Carrie English (artwork)

Contents

Unit Subject *The Big Question*	Functions Language Banks	Grammar	Lexis / Vocabulary
Trinity College, London (Graded Examinations in Spoken English) **GESE Grade 3**			
Cambridge English KET (Key for Schools)			
1 **Home life** What's your family like?	Describing daily routines and times **LB1** Talking about your family and home **LB2** Describing daily routines	Present simple for routines and habits (R), adjectives for home, daily routine collocations, Prepositions of time *on, in, at* **WB:** Present simple	Family members (R), rooms and furniture (R), Daily routines and times, home life **WB:** Adjectives, daily routines (collocations), *My Words*
2 **Cool schools** *What's cool about your school?*	Asking simple questions about everyday life **LB3** Talking about school **LB4** Asking and answering questions	Questions (R) and question words **WB:** Questions	Place of study, school subjects, transport to school, **WB:** School, places in school, school subjects, prepositions, *My Words* **Revision 1 and 2**
3 **Hangouts** *Is your area a good place to hang out?*	Talking about places in the local area, Giving simple directions and locations **LB5** Talking about places in the local area **LB6** Asking for and giving directions	Countable and uncountable nouns, *A lot, much, many, some, any* Prepositions of place *near, in front of, behind, opposite, next to, between* Prepositions of movement *from, to, up, down, along across, past* **WB:** Countable and uncountable, *A lot ...*	Places in local area, in town, directions **WB:** Hangouts, places in town, directions, prepositions, *My Words*
4 **Not just a job** *What job is right for you?*	Expressing ability and inability **LB7** Talking about jobs **LB8** Talking about skills (ability and inability)	*can* and *can't* **WB:** *can* and *can't*	Words to describe jobs and people, abilities and skills, nouns ending in *–er* **WB:** Jobs, abilities, fire fighters, *My Words* **Revision 3 and 4**
5 **Scary stories** *When were you last scared?*	Giving dates, Describing states in the past **LB9** Talking about the weather **LB10** Describing states in the past	Past tense of the verb *to be (was, were),* Link words *and, and then* for joining ideas and events **WB:** *was* and *were, and, and then*	Weather and temperature, Weather adjectives ending in *–y,* feelings, seasons and months (R), Ordinal numbers for dates **WB:** Weather, seasons, months, dates, feelings, *My Words*
6 **Tech time** *Is technology an important part of your free time?*	Free time, Describing current activities of real people and those in pictures **LB11** Talking about free time **LB12** Describing pictures	Present continuous tense	Gadgets and technical activities, phones, free time activities **WB:** Gadgets, phones, free time, *My Words* **Revision 5 and 6**
The Big Read 1	*Waves* by Sharon Dogar		
The Big Read 2	*I am number four* by Pittacus Lore		

Contents

(R) = Revision WB = Workbook pages Ⓐ = Audio Ⓥ = Video

Contents

Contents

(R) = Revision **WB** = Workbook pages

Ⓐ = Audio Ⓥ = Video

Unit 1

Home life

FACT

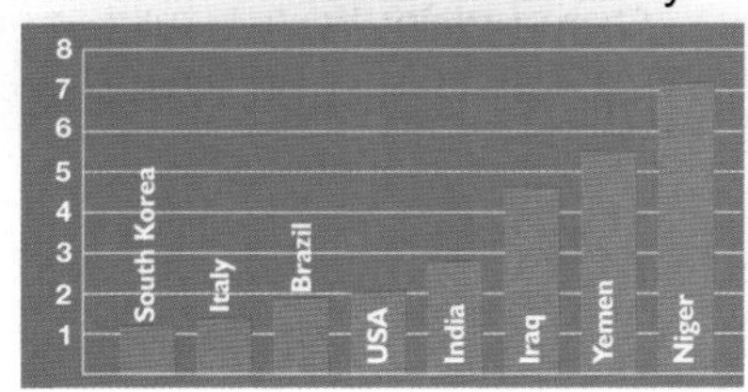

(2) **Laura** I live with my ________, my ________, and my cat. We live in an apartment on the seventh floor. It has a big balcony. My ________, that's my mum's brother, lives next door.

1 The Big Question

What's your family like?

2 VOCABULARY

Family members

(2) 1 Look at the pictures of the two families. Listen.
   a Complete what Laura says above.
   b Complete what Daniel says on page 9.

(3) 2 Can you remember the words for family? Write them in the white spaces. Listen and check.

(3) 3 **Pronunciation:** Listen again and repeat the words. Underline the stress: *mother*

4 Work with a partner. Draw a family tree for Laura's family and for Daniel's family. Ask and answer questions.

Who is Amy's daughter? – Laura.

5 Now draw your family tree. Tell a partner.

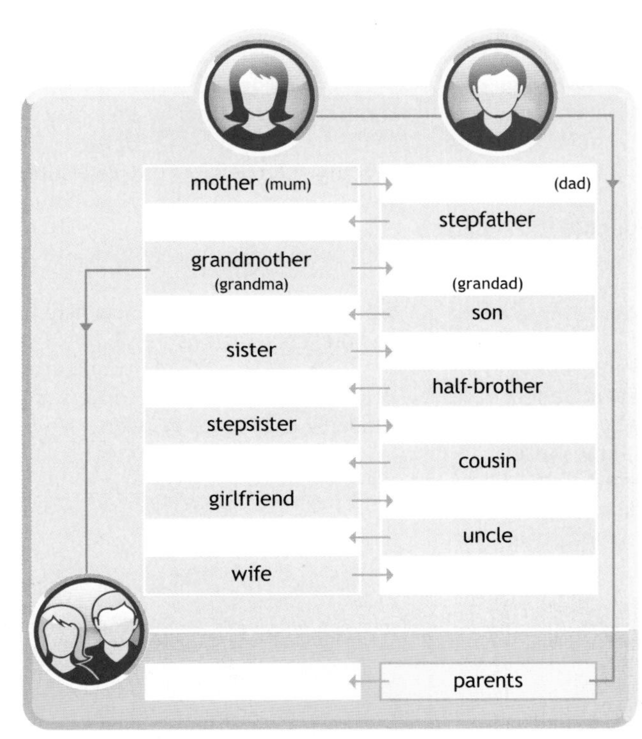

mother (mum)
(dad)
stepfather
grandmother (grandma)
(grandad)
son
sister
half-brother
stepsister
cousin
girlfriend
uncle
wife
parents

YOUR GOALS

Vocabulary: family, home, routines
Communication: talking about time, describing routines
Grammar: present simple for routines and habits
CLIL: genetics

2 **Daniel** I live with my ______ and my ______. My ______ Ryan lives with us and I have two little ______. We live in a new house by the beach.

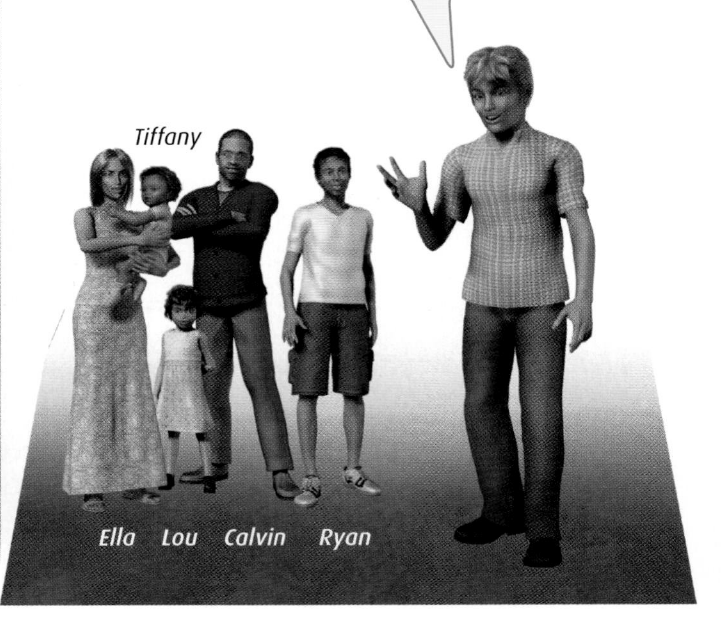

House and home

4 **6** Listen and tick (✓) the number...
of bedrooms 1 ☐ 2 ☐ 3 ☐
and bathrooms 1 ☐ 2 ☐ 3 ☐

4 **7** Listen again and match the names of the rooms with the numbers on the plans.

a living room b kitchen c bedroom
d balcony e bathroom f dining room
g family room h garden / backyard

8 Look in the rooms. What are the names for the furniture and things in the rooms?

Talk about your home

9 Work with a partner. Draw a plan of your home. Talk about the rooms and the things in them.

Ground floor

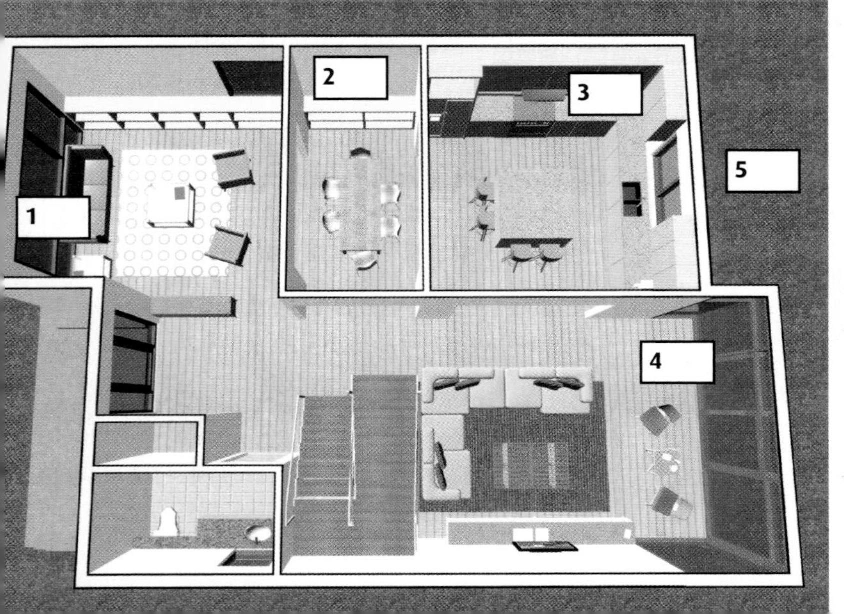

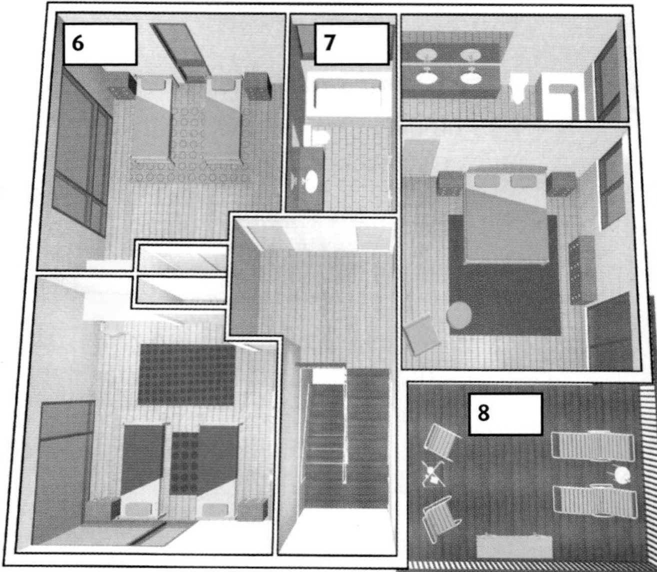

First floor

55 LANGUAGE BANK 1

3 LISTENING

FACT

In the world 24 million children don't live with their families. They live in children's homes or on the streets.

Different families

1. Choose the right words for the pictures. What's your room like?

It's ... tidy | quiet | messy | noisy

a ____________ b ____________ c ____________ d ____________

2. Listen to Aiko and Josh. Who do they live with?

3. Work with a partner. Then listen and check. What does Aiko say about her family life? What does Josh say about his family life? Use the phrases in the boxes.

nice and quiet | feel lonely | noisy | never feel lonely | tidy room | messy room | time alone with parents | do things with others

Aiko

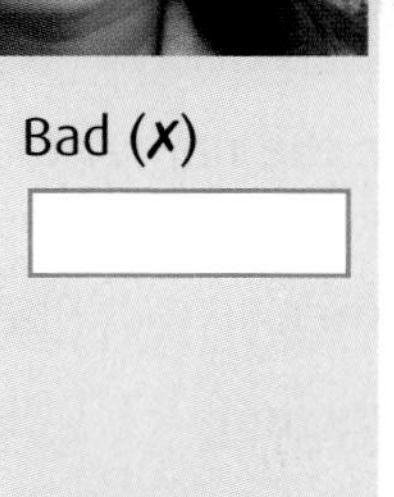

Good (✓)	Bad (✗)

Josh

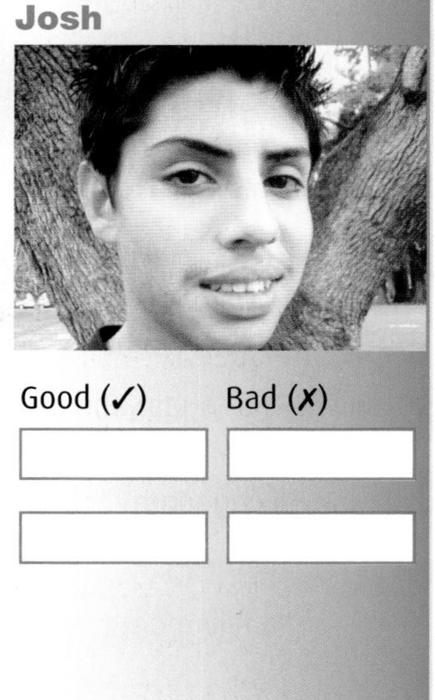

Good (✓)	Bad (✗)

Times and routines

4. Complete the sentences with the correct words.

go | hang | get | come | finish | have (x2) | begin

a My parents ________ **up** at six o'clock.
b They ________ **to work** early in the morning.
c I ________ **breakfast** alone on weekdays.
d School lessons ________ at 9 am.
e I ________ **school** at 4 pm.
f I ________ **home** from school at 5 in the afternoon.
g In the evening we cook and ________ **dinner** together.
h On Saturdays and Sundays, at the weekend, I ________ **out** with my friends.

5. Make time expressions with *in*, *on* and *at* and the words. Use exercise 4 to help you.

________ seven o'clock
________ Monday
________ the morning
________ the weekend
________ Saturdays
________ the afternoon
________ the evening
________ weekdays

On weekdays and at the weekend

6 **6** Listen to Aiko's routines on weekdays and at the weekend. Write the times.

On weekdays Aiko ...
- a gets up at ________
- b goes to school at ________
- c comes home at ________
- d goes to bed at ________

At the weekend Aiko ...
- e gets up at ________
- f has lunch at ________
- g hangs out with friends at ________
- h goes to bed at ________

7 When do you do the things in exercise 6?

On weekdays I get up at ...
At the weekend I ...

7 **8** Read and listen to the poem.

- a Who says the first part?
- b Who says the second part?
- c Is it the morning or evening?
- d What time is it?
- e What is the problem?

Get up, get up, get up	*Oh, mum, stay cool*
It's late, late, late	*I have half an hour*
It's half past eight	*Time to take a shower*
You're late for school	*No problem, mum, stay cool*

9 Work in small groups.

- a Change the poem to evening. Use other words.
- b Share with the class.

4 ROLE PLAY

Describing daily routines

1 **Partner A:** Interview a football player (Partner B) and complete the notes below. Start like this: *Tell me about a day....*
Partner B: Look at page 117. Tell Partner A about a day in your life as a football player. Start like this: *Well, I get up ....*

2 Now swap roles.
Partner B: Interview a pop star (Partner A) and complete your notes on page 117.
Partner A: Look at page 112. Tell Partner B about a day in your life as a pop star.

Notes for Partner A

(A day in the life of a football player)

I get up ________ and go running.
I have breakfast ________.
In the morning I ________.
At 1 pm I ________.
________ I go to the gym.
At 7 pm I ________ at home.
________ I watch TV or play computer games.
At 10 pm I ________.

3 Tell another partner about your daily routine. Use the language bank.

8 Life in the circus

Fourteen-year-old Antony lives in Australia with his mother Rosita and father David, and his two sisters Harmony and Melody. But his family is different from other families. Antony, his parents and sisters, his aunt Caroline, his uncle Gary and his cousins Bonita, Jessinta and Sascha are the performers in Circus Sunrise. Their circus travels all over Australia.

David Rosita Melody Harmony *Antony*

Antony doesn't go to school. He learns at home. In the morning he does his school work and practises for the performance. In the afternoon and the evening he puts on his costume and performs in the circus. They don't have animals in Circus Sunrise. It's only people. Each family member has a special act. Antony is a juggler. He, his father and his uncle also perform as clowns. They sell tickets and drinks too. It's hard work.

The two families live in caravans. When they aren't in the circus, the family hangs out together in the big family caravan and watches films. Does Antony like his life? 'I love it,' he says. 'It's hard work but it's never boring.'

5 READING

A circus family

1 Look at the photos. What do you think is true (**T**) or false (**F**) about Antony?

a He has two sisters.
b He performs as a clown.
c He works with animals.
d He works hard in the circus.
e He lives in an apartment.
f He has a boring life.

2 Read the text and check your answers.

3 Read the text again. Which of these things does Antony do on most days? Tick (✓) them.

a He does school work at home.
b He practises as a juggler.
c He wears a circus costume.
d He performs in the circus.
e He hangs out with his family.
f He watches films in the caravan.

4 Choose the correct words.

a Antony's family is ...
 the same as other families.
 different from other families.
b Performing in a circus is ...
 hard work.
 easy.
c Antony's life is ...
 fun.
 boring.
d Antony does his school work ...
 in the morning.
 in the afternoon.
e The family caravan is ...
 big.
 small.

1 5 Watch the video. What do you think? Is the circus life for you?

(✓) *Yes, it sounds great.*
There's no school.
It's never boring.
(✗) *No. It's not for me.*
It's too hard.
I don't like the circus.

Antony's aunt, uncle and cousins

6 GRAMMAR

The present simple

1 Complete these sentences from the text.

a ________ lives in Australia.
b ________ learns at home.
c ________ sell tickets.
d ________ watches films.
e ________ love it.

2 Look at the sentences in exercise 1. When do we put an *–s* on the end of a verb?

9 3 **Pronunciation:** Listen to these verbs. Does the *–s* sound different? Repeat the words. Say all the words fast, then faster and faster…

/ z /	/ s /	/ ɪz /
lives	puts	watches
learns	works	practises

Antony's sisters

4 **Partner A:** Write about Antony's sister Harmony.
Harmony …

(mouth icon)	curry and pizza
(ear icon)	to music
(phone icon)	friends

Partner B: Look at page 117. Write about Melody.

Read your sentences to your partner (remember the *–s* sound).
What do they both do? *They both …*

Questions and negatives

5 Read sentences (**a–d**). Underline the verbs.

a Antony doesn't go to school.
b They don't have animals.
c Does Antony like his circus life?
d What do you think?

Jessinta

1 10 6 Write the questions for Antony's cousin Jessinta. Listen to or watch the interview with her and check.

a do / What / do / in the circus / you
________________________?
b you / like / the circus / Do
________________________?
c live / do / Where / you
________________________?
d school / you / or friends / Do / miss
________________________?

1 10 7 Listen or watch again. Choose the correct answers to the questions in exercise 6.

a I'm a clown. / I do lassos and whips.
b Yeah, I love it. / No, I don't like it.
c We live in a house. / We live in caravans.
d Yeah, I miss school. / No, I don't miss school.

7 CONVERSATION

1 Work with a partner. Write five questions for your partner.

Does your grandmother live with you?
Do you play computer games?

2 Ask your partner the questions. Answer your partner's questions.

No, she doesn't.
Yes, I do. / Yes, I like computer games.

3 Choose two things about your partner and his / her family. Tell the class.

8 CLIL: Genetics

It's in the family

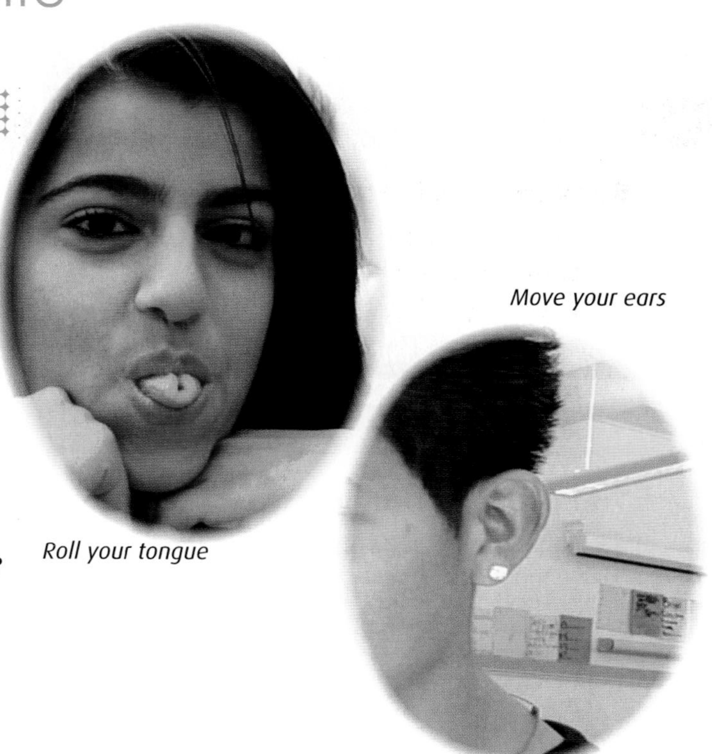

Move your ears

Roll your tongue

2 ① Members of a family often share special skills. Look at the photos and watch the video. Try to roll your tongue and move your ears.

a Is it hard? It's only possible for some people.
b Is it easy? Show the class.

② Now answer these questions.

a Do you look like your parents?
Do you look like other people in your family?
Yes, I look like ... No, I don't look like ...
b Do you have photos of your family?
Show the class.
This is ... . We all have brown hair / blue eyes / big ears ...

11 YOU AND YOUR GENES

Human cells have 46 chromosomes: 22 pairs and an XY pair for a boy, or an XX pair for a girl. Chromosomes contain your genes. Your genes make you who you are. They contain your DNA. Every person (except identical twins) has different DNA. A baby gets half of its chromosomes from the father and half from the mother. The genes in the chromosomes decide lots of things about you – from the colour of your eyes to how tall you are. They decide some of your personality and some of your skills. They often decide how healthy you are too.

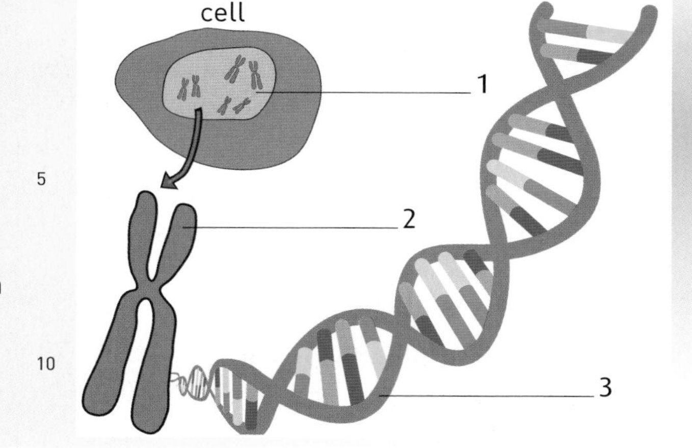

③ Read the text. What do your genes do? Answer true (**T**) or false (**F**).

a They keep you healthy. ☐
b They decide how you look. ☐
c They decide lots of things about you. ☐

④ Read the text again.

a Complete these sentences with *girl* or *boy*.

22 pairs + XY = ________
22 pairs + XX = ________

b Then complete the diagram above with these words.

DNA | chromosomes | genes

FACT

There are 20,000 to 25,000 genes in human DNA.

Short and tall

9 WRITING

Susana's perfect day

1. **Read**: Look at Susana's online poster. Read about her perfect day. What do you like about her day?

Your perfect day

2. **Prepare:** Think about your perfect day. Use the boxes to help you.

In the morning

I get up at 6.00 / lunchtime ...
For breakfast I eat fruit / pizza ...
I hang out with ...

In the afternoon

I visit ...
I play football / listen to music ...
I go to the beach / shopping ...

In the evening

I have dinner at a ... restaurant.
I go out with ...
I go to bed at ...

3. **Write and share**: Make your poster. Take photos, find menus and draw things.
Do it online! Make an online poster with music and videos.

My Perfect Day
I get up at 8:00 in the morning.
For breakfast I have enchiladas.
In the morning, I hang out with my friends. We have a party!
In the afternoon, I visit Angelica Vale. She gives me her autograph and takes pictures with me.
For dinner I go to a Mexican restaurant with my family.
In the evening, I go to a lake with my family. We rent a boat and we go around the lake.
I go to bed at 11:00 at night.

Susana, Mexico

10 Your Answer

What's your family like?

Do you have a big or small family?
Do you live in an apartment / a house / a caravan?
Is your family quiet or noisy, tidy or messy?
What is your family routine like?
What is special about your family?
Do you look like people in your family?

YOUR SCORE

Can you use all the language below?

Yes ☺, *No* ☹ or *Almost* 😐

Vocabulary: family ☐ home ☐ routines ☐
Communication: time ☐ describing routines ☐
Grammar: present simple for routines and habits ☐
CLIL: genetics ☐

Unit 2

FACT

There are English-speaking international schools in over 160 countries.

Cool schools

This school in Denmark has classes in English for international students.

1 The Big Question

What's cool about your school?

2 VOCABULARY

Ida and Rune's school

1. Look at the photos of the school. Do you think it's modern or traditional?

3 12

2. Watch the film or listen about Ida and Rune's school. Check your answer from exercise 1.

3 12

3. Read the sentences (**a–j**). Watch or listen again. Circle the correct words or phrases.

a Our school is quite **big** / **small**.
b There are **475** / **1475** students.
c It's a **public** / **private** school.
d Our school is for students from age **6 to 16** / **11 to 16**.
e The school is very **old** / **new**.
f There are **two** / **four** school buildings.
g There are about **23** / **32** students in each class.
h The teachers are **very strict** / **not very strict** and there aren't many rules.

Ida and Rune

i We call our teachers by their **first** / **last** names.
j We wear **school uniforms** / **normal clothes**.

4. Work with a partner. Write the answers to exercise 3 for your own school. Then read your answers to your partner. Start like this.

I go to ... School. I'm in class ...

YOUR GOALS

Vocabulary:	place of study, school subjects
Communication:	talking about school, asking questions
Grammar:	questions and question words
CLIL:	education

1

2

Places in school

5 Watch or listen. Match *five* of these sentences with the photos.

a Our school has a beautiful **main hall**. There is a lot of art there.
b There isn't a **cafeteria**, but the school has a little **shop**.
c Students eat their lunch in the **classroom**.
d The school has a **gym** where we do sport, but it doesn't have a **swimming pool**.
e Our school doesn't have a **football pitch** or **tennis courts**. But there's a school **playground** where students hang out.
f The school has a **cinema**. The chairs are from an old plane.
g There's a small **library**. The sofas are great!

14 **6** **Pronunciation:** Listen to the words in **bold** in exercise 5 and repeat them. Listen again and underline the stress in each word or phrase.

main *<u>hall</u>*

Talk about your school

7 Work with a partner. Use the words in **bold** in exercise 5.

In our school there's / there isn't ...

3

4

5

57 LANGUAGE BANK 3

3 LISTENING

What's your favourite subject?

15 ❶ Listen to the names of school subjects. Match them to the pictures. Listen again and repeat the names.

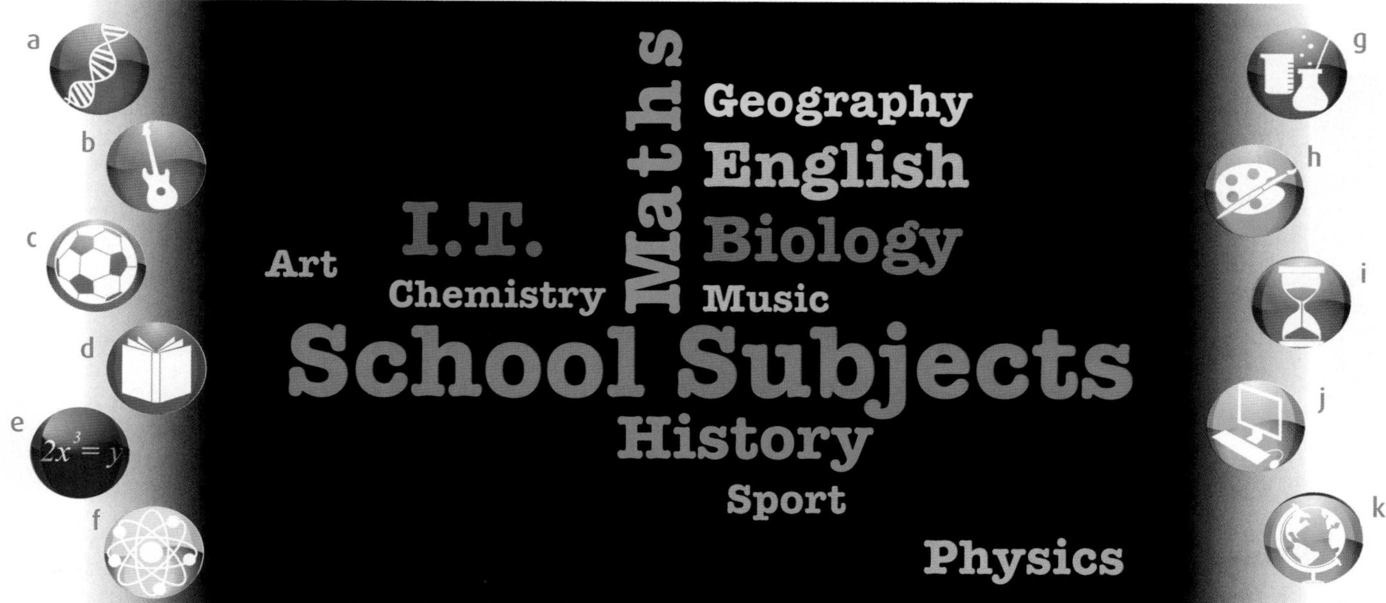

16 ❷ Karoline is in Ida and Rune's class, 7B. She likes some subjects and doesn't like others. Draw the correct face for each subject in her timetable.

I love it.  *I like it.*

It's OK.  *I don't like it.* 

Karoline's Timetable

	Monday	Tuesday
8.15	Chemistry	I.T.
9.10	Biology	Physics
10.10	Music	Art
11.35	Maths	History
12.20	English	Sport
13.20	Geography	Sport

Karoline
_______ is my favourite subject because it's _______ and the teacher is _______

17 ❸ Listen again. Complete what Karoline says.

❹ Write a list of your school subjects. Which are your favourites? Draw faces for each subject.

❺ Work with a partner. Discuss your school subjects. Do you like the same subjects?

I love / like / don't like ...
... is OK / is my favourite subject, because ...

❻ Class 7B's favourite subject is Maths. Make a chart of the favourite school subjects in your class.

How do you go to school?

7 Match the words with the pictures.

by bike | by car | by train | I walk | by tram | by bus

8 How do you go to school? Tell the class. *I go by ... / I walk.*

a ____________________

b ____________________

c ____________________

d ____________________

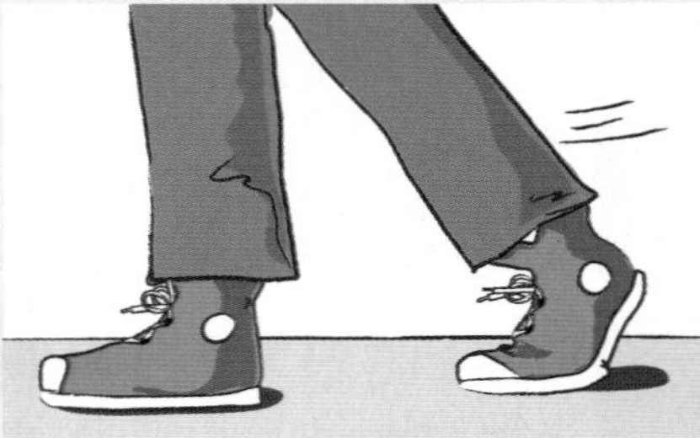

e ____________________

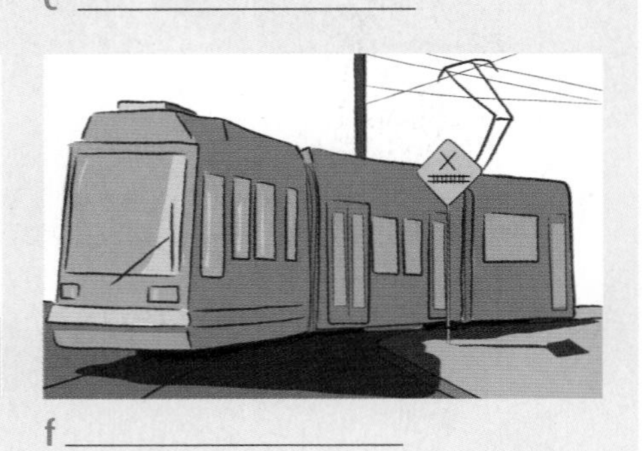

f ____________________

17 9 There's a new boy at Ida and Rune's school. Listen and complete the information. Then check with a partner.

Name:	*Philip*
From:	
Lives:	
Transport to school:	
Likes school:	
Favourite subject:	

17 10 Listen again to Philip's replies. Write Helena's questions. Then listen again and check.

a where / you / from? ....
b where / you / live? ....
c how / you / go to school? ....
d you / like / school? ....
e what / your favourite subject? ....

4 ROLE PLAY

Asking and answering questions

1 **Partner A:** Partner B is a new student. Ask the questions in exercise 10.
Partner B: Look at your notes on page 117. Answer Partner A's questions.

2 Now swap roles.
Partner A: You are the new student. Look at your notes on page 112. Answer Partner B's questions.
Partner B: Ask Partner A the questions in exercise 10.

3 Now ask and answer the questions about you.

58 LANGUAGE BANK 4

5 READING

School on the river

1 Look at the photos. What is different about Jessica's school? Then read the text and check.

18 New River Academy

Interviewer:	Jessica:	
What is the name of your school?	New River Academy. It's for students from 14–18.	
Is New River Academy a public or private school?	It's a private school. And it's very special. We learn in different countries – Chile, Canada or in Uganda … our classroom is the world. We see lots of beautiful places and meet different people. But sometimes it's hard when we have to speak Spanish.	5
Wow! Why does your school move around?	The school sport is kayaking. We go kayaking every day after classes. So we travel to places with good kayaking rivers. Kayaking is great but the water is usually really, really cold.	10
What subjects do you study at the Academy?	English, Spanish, physics, IT … all the usual school subjects. We also learn other things, like how to cook, take photos and make films.	
When do you have classes?	We have six classes in the morning and early afternoon.	15
Where do you learn?	We usually study outside. But sometimes we work inside too.	
How many students are in your class? And who is your teacher?	We work in small groups. There is one teacher for a group of three or four students.	20
That's small! Is it a good way to learn?	Yeah, I learn a lot because it's never boring.	
What do you do in the evening?	Homework, of course. And then we have about an hour of free time before bed. There's usually no internet or TV, so we play cards and talk.	25

2 Complete these sentences with the correct words. Then read the text again and check.

a New River Academy is a *p*... school.
b The students' classroom is the *w* ... .
c Students go *k* ... every day after classes.
d Students learn all the *u* ... school subjects.
e Classes sometimes study *o* ....
f They work in small *g* ... of three or four students.

3 What do you like about this school? What don't you like?

(✓) *Students study outside.*
(✗) *They are in the water a lot.*

4 (video 4) Watch Jessica's video about her class's trip to Chile. What else do you like / not like about the New River Academy?

It's great to cook together.
I don't like sport early in the morning.

6 GRAMMAR

Questions and question words

1 Look at the questions from the interview with Jessica. Put in *is / are* or *do / does*. Then check your answers in the interview.

a What ... the name of your school?
b ... New River Academy a public or private school?
c Why ... your school move around?
d What subjects ... you study?
e Where ... you learn?
f When ... you have classes for your school subjects?
g How many students ... there in your class?
h Who ... your teacher?

2 Underline the question words in the sentences in exercise 1.

3 Write question words for:

a ... time?		*When*
b ... place?		
c ... a person?		
d ... a thing?		
e ... a reason?	?	
f ... a number?	123	

4 Complete these questions for Jessica with the correct question words. Then write one more question.

a ... do you like your school?
b ... is your favourite subject?
c ... people are in the school?
d ... do you sleep – in a tent?
e ... do you go to bed?
f ... is your favourite teacher?
Your question: ...?

19 5 **Pronunciation:** Listen to the questions below. In which sentences does the voice go up?

Put an arrow (↗) above the sentences.

a Do you like to visit new countries?
b Do you learn to cook at school?
c When do you have lunch at school?
d What sports do you do at your school?
e Do you do sports after school?
f Where do you do your homework?

19 6 Listen again and repeat. Then work with a partner and ask and answer the questions in exercise 5.

7 CONVERSATION

1 Look at the questions in the box. Write the answers for you.

2 Work in pairs. Ask your partner. Are your answers the same or different?

3 Share your answers with the class.

HOW DO YOU LEARN?

a Do you prefer to learn in a classroom or outside?
b Do you prefer to learn in a small group or in a big class?
c Do you prefer to learn with computers or books?
d Do you prefer to move around or sit at a desk?
e Do you prefer to listen to music? Or do you like a quiet room?

FACT

All children have the right to free education.
United Nations Declaration of Human Rights

8 CLIL: Education

1 Look at the photos and the titles of the two texts. Find out where Tanzania is on a map.

A Public education in Tanzania

- Primary school is free; secondary school is *not* free.
- 80% of children start primary school; 50% finish it.
- Parents pay for uniforms, lunch and books.
- Some children walk over 10 kilometres to school.
- Up to 150 students in a class; usually no computers. 5
- Classes are in the Kiswahili language.

B Private education at St Jude's

- Free and only for children from very poor families.
- Free books, uniforms, food and free buses to school.
- Secondary students have a free place to live.
- Sponsors from other countries pay for everything.
- Only 25 students in a class; computers in every classroom. 5
- Classes are in English (the language of the universities); international exams.

		Public schools Tanzania	St Jude's Tanzania
a	Is education free?		
b	Who pays for books, uniforms and food?		
c	How do children go to school?		
d	How many students are in a class?		
e	Are there computers?		
f	What language are classes in?		

2 Work with a partner.

Partner A: Read text A. Answer the questions for public schools in Tanzania. Then ask your partner for the answers for St. Jude's.

Partner B: Read text B. Answer the questions for St Jude's. Then ask your partner for the answers for public schools in Tanzania.

Talk about education

3 What about education in your country? Talk about the questions.

a Is there free education for all children? At all ages?
b What age do children leave school?
c Are there private schools? Who are they for? Are they expensive?
d Are private schools a good thing? Why or why not?

9 WRITING

Isabella and Iben's fantasy school

1. **Read:** Read Isabella and Iben's presentation about their fantasy school. Do you think this school sounds good?

Your fantasy school

2. **Prepare:** Think about your fantasy school. Use the boxes to help you.

Where is your fantasy school? What is it like?

My fantasy school is *in the country / in the city ...*
The buildings are *old / new.*
The walls in the school are *blue / ...*

What does your fantasy school have?

My fantasy school has *a garden / swimming pool / football pitch / tennis court / cinema / ...*
In the school there are *clean toilets / a lot of computers / sofas in the hall / nice teachers / ...*

What doesn't your fantasy school have?

My fantasy school doesn't have *rules / uniforms / strict teachers / homework / hard chairs / ...*

How do the students learn?

School starts at *6.30 / 10.00 and finishes at 12.00 / 15.00 / ....*
Students use *computers / new books / ...*
Students work *in small groups / in big classes / outside / by the pool / ...*

3. **Write and share:** Write about your fantasy school. Draw pictures and use photos to make a presentation to the class.
Do it online! Use an online presentation tool and present your work.

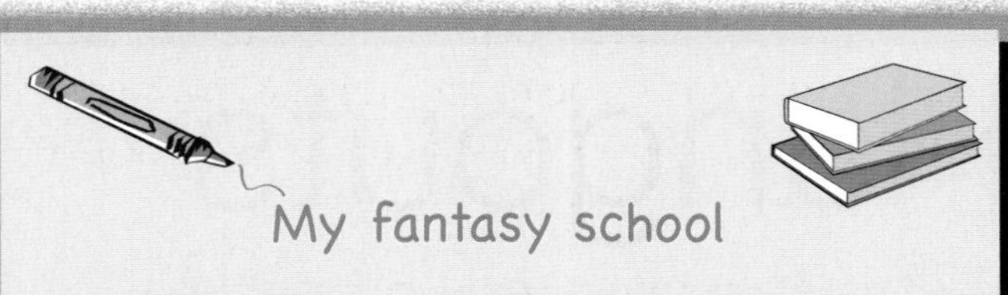

My fantasy school is in the middle of a city. The buildings are very new and modern. The walls in my cool school are many different colours. Around the school there is a big schoolyard with colourful flowers.

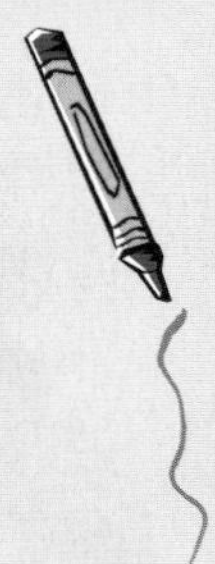

The school has a big garden where the students can relax after class. It also has a swimming pool, a mini-cinema, and a little café for the lunch breaks. In the school there are sofas in the hall and every student has their own brand new computer.

The school doesn't have strict teachers or uniforms, so the students can wear what they want. The school starts at 8:15 and finishes at 14:00. The students usually use computers, but they have some books. They work outside when it's summer, but in the winter they sit in a classroom. They listen to music in the lessons.

School is Cool!

Isabella and Iben, Denmark

10 Your Answer

What's cool about your school?

What is your place of study like?
How do you go to school?
What subjects do you study?
What's your favourite subject?
Do you like school?
What would you like to have at your school?

YOUR SCORE

Can you use all the language below?

Yes ☺, *No* ☹ or *Almost* 😐

Vocabulary:	place of study	☐
	school subjects	☐
Communication:	talking about school	☐
	asking questions	☐
Grammar:	questions	☐
	question words	☐
CLIL:	education	☐

Unit 3
Hangouts

FACT

So many people hang out with friends online that Facebook has over 600 million members.

a *the café*

b *the shopping centre / shopping mall*

c *the street*

d *online*

e *the library*

1 The Big Question

Is your area a good place to hang out?

2 VOCABULARY

Places

20 ❶ Look at the pictures of places on these two pages. Listen to the names of the places (**a–j**) and repeat.

20 ❷ **Pronunciation:** Listen again. Underline the main stress for each place.

the café

21 ❸ Now listen to ten teenagers. Where do they hang out? Write **1–10** in the correct pictures.

❹ Look at the pictures again. For each place, write down one or two words.

the café
food, chat ...

❺ Work with a partner.

Partner A: Say a word from your list in exercise 4.
Partner B: Say the correct place.
Now swap.

YOUR GOALS

Vocabulary: places, prepositions of place and movement
Communication: giving directions, talking about your area
Grammar: countable and uncountable nouns, *a lot, much, many, some, any*
CLIL: street art

f *the skate park*

More places in a town

22 **6** Match the names of places with the pictures (**a–h**). Then listen and check.

museum | bank | cinema | train station | hospital | restaurant | theatre | police station

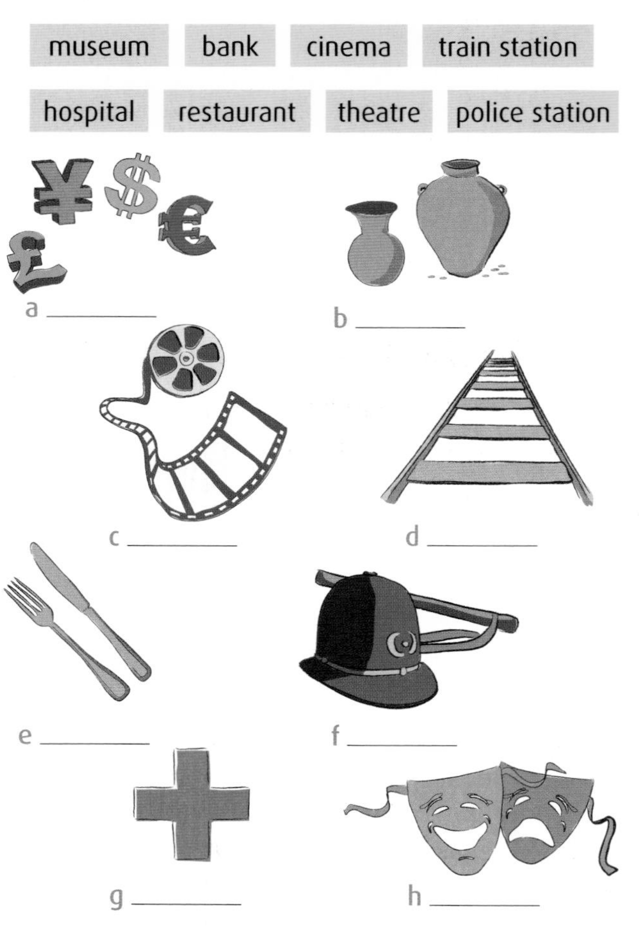

a ______ b ______ c ______ d ______ e ______ f ______ g ______ h ______

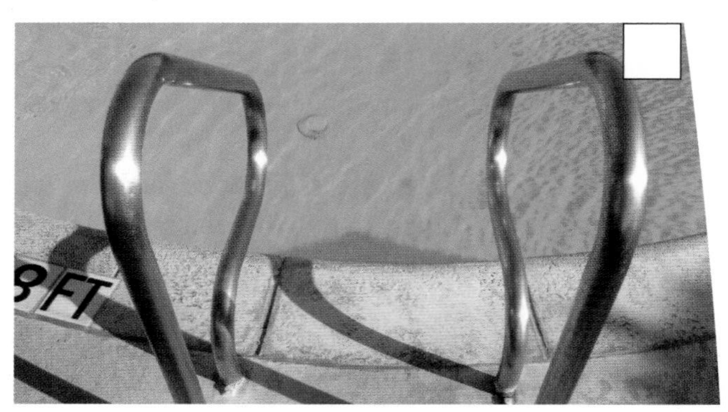

g *the swimming pool*

h *the beach*

i *my house*

j *the park*

7 Which of the places in exercise 1 and exercise 6 do you have in your area? Which don't you have? Make a list.

There's a ...
There are some ...
There isn't a ....

8 Where do you usually hang out? Where do you sometimes go? Tell your partner.

I / My friends and I usually hang out at the ...

59 LANGUAGE BANK 5

3 LISTENING

How do I get there?

23 ① Look at the pictures. Listen. Then listen and repeat.

Turn right.

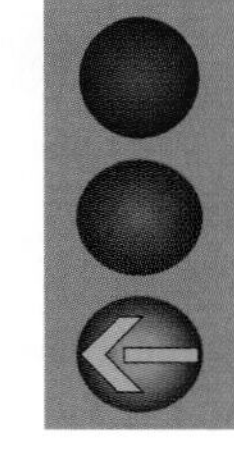

Turn left.

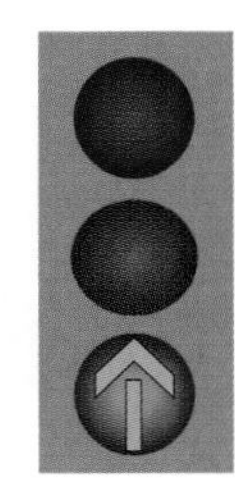

Go straight on.

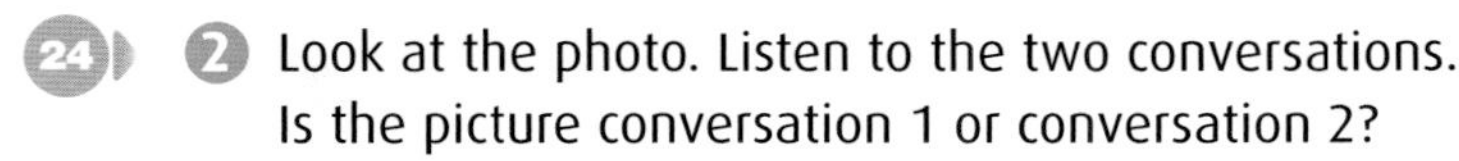

24 ② Look at the photo. Listen to the two conversations. Is the picture conversation 1 or conversation 2?

24 ③ Listen again. Pick the right maps (**a–d**) for conversation 1 and conversation 2. Say the directions for all the maps.

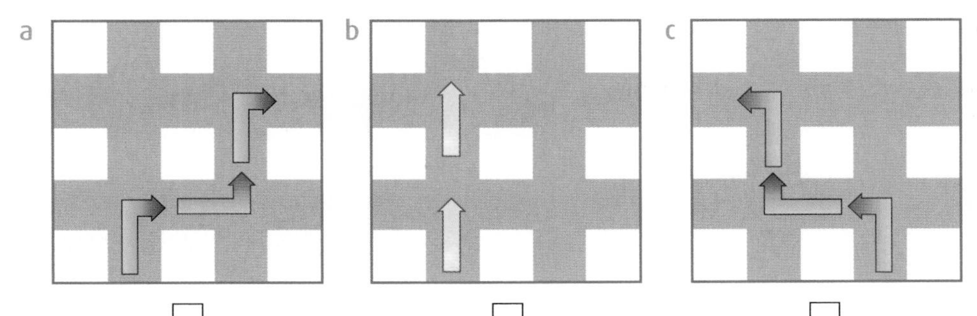

④ Look at the directions (**a–e**). Match them with pictures (**1–5**).

a Go **along** the road.
b Go **across** the road.
c Go **up** the hill.
d Go **down** the hill.
e Go **past** the park.

⑤ Read the conversation. Write down the order of pictures (**1–5**) in the conversation. Then read the conversation with a partner.

A Excuse me, how do I get from here to the museum?
B Go across the road here and then go down the hill. ☐ ☐
A OK.
B Then go along the road and past the park. ☐ ☐
A Past the park – OK.
B Then there's a little hill. Go up the hill and the museum is on the right. ☐
A Thank you.

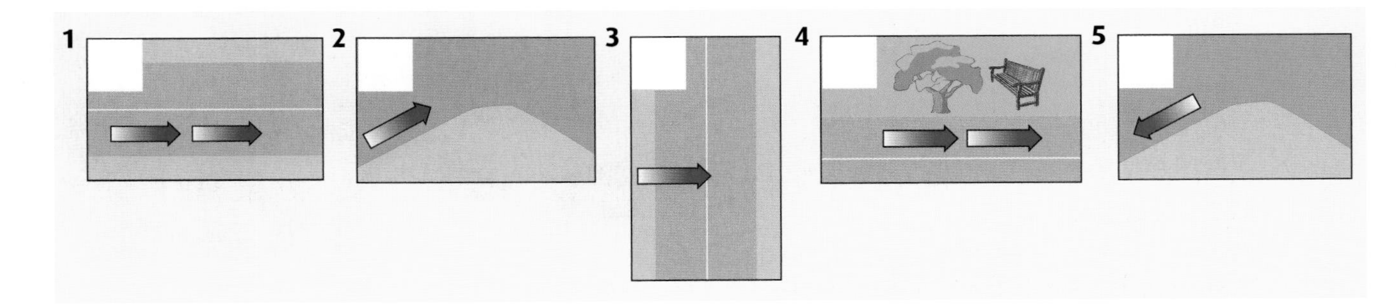

Where is it?

6 Look at the map of the street. Complete the sentences.

a There is a ... **next to** the restaurant.
b There are some ... **in front of** the restaurant.
c There is a ... **behind** the restaurant.
d There is a ... **opposite** the restaurant.
e **Between** the restaurant and the bank is a ....

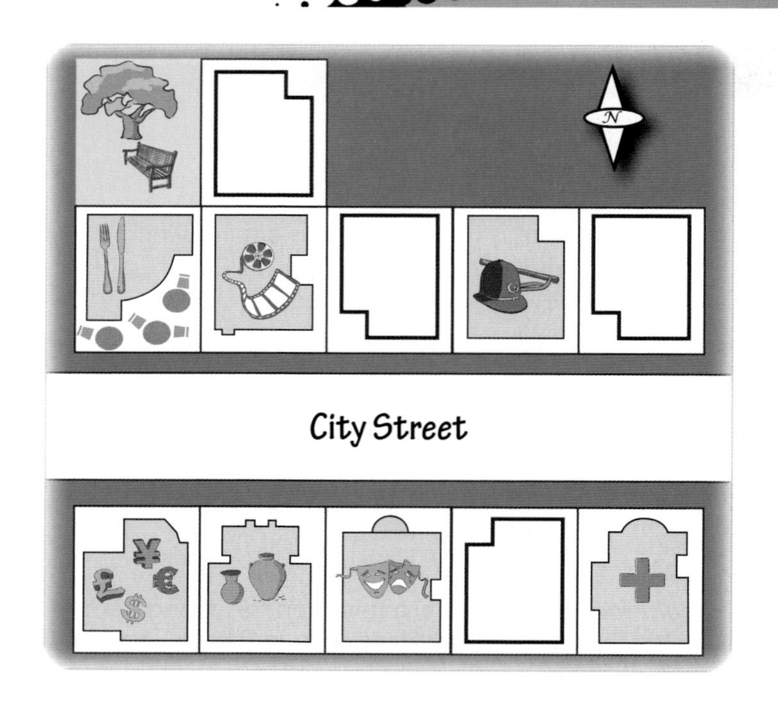

7 Look at the map again and the names of the places below. Where do these places go? You decide! Write the names in the spaces on the map.

museum | sports centre | school | train station

8 Work with a partner. Talk about your buildings. Where are they?

Where's the school on your map? – It's ...

4 ROLE PLAY

Giving directions

1 Work with a partner. Look at the map.

Partner A: Choose a place to start. Describe a route to a place *but* don't tell your partner the place. Start like this:
You're at (Dinner Square / Biology Road).
Go straight on. Turn right / turn left ...
Where are you?

Partner B: Follow the route. Say where you are.

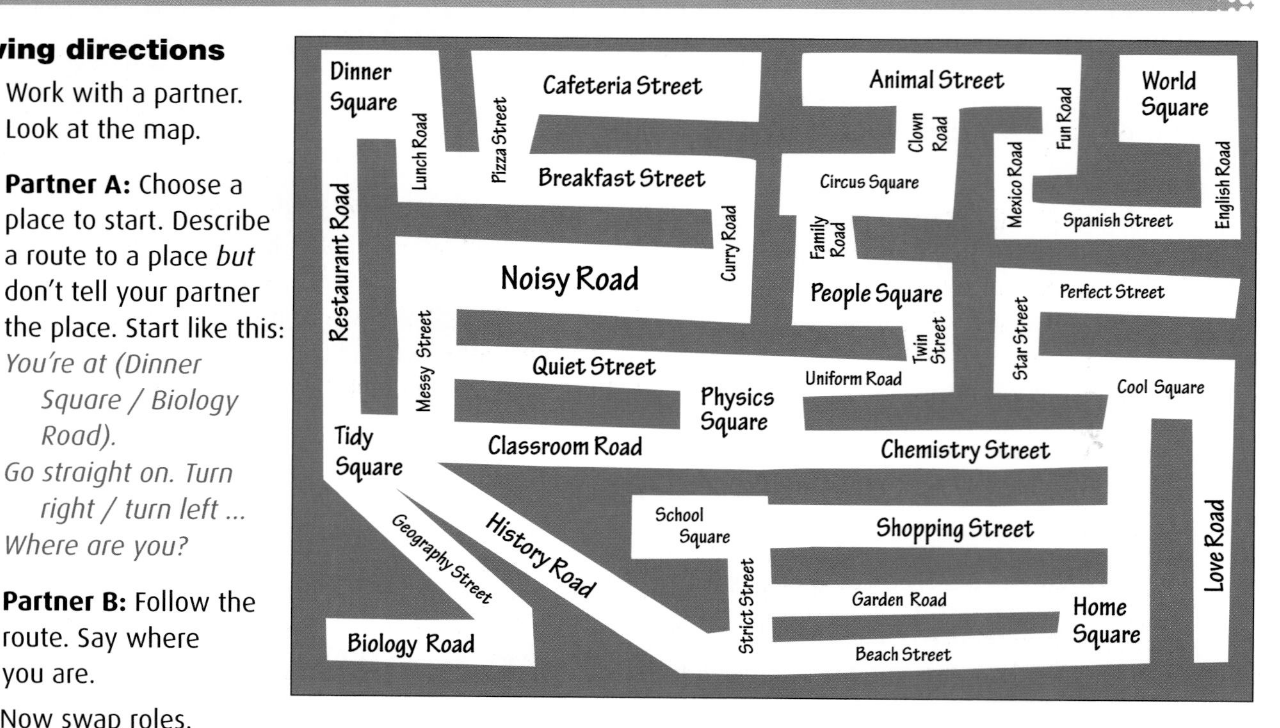

2 Now swap roles.

3 Your partner wants to visit you at home. Think about the route from the nearest bus stop or station to your home. Give your partner directions.

60 LANGUAGE BANK 6

FACT

There are four guns for every ten men in Rio de Janeiro.
One in ten schoolchildren in London has a knife.

5 READING

1 Look at the photos. Read the sentences in red and the first paragraph.

a What is the name of this organisation?
b Where are the two centres?
c Who goes to them?
d What do people do there?

25

FIGHT FOR PEACE

"Coming here is a good place for me."

"This place is like my second home."

Fight for Peace is an organisation for young people against violence. It has two centres, one in Rio de Janeiro, Brazil and one in London, UK. In the two places, young people from age seven to 23 learn boxing and martial arts. They get away from the streets, crime and other problems. 5

Some areas in Rio are dangerous. There are big problems with guns and drugs. Some young people have guns when they are only 12 or 13. The *Fight for Peace* Centre in Rio is a safe place, and teenagers can hang out together. 10

In London the problems are a bit different. Young people want a place to go, but there aren't many places for them. So they get bored, and gangs and knives are a problem. About 20 teenagers die and about 1,000 get hurt every year. At the *Fight for Peace* Centre they can meet friends and become interested in something new. 15

Rio and London offer the same help. Young people train there and get fit. They also have lessons and get help with jobs. They have fun and prepare for their future – without violence and crime. 20

Martial arts

A place to hang out

Boxing

2 Choose the right meanings for the words.

a **Violence** is when you *hurt / help* people.
b **Crime** is when you do something *right / wrong* like use a gun.

3 Now read all the text. Complete the sentences.

a *Fight for Peace* is against ... .
b In Rio there are some problems with ... and ... .
c In London there are some problems with ... and ... .
d The *Fight for Peace* centres help kids to prepare for their ... .

4 Match the opposites.

a	fit	1	interested
b	dangerous	2	old
c	bored	3	unfit
d	young	4	safe

5 5 Now watch the video. Do you think these centres are a good idea?

Yes! They give kids a place to go. / They give kids a future.
I have a different idea for a place for teenagers ...

6 GRAMMAR

Countable and uncountable

1 Look at the countable and uncountable examples. Tick (✓) the right box in the rule.
Rule: We don't use *a* or *an* or plural *-s* with **countable** words ☐ **uncountable** words ☐

countable		**uncountable**	
area – an area (✓)	some areas (✓)	help – ~~a help~~ (✗)	~~helps~~ (✗)

2 Are these words countable or uncountable? Write **C** or **U**.

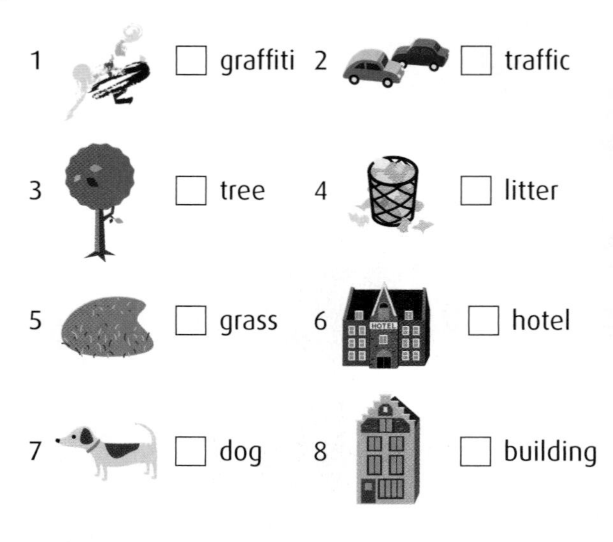

1 ☐ graffiti
2 ☐ traffic
3 ☐ tree
4 ☐ litter
5 ☐ grass
6 ☐ hotel
7 ☐ dog
8 ☐ building

A lot, much, many, some, any

3 Look at the picture. Put the sentences (**a–h**) in the correct place on the scale.

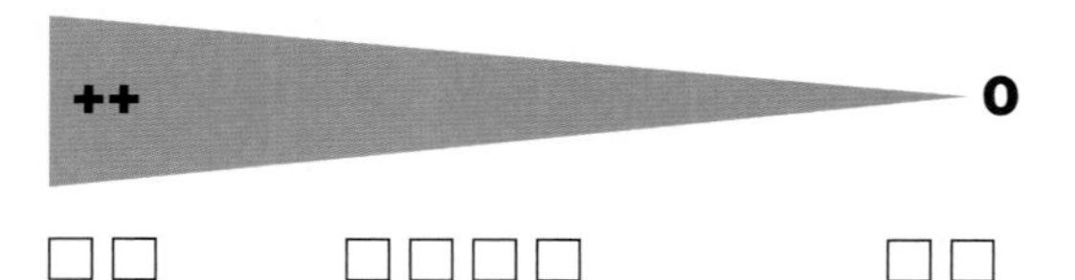

☐☐ ☐☐☐☐ ☐☐

a There aren't **many** shops.
b There isn't **much** graffiti.
c There's **some** traffic.
d There are **some** hotels.
e There isn't **any** grass.
f There aren't **any** trees.
g There are **a lot of** buildings.
h There's **a lot of** litter.

4 Mark the **bold** words in exercise 3 (**C**) or (**U**).

26 5 **Pronunciation:** Listen to the sentences in exercise 3. Underline where sounds join together. Listen again and repeat.

There aren't many shops.

6 Work with a partner.

Partner A: Look at your picture on page 112.
Partner B: Look at your picture on page 118.
Find five differences. Ask and answer like this.

How many hotels are there?
– A lot / Not many / There aren't any hotels.
How much traffic is there?
– A lot / Not much / There isn't any traffic.

7 CONVERSATION

1 Work with a partner. Ask and answer questions about your area.

What's your area like?	*It's nice / messy / safe / dangerous / noisy / quiet / ...*
Are there some fun places?	*Yes, there's a (great swimming pool).*
Are there any ...?	*Yes, there are (some problems).*
How many ... are there?	*There are lots of (shops).*
Is it a good place to live?	*Yes, it is. / I like it. / It's OK. / No, it isn't.*

Graffiti is not new. There are examples of graffiti from ancient Greece and Rome.

8 CLIL: Street art

1 Look at the photos of street art. Which do you prefer? Why?

I prefer ...
I like the colours / the picture / the idea.
I don't like ... / It's messy. / It isn't a good picture.

Political message

27 WHAT IS STREET ART?

Tag

Street art is art on the streets. It has lots of different forms: graffiti tags (the artist's name), spray-paint pictures, stencils, and sticker art. Sometimes street art has words. Sometimes it only has pictures. Often street art has a political message and bright colours.

A street artist usually only works in one area, but some put the same tag, stencil or sticker in lots of different cities around the world.

Street art is usually against the law. Artists use buildings, walls or trains – and these usually belong to other people. People often think graffiti is ugly and messy. They don't think it is art.

Sometimes there are special classes for young street artists, like the *Youth Together* project in Oakland, California. Students learn to create their own style. They tell stories and write messages on walls in the city. They communicate through their art.

Stencil

Spray-paint picture

2 Read the text about street art. Tick (✓) the answers.

	usually	often	sometimes
a Street art uses words and pictures together.	☐	☐	☐
b It has a political message.	☐	☐	☐
c Artists work in different areas.	☐	☐	☐
d It is against the law.	☐	☐	☐
e It's ugly and messy.	☐	☐	☐
f You can learn street art in a school.	☐	☐	☐

6 3 Watch the video about students and street art. What do you think of street art?

4 Make your own street art in the classroom. Use a large sheet of paper on the wall. Write your own tag and a message in English.

9 WRITING

Donislav's favourite place

1. **Read:** Read about Donislav's favourite place. Would you like to go there?

Your favourite place

2. **Prepare:** Think about your favourite place. Use the boxes to help you.

What is it?

My favourite place is *the café / the beach / the park ...*

Where is it and what's it like?

It's *near my house / about five kilometres from my house ...*
It's *in town next to the bank / opposite our school ...*
It's *quiet / noisy / exciting ...*

When do you go there?

I go there *every week / on Saturdays / in the summer / now and then ...*

Why is it your favourite place?

It's my favourite place because I love *the sea / the food / the music / ...*
I hang out with friends there ...

3. **Write and share:** Take a photo of your favourite place, or find a photo like it. Write about your place and present it to the class.
   Do it online! Publish your photo and description online.

pictr

Home | Your Photos | Search | Upload

My Favourite Place

My favourite place is Lozen Mountain. It's a small mountain in western Bulgaria and it's near my village. In our area there are four monasteries. They are very old. One of them is from the thirteenth century.

Every week in the summer my friends and I go to the mountain by bike. We have a picnic and then play football and other interesting games. After that, we cycle down to the village. It's fun because we love extreme cycling.

Lozen Mountain is my favourite place because the air is very fresh. We always have wonderful adventures there.

Post Comment | Preview

Donislav, Bulgaria

10 Your Answer

Is your area a good place to hang out?

Is your area exciting or boring?
Is it noisy or quiet? Safe or dangerous?
Are there many places for young people in your area / neighbourhood?
Where do you hang out with your friends?
What does your area need?
Is there street art in your area?

YOUR SCORE

Can you use all the language below?
Yes ☺, *No* ☹ or *Almost* 😐

Vocabulary:	places	☐
	prepositions of place and movement	☐
Communication:	giving directions	☐
	talking about your area	☐
Grammar:	countable and uncountable nouns	☐
	a lot, much, many, some, any	☐
CLIL:	street art	☐

Unit 4

Not just a job

FACT

In many countries, young people can work at age 16 (China and Sweden). In some countries, they can work at 14 (Russia and Mexico).

1 The Big Question

What job is right for you?

2 VOCABULARY

What do they do?

28 ❶ Listen to some teenagers talk about jobs. Write the jobs below the pictures.

actor | cleaner | doctor | driver | engineer | explorer | farmer | nurse | police officer | shop assistant | spy | waiter / waitress

29 ❷ **Pronunciation:** Listen and underline the stress for each job: *actor*
Then listen again and repeat.

❸ Where do the people work? Say the places. Use *at, in* or *on*.

at *a hospital / a police station*
in *an office / a factory / a restaurant*
a theatre / on *a farm / lots of different places*

An engineer works in a factory.

a She's ______________________

b She's ______________________

c He's ______________________

d He's ______________________

e He's ______________________

f She's ______________________

YOUR GOALS

Vocabulary:	jobs, adjectives to describe jobs and people
Communication:	talking about ability and inability
Grammar:	*can* and *can't*
CLIL:	the music industry

g She's ______________________________

h He's ________________

i She's ________________

j He's ________________

k He's ________________

4 Write these jobs from Units 1 to 3.

a This person works in a school. *t...*
b This person sings and dances. *p... s...*
c This person plays football. *f... p...*
d This person paints pictures. *a...*
e This person works in a circus. *c...*

5 Work with a partner. What are your parents' jobs? What do other people in your family do?

My mum / dad / brother / cousin / ...
... is a nurse / ...
... works for a big company / works in an office / at a police station / ...
... works with children / with old people / with animals / ...
... doesn't work / doesn't have a job

l She's ______________________________

61 LANGUAGE BANK 7

3 LISTENING

Alex Rider's exciting job

1. Alex Rider is a character in books and films. Look at the photos. Answer the questions.

   a How old do you think Alex Rider is?
   b What do you think Alex Rider's job is?

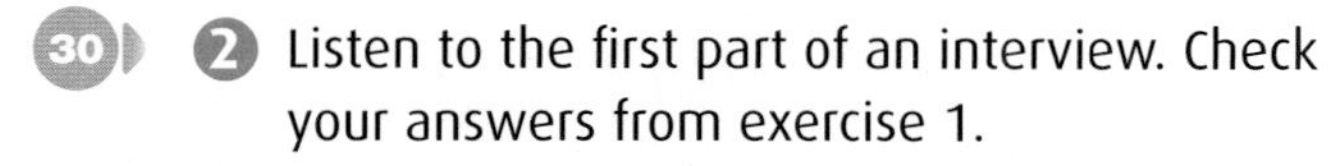

30 2. Listen to the first part of an interview. Check your answers from exercise 1.

30 3. Listen again. Circle the correct answers.

   a Alex lives with his *father / uncle.*
   b Alex's uncle works for the *British / American* government.
   c Alex thinks his uncle works in a *bank / office.*
   d They say his uncle is *dead / in hospital.*
   e Alex *believes / doesn't believe* them.
   f He becomes a spy because he wants to find *a girlfriend / his uncle.*

Words for jobs and people

4. Which words do you think describe Alex's job? Circle them.

exciting	fun	easy	boring
dangerous	safe	hard	cool

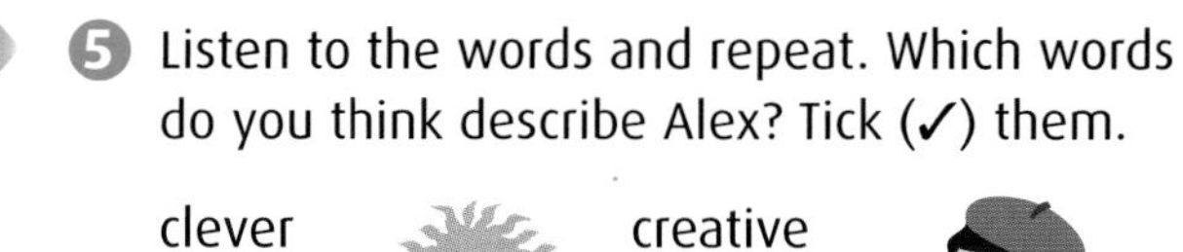

31 5. Listen to the words and repeat. Which words do you think describe Alex? Tick (✓) them.

clever ☐ creative ☐
brave ☐ friendly ☐
confident ☐ calm ☐

6. Look at the jobs on pages 32–33. Describe the jobs. Use the words from exercises 4 and 5.

A police officer's job is ...
A good police officer is ...

Alex's abilities

7 Read the activities in **bold** (**a–j**). Write the letter next to the correct picture.

- a He can **speak French** and **German**.
- b He can **speak Japanese**.
- c He can **do martial arts**.
- d He can **climb mountains**.
- e He can **drive a car**.
- f He can **ride a mountain bike**.
- g He can **ride a quad bike**.
- h He can **ride a horse**.
- i He can **fly a plane**.
- j He can **scuba dive**.

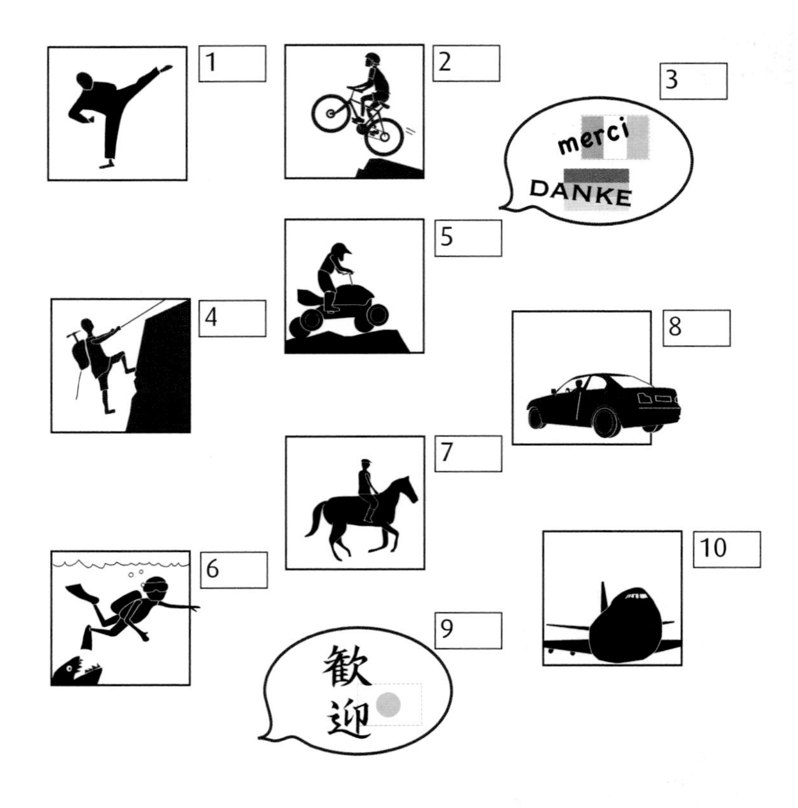

8 Now listen to the second part of the interview.

- a Which sentences in exercise 7 are correct for Alex Rider? Tick (✓) them.
- b Then listen again and check.
- c Which activity **can't** (✗) he do?

Your abilities

9 Work with a partner. Look at exercise 7. Tell your partner what you **can** do (✓) or **can't** do (✗).

I can speak German.
I can't speak Japanese.

10 **Word building:** Look at the example. Use the verbs in sentences (**a–d**) to make nouns.

*Alex can **scuba dive**.*
*He's a really good **scuba diver**.*

- a He can speak French. He's a good French ... .
- b He can ride a horse. But he isn't a good horse ... .
- c He can climb mountains. He's a good mountain ... .
- d He can drive. He's a good ... .

11 Write two sentences about you on a piece of paper.

I can ... .
I'm a good ... .

12 Collect the sentences in exercise 11. Read out the sentences. The class says the person.

4 ROLE PLAY

Expressing ability and inability

1 Work with a partner. You are both spies. Compare what you can do.

Partner A: Look at your spy card on page 113.
Partner B: Look at your spy card on page 118.
Start like this:

Partner A: *I can ...*
Partner B: *I can ... too.*
Partner A: *I can ... and...*
Partner B: *I can ... but I can't ...*

2 Who is the super spy? Partner A or B?

5 READING

Mariah, fire fighter in training

1. Look at the photos. Do you think this job looks exciting / dangerous / fun?

2. Read the text about Mariah. Where is she? Is she confident she can do the job?

33 I CAN SAVE YOUR LIFE!

Mariah Carter is a fire fighter in training.

Some people think girls can't be fire fighters. That isn't true! I'm at a fire fighter training camp for girls. There are 22 of us at Camp Blaze and the teachers are all women fire fighters. The job is very hard and can be quite dangerous sometimes. We learn to put (5) out fires and to save lives. Sometimes I'm scared because our lives are in danger too.

Fire fighters can't work alone. They always work in a team. Fire fighters also help people in accidents, with medical emergencies and in other dangerous (10) situations. They teach people about safety – so fires and accidents don't happen.

At Camp Blaze we train hard. I'm really tired sometimes and I want to sleep – I don't want to check the equipment or carry heavy things. But you (15) can't stop in this job. At the camp we learn to be confident about our skills. Now I always ask myself 'Can I do it?' And the answer is never 'No, I can't' – it's always, 'Yes, I can!'

3. Read the text again. Complete the facts about fire fighters.

   a How do fire fighters work?
   They work in a ...

   b What do fire fighters do?
   They put out ...
   They help people in ...
   They teach people about ...

   c What's the job like?
   It's hard and ... sometimes.

4. Answer true (**T**) or false (**F**). Good fire fighters:

		T / F
a	are always men.	☐
b	are OK in dangerous situations.	☐
c	always work with other people.	☐
d	don't sleep a lot.	☐

A job as a fire fighter – Can you do it?

- Can you stay calm in a dangerous situation?
- Can you follow instructions fast?
- Can you work in a team?
- Can you carry heavy equipment?
- Can you work hard when you are tired?

5. Do you have the skills to be a fire fighter? Answer the five questions for yourself with *Yes / No*.

6. [7] Watch the video. Is the job of a fire fighter right for you? Tell the class.

   Yes! I have the skills and I like dangerous situations.
   I have the skills but I'm not sure about the job.
   No! It's not the right job for me.

6 GRAMMAR

can and *can't*

1. Read the examples (**a–e**) from the text. Match them to the correct rules (**1-5**). Write the letter of the example in the box next to the rule.

a Fire fighters can't work alone.
b I can save your life!
c The answer is never 'No, I can't.' It's always 'Yes, I can.'
d Some people think girls can't be fire fighters.
e Can I do it?

1 We use **can** + verb to talk about ability – skills we have. ☐
2 We use ***can't*** + verb to talk about inability – skills we don't have. ☐
3 We use ***can / can't*** to talk about permission – things it is OK or not OK to do. ☐
4 In questions we use *can* + *(I / you / she)* + verb. ☐
5 To answer questions, we can use short answers. ☐

34 2. **Pronunciation:** Listen to the examples in exercise 1 and repeat. We also say *can't* with a long *a*. How do we say *can* in these sentences? Listen and repeat again.

3. Write sentences about Mariah with *can* (✓) or *can't* (✗). Then work with a partner. Read out your sentences and check.

(✓) (put out fires) *She can put out fires.*

a (✓) (help people in accidents) ________
b (✓) (carry heavy equipment) ________
c (✗) (run fast with heavy equipment) ________
d (✓) (teach people about safety) ________
e (✗) (drive a fire engine) ________
f (✓) (work in a team) ________

4. A group of fire fighters in training have a lot of questions. Write the questions with *can* or *can't*.

a When / we / put out / fires? ________ ☐
b we / have / a uniform? ________ ☐
c we / work / alone? ________ ☐
d Who / we / ask for help? ________ ☐
e we / have / a break now? ________ ☐

5. Match the answers with the questions in exercise 4. Put the correct numbers in the boxes.

1 Yes, you can. You can have one today.
2 You can ask me – or another fire fighter.
3 No, you can't. We need to finish the job.
4 No, fire fighters always work as a team.
5 After you learn about fire safety.

7 CONVERSATION

Work with a partner. Find out what your partner can do. Ask about sports and games, circus tricks, creative things, food and drink.

Can you play basketball? - Yes, I can.
Can you stand on your head? - No, I can't.

62 LANGUAGE BANK 8

8 CLIL: The music industry

Music jobs

1 Tell the class.

a Are you a fan of a singer or band? Who?
b Do you buy your music online (downloads) or in a shop (CDs / DVDs)?
c Do you go to concerts?

2 Look at the mind map of jobs. Write the descriptions (**a–h**) next to the correct jobs. Then listen or watch the video and check.

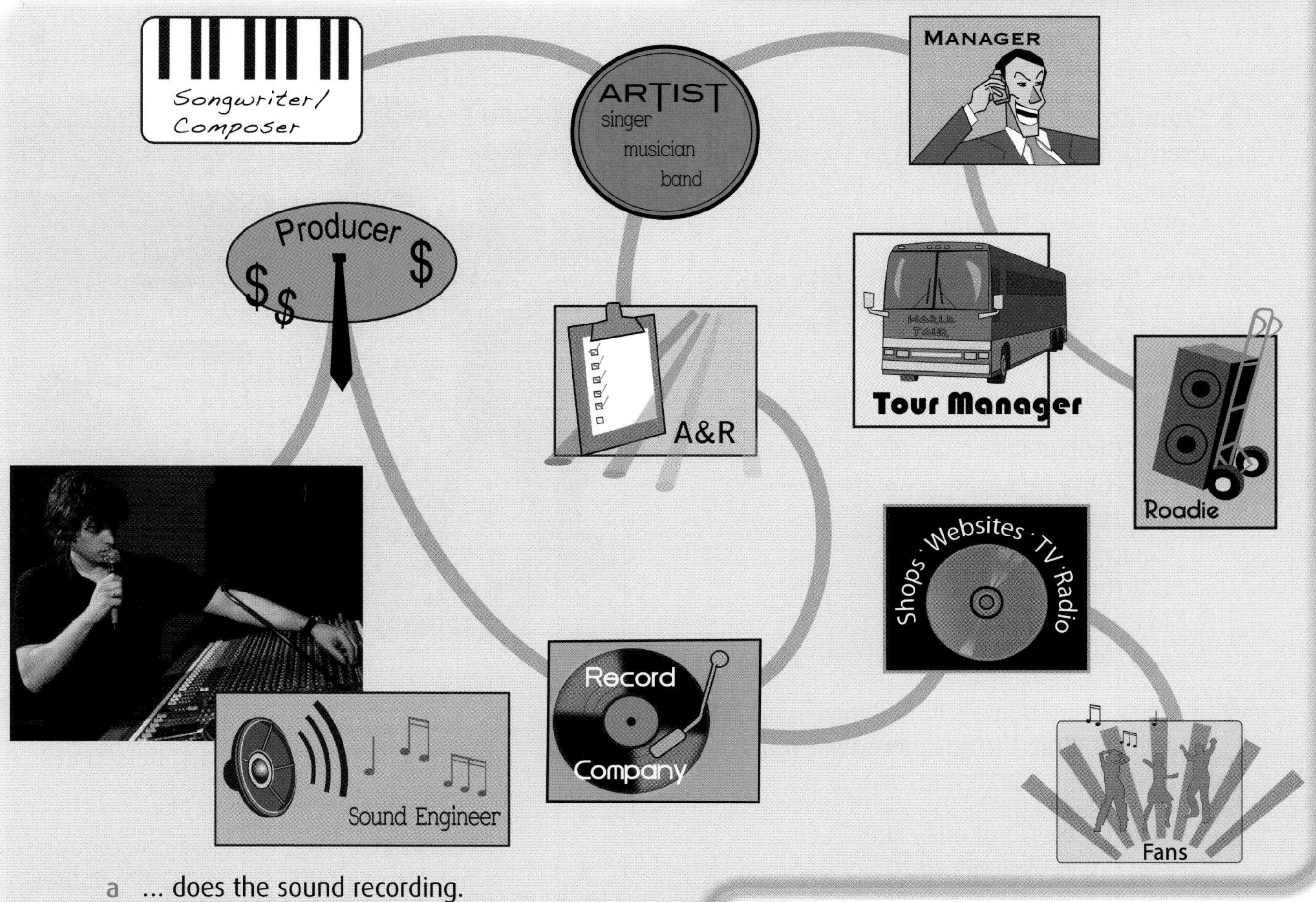

a ... does the sound recording.
b ... organises the artist's career.
c ... performs and records music.
d ... organises concerts in different places.
e ... produces recordings with the artist.
f ... prepares the sound and light equipment for concerts.
g ... writes music or music and lyrics (words).
h ... finds new bands for record companies.

3 Work with a partner. Ask and answer about each job.

What does a (tour manager) do?
– A (tour manager) ...

4 Does a job in the music industry sound interesting to you? Which job(s)?

Yes. / No. / Maybe.
The job of ... sounds interesting.

9 WRITING

Emily's dream job

1. **Read:** Look at Emily's poster. Read about her dream job. Is this a good job for you?

Your dream job

2. **Prepare:** Think about your dream job. Use the boxes to help you.

Where do they work?
A *(doctor /...)* works at *a hospital / an office / different places / ...*

What do they do?
A ... *helps people / travels a lot / teaches students / saves people / works with ...*

What's the job like?
The job is *interesting / dangerous / safe / hard / easy / cool /...*

What skills do they need?
A good ... is *calm / brave / friendly / tidy / clever / creative / ...*
A good ... *can listen / work in a team / stay calm / ...*

Why is it your dream job?
I want to work with *people / animals / children / ...*
I want to work *in a school / at home / ...*

3. **Write and share:** Write about your dream job. Describe it to a partner or to the class.
Do it online! Make an online poster.

My Dream Job
My dream job is to be a musician.
A musician usually works in a studio. He or she writes and records songs.
It's an exciting job because you play for many people.
Musicians travel all over the world. They play music at festivals and concerts.
You need to work in a team and be creative and patient.
It's my dream job because people pay you to do something you enjoy.

Emily, United Kingdom

10 Your Answer

What job is right for you?

What can you do?
Are you a good artist / writer / swimmer / ... ?
What jobs do people in your family do?
Would you like to do the same job as somebody in your family?
What do you think is an interesting or exciting job?

YOUR SCORE

Can you use all the language below?
Yes ☺, *No* ☹ or *Almost* 😐

Vocabulary:	jobs	☐
	adjectives to describe jobs and people	☐
Communication:	talking about ability and inability	☐
Grammar:	*can* and *can't*	☐
CLIL:	the music industry	☐

Unit 5

FACT

At any time, there are over 1,000 thunderstorms in the world.

Scary stories

1

2

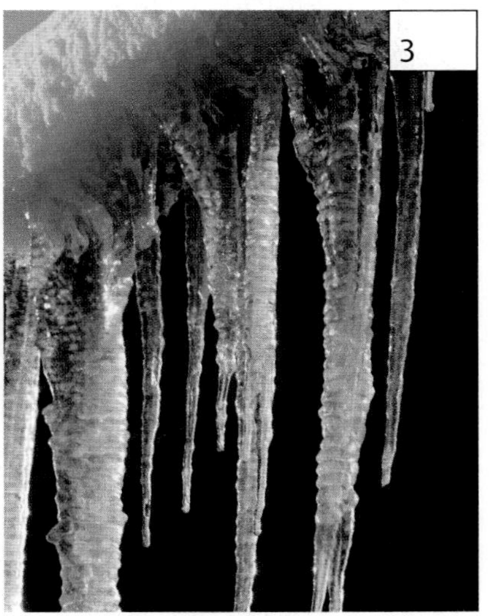
3

4

1 The Big Question

When were you last scared?

2 VOCABULARY

What's the weather like?

36 **1** Listen. Match the weather words (**a–h**) with the weather in the pictures. Then listen again and check.

a wind b fog c ice d rain
e snow f sun g cloud
h storm (thunder and lightning)

37 **2** **Word building:** Complete the table. Listen and check.

	Noun		Adjective
a	snow	It's	*snowy*
b			sunny
c	ice		
d			windy
e	rain		
f			foggy
g	storm		
h			cloudy

37 **3** **Pronunciation:** Listen again and repeat the words and phrases in exercise 2.

a Underline the words in (**a–h**) with a long vowel sound.
b Circle the words in (**a–h**) with a short vowel sound.

4 Work with a partner.

Partner A: Choose a picture. Do an action for the weather. For example, put your hands on your ears and look scared.
Partner B: Say the weather. *It's stormy.* Then swap.

YOUR GOALS

Vocabulary:	weather, dates, feelings
Communication:	describing past states
Grammar:	past tense of *to be*
CLIL:	depression and moods

What's the temperature?

5 Listen. Write the temperatures. Mark them on the thermometer.

a *It's ___ °C (degrees Celsius).* It's hot.
b *It's ___ degrees.* It's quite warm.
c *It's ___ degrees.* It's cold.
d *It's – (minus) ___ degrees.* It's really cold.

6 Work with a partner. Ask and answer questions.

a What's the weather like today?
It's really cold / ...
b What's the temperature today?
It's about .... It's ...
c What kind of weather do you like?
I like rainy / warm / ... weather.
d What kind of weather do you hate?
I hate hot / cold / ... weather.
e Do you think storms are scary? Why?
Yes, because of the thunder...

Wild weather around the world

7 Work with a partner.

Partner A: Look at page 113. Answer Partner A's questions.
Partner B: Ask and make notes about the weather in Yakutsk (Russia), Timbuktu (Mali, Africa), Auckland (New Zealand) and Singapore.

Partner B: Look at page 118. Answer Partner A's questions.
Partner A: Ask and make notes about Cherrapunji (India), Newfoundland (Canada), Mawson Station (Antarctica) and Faro (Portugal).

63 LANGUAGE BANK 9

FACT

Near the equator there are only two seasons: a rainy season and a dry season (with no rain).

3 LISTENING

The seasons

1 Look at the twelve months in the year. Write the months in the correct order.

March	October	January	August	December	June
September	April	May	February	July	November

2 Look at the four seasons. Answer the questions.

a Do you have four different seasons in your country or only two?
b What months are these seasons?
c What's the weather like in these seasons?
d What are the temperatures?
e What's your favourite season? Why?
My favourite season is ...
because I like the summer holidays / winter sports ...

spring

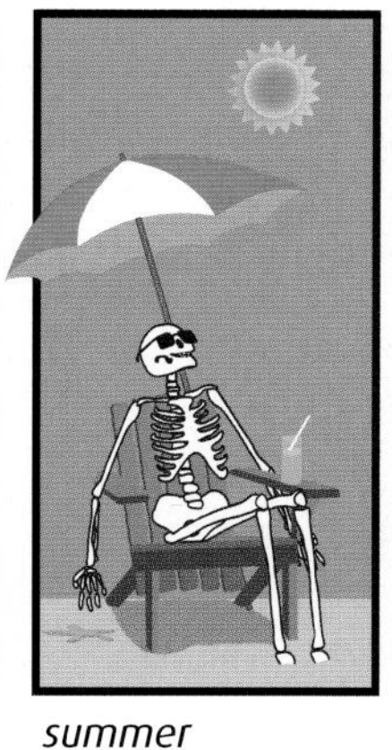

summer

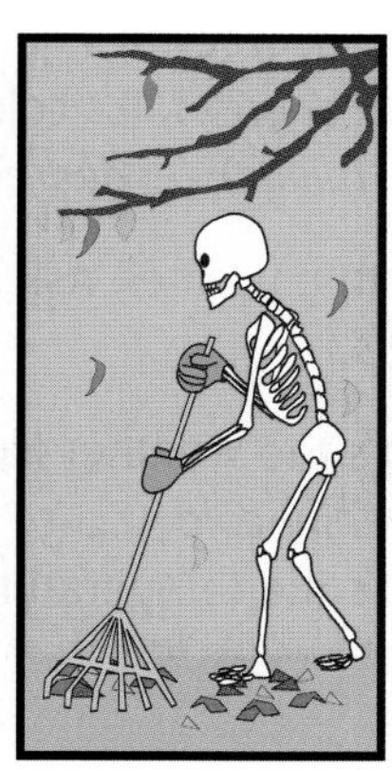

autumn

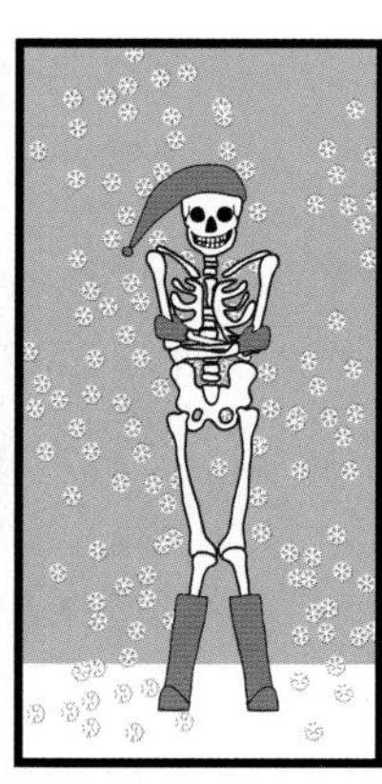

winter

What's the date?

39 3 Read and listen to the poem. Then read it together.

a Which months have 31 days?
b Which month has under 30 days?
c What's a leap year?

Thirty days has September,
April, June and November;
February has twenty-eight alone,
All the rest have thirty-one.
But in leap year that's the time,
When February's days are twenty-nine.

40 4 Look at the dates on the calendar. Listen and repeat.

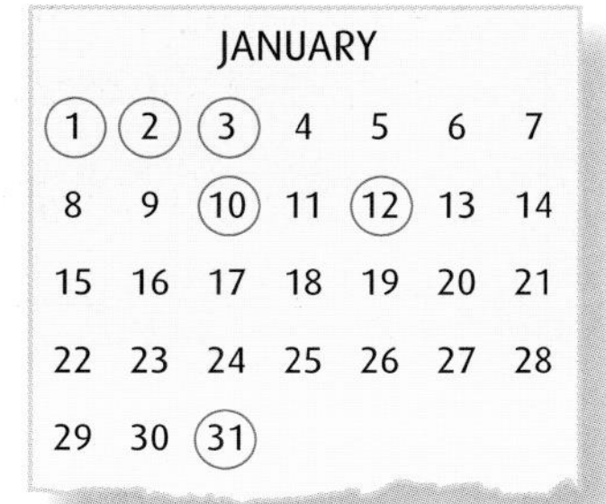

JANUARY						
1	2	3	4	5	6	7
8	9	10	11	12	13	14
15	16	17	18	19	20	21
22	23	24	25	26	27	28
29	30	31				

41 5 **Pronunciation:** Listen to the two *th* sounds in the date. Repeat the different sounds. Then say the tongue twister.

ð ð
The tenth of January.

The things that these things think,
they're the things that these things think.

42 6 Listen to the years and repeat.

1939	1977	1986	2010	1974	2004

7 Work with a partner. Think of five important dates in your life. Write them down.

Partner A: Say your dates. Be careful with the *th* sound!
30th August 1999.
Partner B: Write the date. Ask your partner why it is important.
This is an important date because it's my birthday.
Then swap roles.

Wild weather

43 **8** Listen to four stories of wild weather. Match the stories (**1–4**) with the correct pictures and story titles.

43 **9** Listen again and cross out the incorrect information for each story.

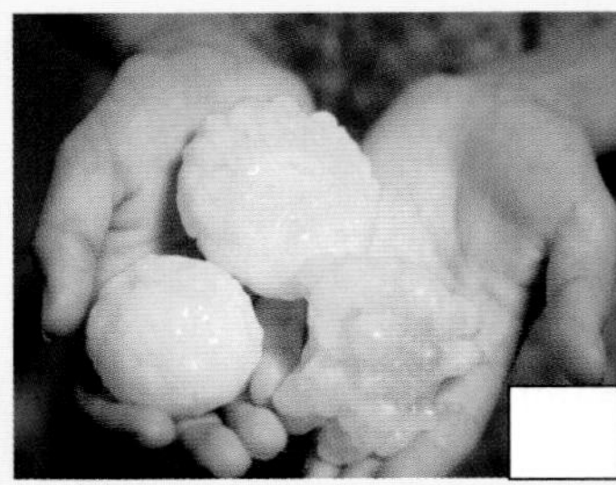

Huge hailstones

Lucky seven times

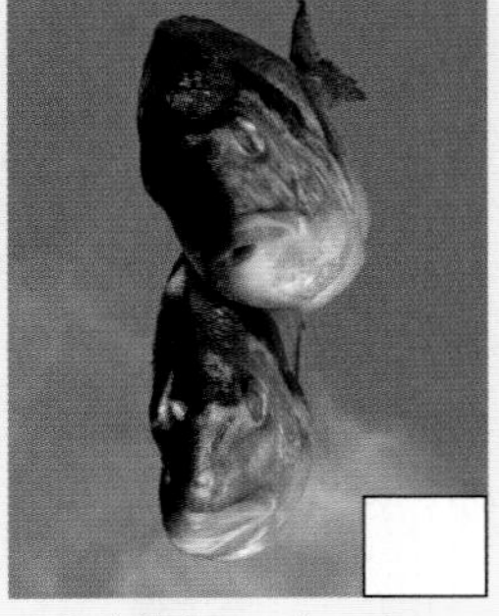

Fish fall from the sky

Story	Date	Place	Information
1	5th June 1977	UK	Roy was still alive.
2	16th June 1939	Scotland	There was a bad storm.
3	28th February 2001	Australia	It was the second time.
4	14th April 1986	Bangladesh	Twenty-two people were dead.

Frog rain

Feelings

10 Now read the sentences from the listening. Match the words for feelings (**a–d**) with the faces (**1–4**).

1  2  3  4 

a After the fourth strike he was very **scared**. ☐
b Mr Ettles was very **surprised**. ☐
c I'm just **happy** it wasn't crocodile rain! ☐
d It was a **sad** day in Bangladesh. ☐

44 **11** Listen to the sentences (**1–4**). Match them with the correct feelings (**a–d**).

1 ☐ 2 ☐ 3 ☐ 4 ☐

a disappointed b excited  c embarrassed  d bored 

12 Write two sentences like this with the words in exercise 10 and 11.

I feel (happy / scared / embarrassed / ...) when ...

4 ROLE PLAY

Describing states in the past

1 Work with a partner.

Partner A: Look at your card on page 113. Phone the local TV station. Tell them your story. Start like this: *It was in /on ... I was at ... It was ... I was ...*

Partner B: You are the reporter. Listen and make notes for a story about wild weather.

2 Now swap roles. **Partner B**: Look at the card on page 119. **Partner A**: Listen and make notes.

When? *Where?*
Weather? *What?*
Feeling?

64 LANGUAGE BANK 10

5 READING

The Tower of London

9 ① Read **Facts about the Tower** and look at the photos. What is scary about this place? Watch the video. Would you like to visit the Tower of London?

② Read the story *Murder in the Tower*. Was it murder?

Yes, it was murder. / No, the boys were ill. / Nobody knows.

45 MURDER IN THE TOWER?

Visitors to the Tower sometimes see two small boys together. They look scared. Who are they? ... Or is the question who were they? Some people say the boys are the ghosts of the Little Princes ...

The Little Princes

It was the year 1483. Twelve-year-old Prince Edward and his younger brother Prince Richard were the sons of King Edward IV of England. Their father was dead and the next king was Edward. But their uncle, the Duke of Gloucester, wasn't happy. His plan was to be king himself.

The princes were the only thing between their uncle and power. The story goes that there was an order from the Duke: 'Take the boys to the Tower!' – and then the princes were prisoners.

Nobody knows the rest of the story. But we know the princes weren't alive for long – maybe only a few weeks. Many years later there was a sad discovery in the Tower: two small skeletons. The skeletons were boys aged 10 and 12. ... So were the boys ill? Or was it murder?

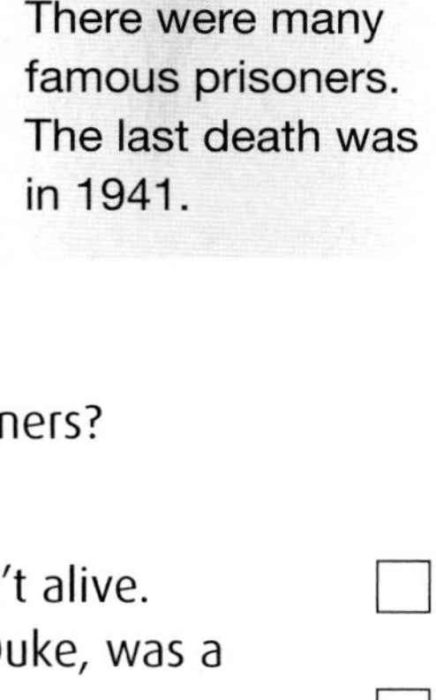

FACTS ABOUT THE TOWER

- The Tower of London isn't just one tower – there are lots of different buildings.
- The Tower has two million visitors every year.
- Many years ago, the Tower was a prison. There were lots of horrible deaths and murders here.
- There were many famous prisoners.
- The last death was in 1941.

③ Look at the pictures. Write the correct word in the sentences.

a The two boys were ________s. Their father was king.
b They were ________s in the Tower.
c There were two small ________s in the Tower.
d Are the two scared boys in the Tower ________s?

prisoner

prince

ghost

skeleton

④ Why were the boys prisoners? True (**T**) or false (**F**)?

a The boys' father wasn't alive. ☐
b The boys' uncle, the Duke, was a nice man. ☐
c The Duke wasn't interested in power. ☐
d After the princes, the Duke was the next king. ☐
e The princes were a problem for the Duke. ☐

6 GRAMMAR

was / wasn't and *were / weren't*

1. Underline sentences in the story with *was / wasn't* and *were / weren't*.

2. What's the rule? Choose the right words for the sentences.

was / were in **positive** / **negative** sentences
wasn't / weren't in **positive** / **negative** sentences
was / wasn't with ***I*** and with ***he***, ***she***, ***it*** / ***they***

46 3. **Pronunciation:** Listen to *was / wasn't* and *were / weren't* in these sentences. Listen again and repeat.

a The next king *was* Edward. But his uncle *wasn't* happy.
b The princes *were* prisoners. But they *weren't* alive for long.

4. Complete this story with *was / wasn't* or *were / weren't*.

In 1553, after the death of Edward VI, there (1) ______ questions about the new queen, Lady Jane Grey. She (2) ______ Edward's favourite cousin. But she (3) ______ queen for long. After nine days, Jane and her husband (4) ______ suddenly prisoners in the Tower, but they (5) ______ in the same place. This graffiti of Jane's name (6) ______ on a wall in the Beauchamp Tower. But she (7) ______ a prisoner there. Maybe it (8) ______ her husband's goodbye to her.

The Traitors' Gate

Questions with *was* and *were*

5. Make questions with *was* and *were* for this quiz. Put the words in the correct order.

the Tower / a prison / was
Was the Tower a prison?

a a nice place / was / to stay / it
b there / any famous prisoners / were
c a lot of deaths / there / at the Tower / were
d murders / were / here / there / any
e the last death / was / in the nineteenth century

6. Work with a partner. Ask and answer the questions in exercise 6.

Yes, it was. / No, it wasn't.
Yes, there were. / No there weren't.

and, and then

7. Look at these sentences from the story. Complete the rule with the words in bold.

a Their father was dead **and** the next king was Edward.
b There was an order from the Duke **and then** the princes were prisoners.

To link two ideas or events, use ______ .
To show two events happen one after another, use ______ .

7 CONVERSATION

Work with a partner. Talk about your day yesterday. Ask and answer the questions.

What was the date yesterday?
What was the weather like?
Where were you?
Who were you with?
Were there any special events or problems?

FACT

One in eight teens are depressed.

8 CLIL: Depression and moods

Depression

1 Read the fact and the FAQs. When you feel depressed, do you feel good or bad?

FAQs: Depression

Q What is depression?

A When you are depressed, you feel sad. It isn't just a mood. You feel sad all the time – for a long time. You often want to cry. Sometimes you don't want to see your friends or other people. You are tired and you don't have any energy. You can have problems with school work. 5

Q Is depression genetic?

A People with depressed family members often get depression too. But there are other reasons, like family problems at home. Violence, family money problems or problems with step parents can also cause depression. 10

Q Can weather make you depressed?

A Yes, sometimes. Some people in northern places like Scandinavia often feel sad and tired in the winter months because there isn't much sun. 15

Q A friend is depressed. How can you help?

A Talk to your friend. Tell them to talk to their parents or another family member. Then a doctor can help them. 20

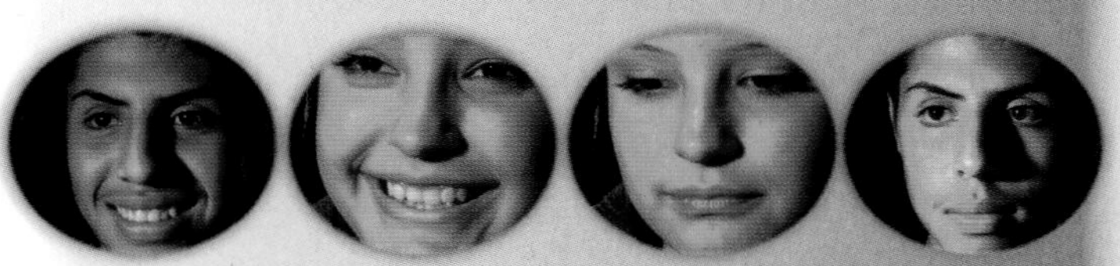

Good mood *Bad mood*

2 Read the FAQs again and tick (✓) the correct answers.

a When you are depressed
  1 you feel sad sometimes. ☐
  2 you always feel sad. ☐
b People with depression have no
  1 friends. ☐
  2 energy. ☐
c Depression
  1 can be genetic. ☐
  2 is never genetic. ☐
d Other reasons are
  1 family problems, no sun. ☐
  2 a bad day at school, bad weather. ☐
e When someone has depression
  1 he/she can get help. ☐
  2 he/she can't get help. ☐

Your moods

3 Work with a partner. Ask and answer the questions. Use the ideas to help you.

nice message from friend
boring lessons
happy music
nothing to do
problems with friends
problems with parents
bad day at school
good news
sunny day
rainy day
no money
good day at school
no homework

a What puts you in a good mood?
... puts me in a good mood. / I feel in a good mood when ...

b What puts you in a bad mood?
... puts me in a bad mood. / I feel in a bad mood when ...

c Are you in a good mood or a bad mood today? Why?
I'm in a good / bad mood because ...

10 4 Watch the video about people's good and bad moods. Do you share any of their ideas?

9 WRITING

Daniela, Bernardo and Francisca's scary story

1. **Read:** Look at the pages of their story. Read the story. What is scary about it? Is it a good story?

Your scary story

2. **Prepare:** Think about your scary story. Use the boxes to help you.

Set the scene! Describe the place, time, weather, and people.

I was *at home / in my bedroom / at my grandma's / at school / ...*
It was *my birthday / 31st October / ...*
It was a *stormy / windy / foggy / sunny / dark / ...* day/night.
My family was there / I was alone / I was with my brother / ...

Describe the scary things and your feelings.

There was *a strange person / a black cat / a hand / something / ...*
And there was *a horrible sound / voice / ...*
I was *cold / scared / ...*

Write the ending.

And then suddenly, ...
To this day, I don't know what it was.
I can't forget that *night / that day.*

3. **Write and share:** Draw or find pictures for your story. Write your story. Then swap your story with a partner.
Do it online! Visit an online story website and publish your story.

10 Your Answer

When were you last scared?

What was the date?
Where were you?
Who were you with?
What was the weather like?
Why were you scared?

Dancing Ghost

In a small town at 11:30 pm, it was Friday the 13th.

It was a dark night with rain, lightning and thunder.

◀ 1 ▶

I was alone in my house and suddenly there was no light. I was in the dark and I was very scared.

There was a strange noise and footsteps outside my bedroom.

◀ 2 ▶

At the door there were two ghosts - dancing ghosts...

And then suddenly I was awake. I was in bed and it was morning.

◀ 3 ▶

Daniela and Bernardo, Brazil; Francisca, Chile

YOUR SCORE

Can you use all the language below?
Yes 🙂, *No* ☹ or *Almost* 😐

Vocabulary:	weather	☐
	dates	☐
	feelings	☐
Communication:	describing past states	☐
Grammar:	past tense of *to be*	☐
CLIL:	depression and moods	☐

Unit 6

FACT

The first computer (1946) was the size of a large room.

Tech time

1 The Big Question

Is technology an important part of your free time?

2 VOCABULARY

Gadgets

1. Work with a partner. Match the pictures (**a–h**) with the correct words.

2. What can you do with gadgets? Use the verbs to make phrases.

chat	check	listen	play
send	take	go	watch

watch my favourite series

a ________ on the internet
b ________ to music
c ________ with friends
d ________ films and music videos
e ________ games
f ________ email
g ________ the time
h ________ pictures and videos
i ________ messages

47 3. **Pronunciation:** Look and listen to the sounds in these two words. Listen again and repeat.

/ æ /	/ eɪ /
g**a**dget	g**a**me

48 4. Now listen to these words. Put them in the correct column in exercise 2.

play	camera	take
favourite	email	chat

5. Work with a partner. Match the gadgets in exercise 1 with the activities in exercise 2. Write sentences.

I watch my favourite series on television.

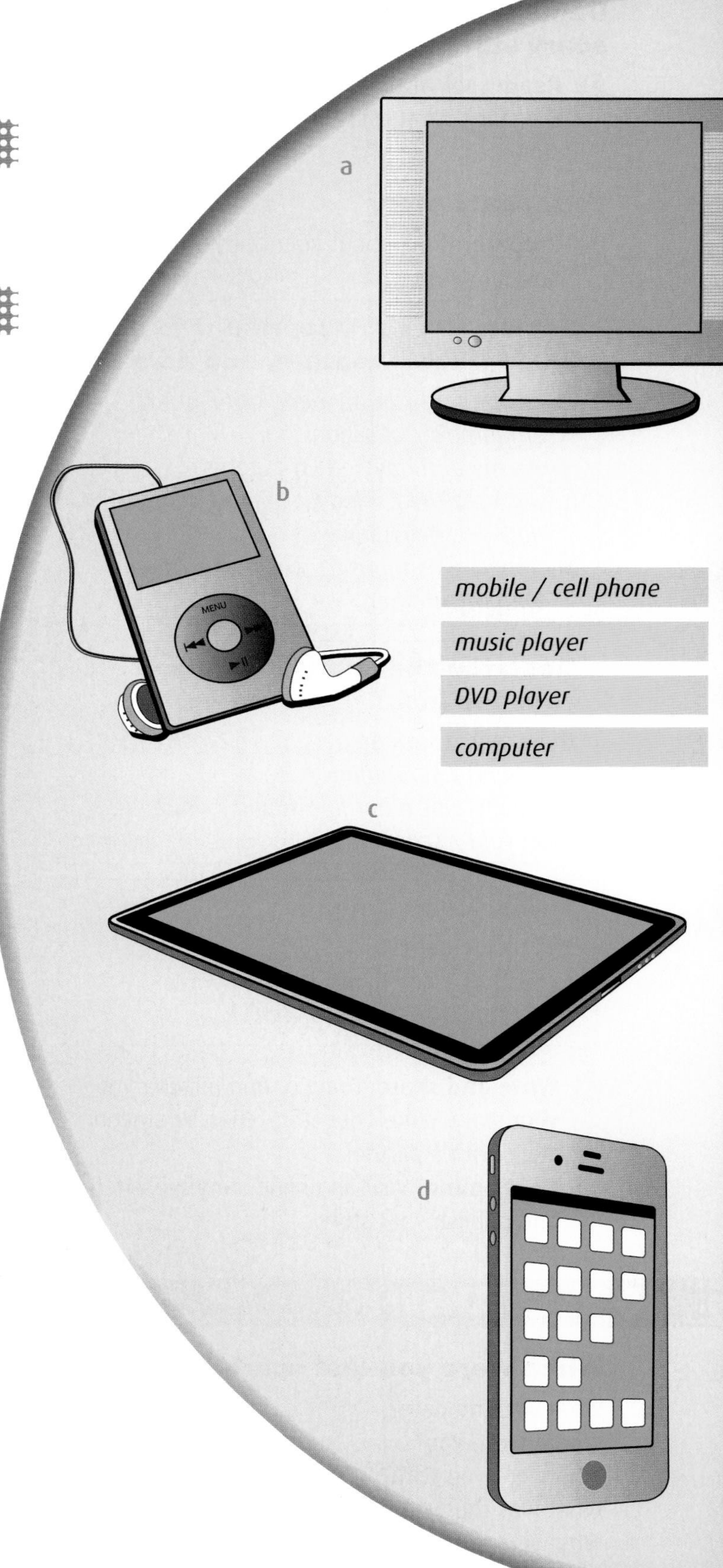

YOUR GOALS

Vocabulary:	gadgets, free time activities and interests
Communication:	describing current activities
Grammar:	present continuous
CLIL:	IT / animation

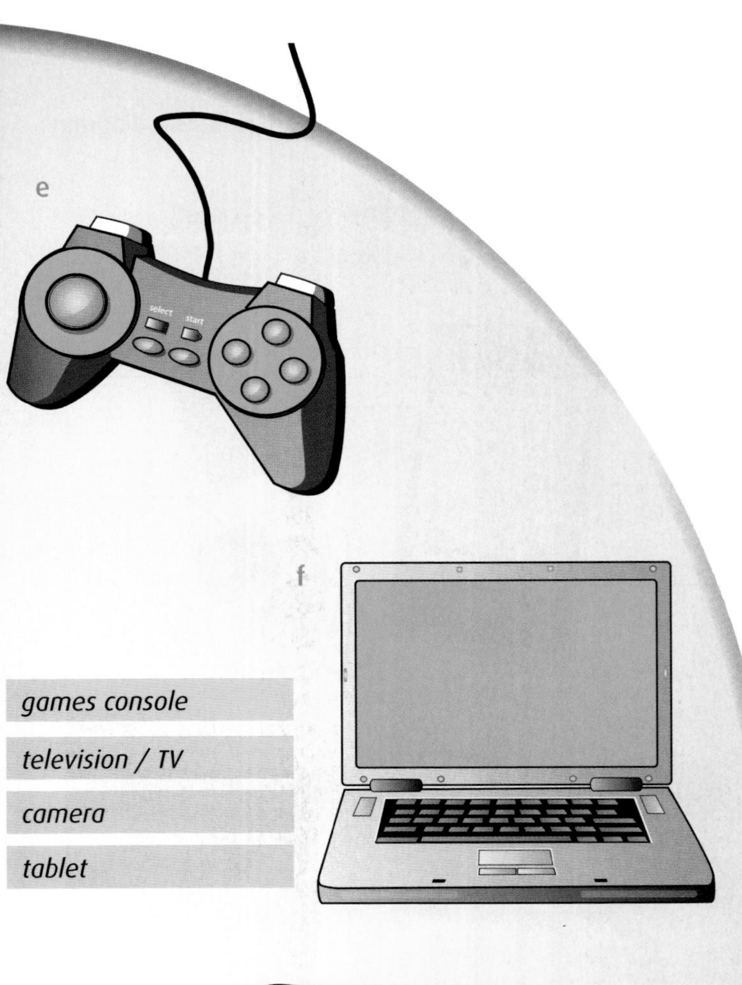

games console

television / TV

camera

tablet

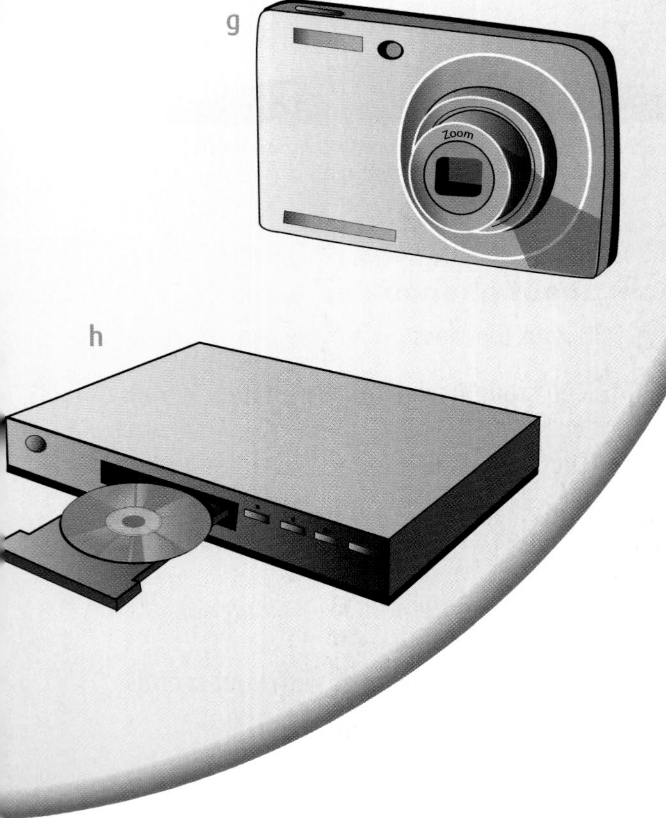

Our gadgets

49 **6** Listen to five teenagers. Which gadget are they talking about?

49 **7** Listen again. What do they use their gadget for?

Your gadgets

8 Work with a partner. Ask and answer:

a Do you or people in your family have any of the gadgets in exercise 1?
I have ... / We have ... at home.
My brother / mum has ...

b What do you / they use it for?
I use it to ...

c Would you like any of these things?
I'd like a ...

9 Draw a picture or find a photo of your favourite gadget. Write three or four sentences about it.

10 Show your work to a partner. Or record your description and publish it online.

This is me and my friend on my games console. We play car racing and sports games. My sister likes the sport games too.

3 LISTENING

FACT

In South Korea 87% of kids have a mobile phone. They use their phone for 75 minutes a day.

Tech activities

1 Read the fact. Find out about phones in your class.

a How many students in your class have a phone?
... students have a phone.

b How many per cent is that?
... % (per cent)

c How often do they use their phone?
... uses his / her phone for about ... minutes a day.

50 2 Listen to the dialogue. Complete the diagram with the words.

apps	battery	charger
keyboard	screen	type

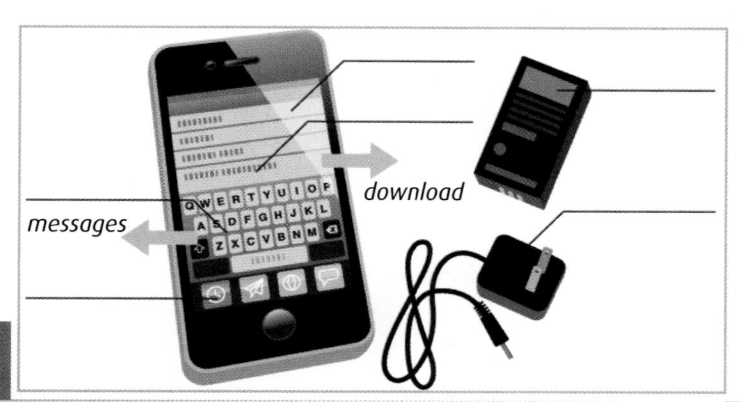

51 3 Listen. Complete the sentence below the photo.

Competition winners

Mok-Min Ha and Yeong-Ho Bae from South Korea were the winners of an international competition in ...

51 4 Listen again. Circle the correct answers.

a Mok-Min sends **50–100** / **150–200** messages a day.

b Some of her friends send **400** / **500** messages.

c Mok-Min texts under the table **at dinner** / **in class**.

d Yeong-Ho sends **200–300** / **300–400** messages a day.

e He can type **4** / **8** letters a second.

f Yeong-Ho likes text messages because they are **cheap** / **fast**.

Talk about phones

5 Talk with the class.

a Can students use mobile phones at your school?
Yes, all day. / Only in breaks. / No, we can't.

b Do students text in lessons?
Yes, sometimes. / No, never.

c What other things do students do on their phones?
go on the internet / download apps / watch music videos / ...

d How do you talk most with your friends?
face to face / online / by phone / on Facebook / with instant messages

Non-tech activities

6 Complete the words for the activities in the pictures. Use *a, e, i, o* and *u.*

a *play basketball / football*
b dr_w and p_ _nt ☐
c d_ my h_ _r and n_ _ls ☐
d r_ _d b_ _ ks or m_ g_z_n_s ☐
e wr_t_ in my j_ur_al ☐
f pl_y_ th_ g_ _t_r ☐

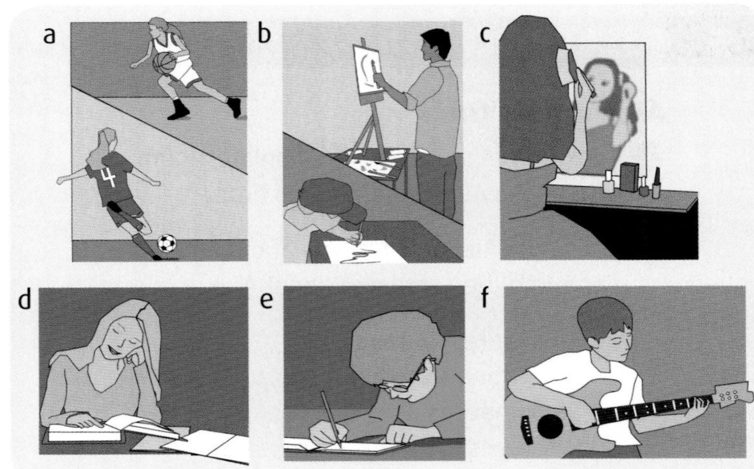

7 Work with a partner. Ask and answer about the activities:

In your free time, do you ...?
No, I don't. / Sometimes. / Yes, I often do that.

Your free time

8 Look at the cartoon. What does it say about boys and girls?

In their free time, boys ... They don't ...
Girls ... and they ... They don't ...

9 Do you think the cartoon is right?

What do boys in your class do in their free time? What do girls in your class do? Are your interests the same or different?

4 ROLE PLAY

Talking about free time

1 Work with a partner.
Partner A: Use the free time questionnaire to ask about Partner B's activities and interests.
Partner B: Look at page 119. Answer Partner A's questions.

2 Swap roles. **Partner A:** Look at page 114.

3 Now ask and answer about your free time.

FREE TIME QUESTIONNAIRE

1 What do you do in your free time?
2 Where do you do these activities?
3 Are you good at them?

65 LANGUAGE BANK 11

5 READING

Alex's free time

1. Look at the photos in Alex's online album. What does Alex do in his free time?

2. Now read Alex's comments about his photos. Complete the sentences about Alex.

   a Alex writes ... about ...
   b His writing starts with his ...
   c He composes ...
   d He shares his songs with ... and ...
   e He loves to ...
   f Alex and his friends want to ...

Photo 1

Here I'm working on a song with a friend. We write poetry to music – or raps. I have a journal and I write about the world around me – things like unity and peace. I write to express myself to the world. My writing starts with my feelings – like when I feel happy, depressed, or even embarrassed. I always carry my journal, so I can write anywhere.

Photo 2

I also compose the music for my raps. I remix old music with new sounds, so it sounds fresh. In this photo I'm working in a studio with a sound engineer. We're mixing the music for a new song. The sound engineer is helping me with the sound levels. I always share my songs with my mom and dad – they're creative people and they like my work. I also upload my songs to free music sites on the internet. So my friends and people all over the world can listen to my music.

Photo 3

I love to perform my songs. Sometimes I feel nervous. But when I'm on stage and I feel the music, I enjoy it. In this photo I'm with my friend Javonte. We're performing with some other very good musicians. My friend Sean isn't singing with us here. Javonte, Sean and I have a band together. It's called 4Real. A lot of rap has a negative message. But our band is trying to make hip hop positive.

11 3. Watch the video about Alex's group *4Real*. What do you think of their music?

I don't like the music / the lyrics.
They want to make hip hop positive – I think that's good.
I think the music is OK, but I don't really like hip hop.

6 GRAMMAR

Present continuous

1 Look at the photos on page 52 again. Complete the sentences. Then complete the rule in the box.

a **Photo 1:** Alex is ...
b **Photo 2:** Alex and the sound engineer are ...
c **Photo 3:** Alex says, 'We're ... My friend Sean isn't ...'

We use the present continuous tense for actions NOW.
We often use the present continuous to describe photos.

We use: ... and verb + ...
For spelling changes, see Workbook page 28.

52 2 **Pronunciation:** In spoken English, we usually shorten the verb *to be* in the present continuous. Listen to the sentences and repeat.

a I am working on a song. → **I'm** working on a song.
b We are mixing the music. → **We're** mixing the music.
c He is helping me with the sound. → **He's** helping me with the sound.
d Sean is not singing with us. → Sean **isn't** singing with us.
e We are not performing together. → We **aren't** performing together.

3 Look at more photos in Alex's album. Complete the sentences with the correct form of the verb.

a This is me and Sean. We (*practise*) _______ on stage. Sean has a broken arm so he (*wear*) _______ a sling.

b Here I (*listen*) _______ to my new song for a performance. I (*sit*) _______ in a window at our hotel in New York.

c Spring break! I (*spend*) _______ it with my family. We (*explore*) _______ the city.

d I (*wear*) _______ my dad's favourite hat in this picture. My friend Javonte (*take*) _______ the photo.

4 Alex has two messages. Complete the messages and Alex's replies.

a **Scarlett** Hi. What ... (*you / do*)?
Alex I ... (*watch*) TV. What about you?
Scarlett Spanish homework. My dad ... (*help*) me.

b **Hakim** Hi. What are you doing?
Alex Not much. I ... (*hang out*) at home. What about you?
Hakim I'm at Joel's house. We ... (*play*) computer games.

5 Work with a partner. Write a message(s) on a friend's social network page. Ask what he / she is doing. Reply to your partner's message.

7 CONVERSATION

1 Work with a partner.
Partner A: Look at page 114.
Partner B: Look at page 119.
Describe what the people are doing in your pictures.

2 Find four differences.

3 Compare pictures.

8 CLIL: IT / Animation

1. Do you like cartoons and animated films? Who or what is your favourite character? What is it like? What can it do?

2. Read the interview. Complete the information about animation.

   To make an animated film you need a (1) c__________ with a clear (2) p__________. You can draw this or make a (3) m__________. Then you make a (4) s__________ about what happens in the film.

Lydia Baillergeau

53

Daniel Machua

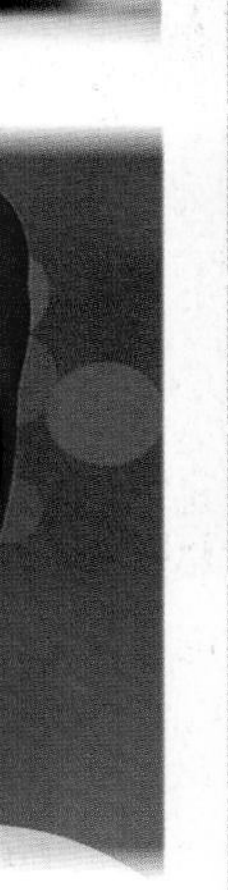

Renee Busse

Interviewer:	Daniel:
You're a student at Ex'pression College of Digital Arts. What course are you doing there?	I'm learning about animation and visual effects.
What is animation? Can you tell us in a few words?	It's really just a series of pictures with a character. Each picture is a little different. When you show the pictures really fast, it looks like they're moving.
What's important about the characters?	They need to have a personality. They need to like some things, not like other things and have habits – just like people.
What exactly do students learn at the college?	Well, we're learning how to make characters, models and storyboards.
What's a storyboard?	A storyboard is like a comic of the film. It shows all the pictures so you can see what happens in the film.
And there's something about the 12 rules of animation. What's that?	They're the important things for animation. So for example there's *squash and stretch*.
What does that mean?	*Squash* means you make a face or body flat. *Stretch* means you make it thin. With a lot of *squash and stretch*, you can make things look very funny.
What do you want to do after the course?	I'd like to work in film or television. But there are lots of jobs in video game production and in science too.

3. Read the interview again. Look at the diagram about *squash and stretch*. Label the three faces with these words:

   stretch | normal | squash

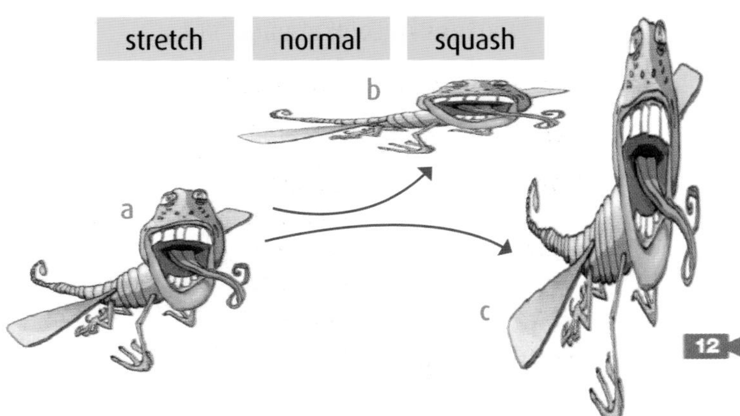

4. Draw a character or find a picture. Give it a name. Think about its personality and its habits. Then tell a partner.

   This is my character. His / her name is ...
   He's / She's happy / always in a bad mood / ...
   Every day / In the morning ...

5. Draw a storyboard for a short video clip about your character. Write short descriptions of what the character is doing.

   Here she's eating breakfast / fighting with ...

6. 12 Watch the video about animation camp. Would you like to go there?

9 WRITING

Pau and Marta's favourite photos

1. **Read:** Look at Pau and Marta's favourite photos from their online albums. Why are these photos their favourites?

Your favourite photo

2. **Prepare:** Find your favourite photo (a photo of you, your family or friends, a famous person etc). Think about the description of your photo. Use the boxes to help you.

Who is it?
This is *me / my dog / my brother / my best friend / the students in my class / …*

Where are you / they?
I'm *in my room at home / on holiday / …*
We're / They're *in the classroom / …*

What are you doing?
I'm *playing video games / laughing with my best friend / sitting on the beach / …*
We're *playing football / celebrating Dani's birthday …*

Why is it your favourite photo?
This is my favourite photo because …
I'm with my best friend / my class / …
It was a special day for me / my family / …
I look really good!

3. **Write and share:** Write the description of your photo. Swap descriptions with a partner. **Do it online!** Publish your photo online. Make an online album or use a photo-sharing site.

I'm competing in the Spanish skiing championships in the Sierra Nevada. This is my favourite photo because I'm very proud of my results in the championships and because I like skiing a lot.

Pau, Spain

This is me with some students from my class. We're in Montgat, a village near Barcelona. We're on a trip. We're spending some time in a beautiful forest. This is my favourite photo because it shows some of my best friends. It makes me remember good moments with them.

Marta, Spain

10 Your Answer

Is technology an important part of your free time?

What gadgets do you have?
What's your favourite gadget?
What do you do after school / at the weekend?
What are you doing now?
Do you often do tech activities?

YOUR SCORE

Can you use all the language below?
Yes ☺, *No* ☹ or *Almost* 😐

Vocabulary:	gadgets	☐
	activities and interests	☐
Communication:	describing current activities	☐
Grammar:	present continuous tense	☐
CLIL:	IT / animation	☐

The Big Read 1

1 This story is about Cornwall in the UK. Look at the photos and read the information about Cornwall. Which of these words do you think best describes it? Would you like to go there?

wild	exciting	beautiful
calm	boring	ugly

Cornwall is a special place. It has high **cliffs**, amazing **rocks** and beautiful sandy **beaches**. The **sea's** big **waves** are very popular with surfers.

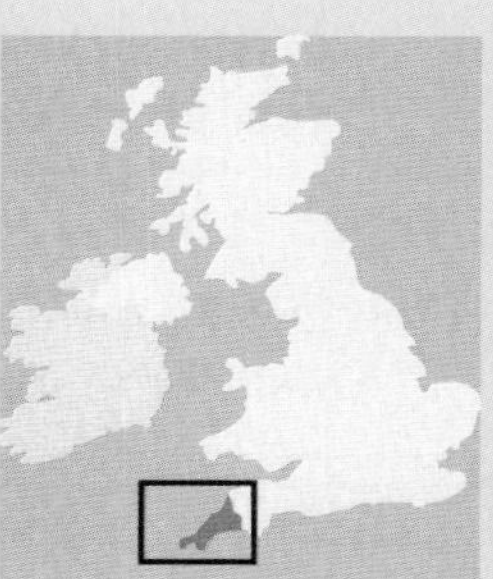

2 Look at the words in **bold**. Write them in the correct places in the pictures.

3 Now read the story. Who is telling the story? Who are the other people?

Charley Hal Sara

4 True (**T**) or false (**F**)? Correct the false sentences.

- a Charley was in an accident on the cliffs in Cornwall. ☐
- b Charley is in hospital. ☐
- c Hal takes Charley's favourite book to her. ☐
- d Charley talks to Hal. ☐
- e The family go to Cornwall without Charley. ☐
- f The family stay in the same place in Cornwall. ☐
- g The family stay in a different house this time. ☐
- h Hal hears Charley's voice all the time. ☐

5 Read the text again. Why does Hal hear Charley's voice? How does he feel? Does he miss Charley? Find places in the story about Hal's feelings.

6 Hal sends Charley a postcard from Cornwall. What does he say? Write his postcard.

Start like this:

Dear Charley,
How are you? We ...

a remarkable novel
both sensuous and sinister
PHILLIP PULLMAN
waves
SHARON
DOGAR

Waves

I'm here at the hospital with a surfboard in my hand. People are looking at me. Who cares? Not me. I have a half-dead sister. I hit the door hard with my hand.

'Hey.' I put the surfboard next to the bed. She doesn't move. Her sheets go up and down, up and down. She's breathing.

'Can't you see it?' I ask.

Up. Down. Up. Down.

No answer.

I take her hand and put it on the board. I don't like touching her.

Suddenly I'm sure she's there. She's right behind those closed eyes and she's listening. I'm angry, really angry. 'WAKE UP. Wake up Charley.'

The nurse comes in. 'All right?' she asks. I smile and nod.

'Hard saying goodbye to your sister?'

'It's only a month.'

'Hard for your parents.'

'Yep.' I get up. 'Bye, sis,' I say to Charley. 'Sorry you can't be on the waves this year.'

***

Help me!

I hear the words as clear as day. My little sister Sara and I are standing outside the hospital waiting for mum. She appears and we walk to the car.

Help me!

Charley's voice. I look around for her.

'All right?' says Mum.

'Fine.'

I look at my watch. It says the day is Friday. It says the time is 4.15. It says the month is July. The date is July 15th, the day we always go to Cornwall.

But never without Charley.

***

I can see the sea below us. I look at it. Everything looks exactly the same. Everything – the cliffs, the sea, the beach – only Charley's not here.

The house is waiting, quiet and empty up on the cliff.

Dad takes the old key from the tin by the door. Mum turns and looks right past me. I wonder what she can see because I can feel something. Something behind my shoulder: Charley's standing behind me, and her voice is whispering in my ear.

Charley? I turn round but there's nothing – nothing but empty space.

***

I can't sleep. Our room's exactly the same. Same beds, same window – but no Charley. I think I can hear her voice. *Hal! Where am I? Help me!*

When morning arrives, it's hard to believe that I'm really here. I open the window.

Over there, Hal, says the voice in my head. *Look over there.*

No. I don't want to look at the rocks where Charley was. I do not want to remember. I look away from the rocks and the sand and the memories.

The Big Read 2

1. Look at the photos on these pages. What sort of story do you think this is?

   a a love story
   b an action story
   c a science fiction story

2. Read the introduction in **bold** on page 59 and check your answer. Complete the information about Number 4.

Name:	
Age:	
From:	
Hiding from:	

3. Read the story. Put the events in the right order (**1–7**).

___ a John follows the football player.
___ b John sees a lot of kids outside the school.
___ c A girl with a camera talks to John.
___ d A football player hits John with his backpack.
___ e John walks away from Mark.
___ f Henri drives John to school.
___ g A boy in a NASA T-shirt tries to help John.

4. Find these phrases in the text. Underline them. Match them with the right meanings.

   1 thick **glasses** — a kind
   2 has a **telescope** — b a bag for your back
   3 **soft** blue eyes — c important
   4 **backpack** — d you wear them in front of your eyes
   5 **a big deal** — e you look through it and it makes things nearer

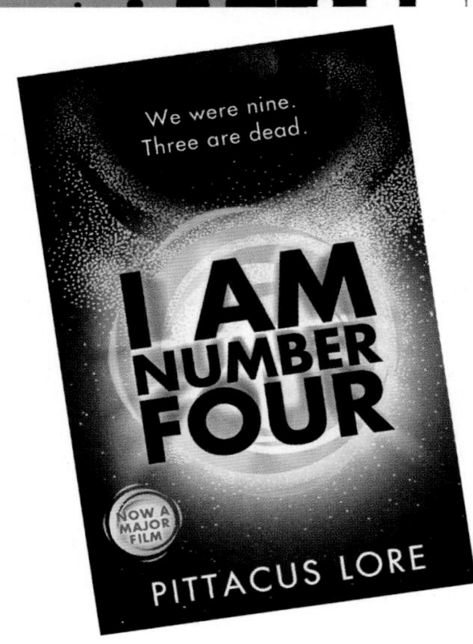

We were nine.
Three are dead.
I AM NUMBER FOUR
NOW A MAJOR FILM
PITTACUS LORE

5. Put the words in exercise 4 with the right person. Add other words or ideas from the text to describe them.

the boy in the NASA T-shirt

Sarah Hart

Mark James

6. Talk about these questions.

   a How do you think John feels at the new school? Why is it especially hard for him?
   b What parts of the text show you John is different?
   c Do you think John likes Sarah? Why do you think that?
   d Why does Mark hit John? Do you think John is right when he walks away?

7. Read the scene with Sarah and John (lines 29–44). Write what they are thinking. Use your own ideas. Start like this:

   Sarah says 'You're John right?'
   (Thinks: He looks ...)
   John says: 'Yeah, how do you know?'
   (Thinks: ...)

I AM NUMBER 4

John Smith is living in a new town with his guardian Henri. They are hiding. John is a 15-year-old alien from the Planet Lorian, three hundred million miles from Earth. After a violent fight with the Mogadorians, only nine children and their guardians were still alive. Now three children are dead and John is Number Four. 5

Another new name, another school. Is it the fifteenth? Or the twentieth? Always a small town, a 10 small school, always the same routine.

The school is three miles away from our house. Henri drives me in the morning.

"You know the routine," Henri says. "Don't show them how clever you are. Don't hurt anybody. And 15 always be ready to leave."

"I know."

"Good luck in there," he says.

I walk towards the building. A lot of kids are hanging around outside. They're in groups, 20 the football players, the band kids with their instruments and the clever kids in glasses with their books. One kid with thick **glasses** is alone. He's wearing a black NASA T-shirt and jeans. He has a **telescope** and is looking at the cloudy sky. A girl is 25 taking pictures and moving from one group to the next. She's very beautiful with straight blond hair and **soft** blue eyes.

She sees me, smiles and walks towards me. I'm nervous and feel embarrassed. She starts taking 30 pictures of me but I put my hands in front of my face.

"You're John, right?"

"Yeah," I say. "How do you know?"

"I'm Sarah Hart, my mother is your real estate 35 agent."

She's holding out her hand. I smile and take it. It's a good feeling.

"Wow," she says.

"What?" 40

"Your hand feels hot. Really hot, like you have a fever or something."

"No, I'm OK."

A bell rings. We say goodbye and she walks away. A moment later, a **backpack** hits the back of my 45 arm. I turn round and a group of football players walk past me. One of them is giving me an angry look. I start to follow him – I don't like bullies. The kid in the NASA T-shirt comes and walks next me.

I want to tell you something," he says. 50

"What?" I ask.

"That's Mark James. He's **a big deal** round here. His dad is the town sheriff and he's the star of the football team. He was Sarah's boyfriend, but he isn't now. He's still angry about that. Be careful." 55

"Thanks," I say.

The kid hurries away. I go to the office so I can register for classes and start school.

Unit 7

Spend or save?

FACT

In the UK, teenagers spend over £1,000 a year on phones, MP3 players and downloads, £240 on haircuts and £300 on trainers.

1 The Big Question

Do you like shopping?

2 VOCABULARY

Your money

1. What's the name of your currency (the money in your country)? How many other currency names do you know? Which countries use them?

2. How much do these things cost in your country? Write a price.

   a a bottle of water [ ]
   b a cinema ticket [ ]
   c a pair of jeans [ ]
   d a music download [ ]
   e a magazine [ ]

3. Read the questionnaire on the next page. Then work with a partner. Ask and answer the questions. Circle your answers. Tell your partner more if you can.

4. Look at the information in the chart above. Do students in your class save more (>) or less (<) than young people in the UK?

How much do young people in the UK save?

9% save all their money

13% save three quarters (3/4)

23% save half (1/2)

29% don't save any money at all

2 ▸ 5. Listen. Write in column 1 how much money each person gets a month.

	1 Money	2 Where from?	3 Spend or save?
a Chloe			
b Jack			
c Andy			

2 ▸ 6. Listen again. Where do Chloe, Jack and Andy get their money from? Do they spend it or save it? Complete columns 2 and 3. Then compare with a partner.

Money words

7. Work with a partner. Complete the sentences with the correct money words.

allowance | prices | charity | currency

a When I buy something expensive, I compare ________________ online.
b I get an __________ every month but it's never enough.
c People use the ____________ of my country in other countries too.
d My school gives money to a local _______ .

spend | cost | earn | save

e I think it's important to work and ________ my own money.
f I ____________ a lot of money on my phone.
g I spend a lot of money and don't _______ much.
h I think music downloads ___________ too much.

8. Rewrite the sentences in exercise 7 for you.

YOUR GOALS

Vocabulary: money, clothes, adjectives to describe clothes
Communication: shopping, making comparisons
Grammar: comparatives and superlatives
CLIL: bank accounts

Questionnaire: You and your money

1 Do you get money every week or month? Where does your money come from?

a
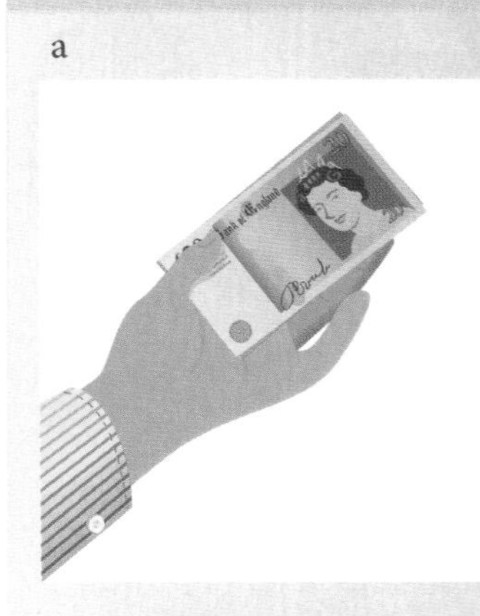
I get an allowance (every week / month).

b

I do extra jobs at home.

c

I earn money from a Saturday job / help my parents in their business.

d
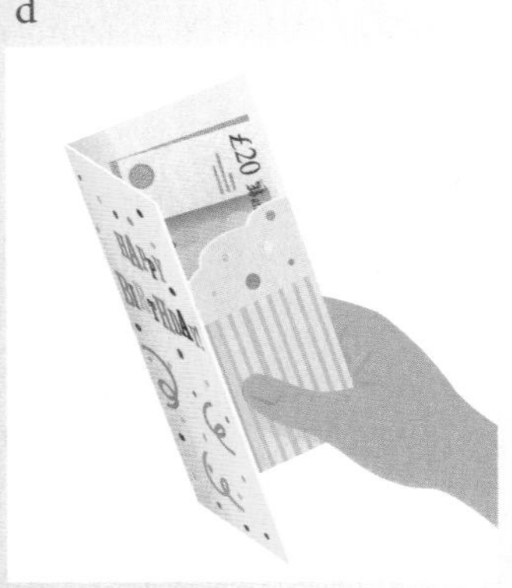
I often get money for my birthday.

2 How much money do you save?
a all of it. b at least half (> ½). c less than half (< ½). d I don't save any money.

3 Do you ever give money to charity (e.g. Greenpeace, the Red Cross)?
a Yes, often. b Sometimes. c No, never.

4 Do you spend money on birthday gifts?
a I buy gifts for my family. b I buy gifts for friends. c I don't usually buy gifts.

5 What do you spend money on for yourself?

a
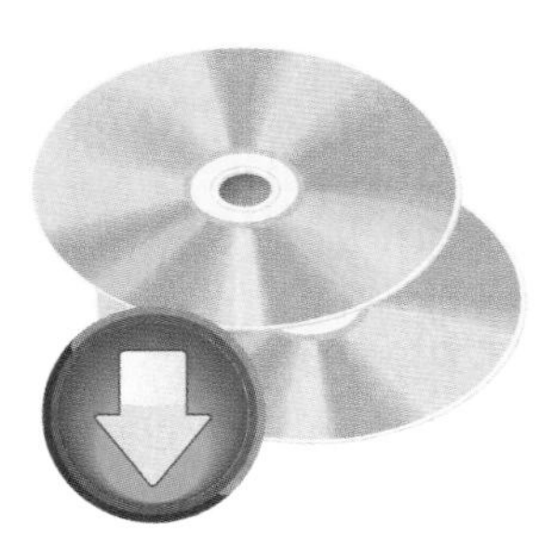
music downloads, DVDs, video games, magazines, comics, books

b

clothes and shoes, jewellery, makeup, sports clothes and equipment

c

phone (phone credit/ phone cards), apps, gadgets

d

cafés and coffee shops, takeaways, cinema tickets, concerts

3 LISTENING

Clothes

1 Can you remember the names of these clothes? Complete the words.

3 2 Listen to two American students. Where are they? What are they doing?

h T-________

k d________

a c________

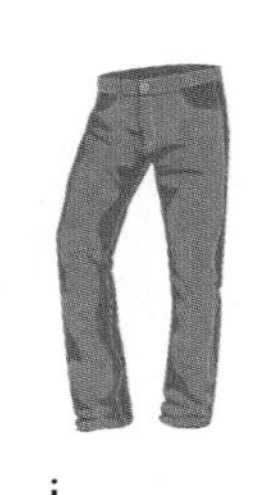
b j________

c s________

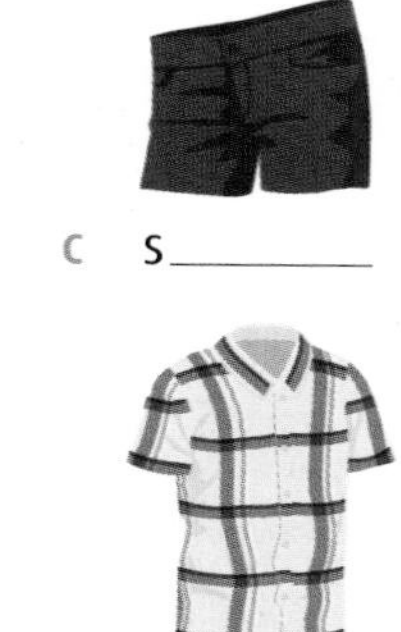
d s________

e s________

f t________

g t________

i s________

l j________

j s________

3 3 Listen again.

a What are the British words for the American words **pants** and **sneakers**?
b What does the second boy need to buy for a family party next week?

4 4 Match the questions and answers from the listening. Then listen again and check.

a How much are these pants?
b Do you have them in a bigger size?
c Can I try them on?

1 Umm, yes. Here you are.
2 Sure, the changing room is over there.
3 They're 25 dollars.

5 5 Four teenagers are describing their clothes. Draw a line from the right clothes to the teenager.

a sandals b glasses c baseball cap d scarf e boots f hoodie g sunglasses h top

Jerez

Marie

Nasreen

June

6 Make six pairs of opposites from the listening.

a expensive	1 light
b tight	2 trendy
c old-fashioned	3 long
d dark	4 comfortable
e short	5 cheap
f uncomfortable	6 baggy

6 7 **Pronunciation:** Listen to these words. Write the correct sound (/ʃ/, /sk/, /sw/) next to the word. Then listen again and repeat.

shorts ____ sweater ____
shirt ____ scarf ____
skirt ____ shoes ____

Your clothes

8 Walk round the class. Choose one student but don't tell him or her. Describe that person's clothes. Other students guess the name.

This person is wearing (a) blue / white / ...

Fashion shopping

9 Look at the photos of London fashion stylist Cristina. What do you think a fashion stylist does? Listen to a report about Cristina and check your ideas.

7 10 Read the sentences. Then listen again and tick the correct sentences.

- [ ] a Fashion stylists give people a strong look.
- [ ] b Stylists are very creative.
- [ ] c Cristina works in a fashion shop.
- [ ] d First, Cristina gets ideas for a style.
- [ ] e At a fashion shoot, she dresses the models.
- [ ] f She buys clothes for private customers.

13 11 Now watch the video. Would you like to have a fashion stylist?

12 Work with a partner. Ask and answer the questions.

a Do you follow fashion or is it important for you to look different? What clothes do you usually wear?
I love fashion! I like to wear different styles.
I like to look different. / I wear the same clothes as my friends.
I usually wear comfortable clothes / jeans and trainers / ...
I'm not interested in clothes.

b Do you often wear clothes from the same brand? Why?
I often wear clothes by ... because they're cool. / I like their style. / Everyone wears them. / ...
I never buy clothes because of a brand.

c Do you like shopping for clothes?
Yes, I love clothes shopping. / No, I hate it!

4 ROLE PLAY

1 Work with a partner.
Partner A: You are shopping. Look at your role card on page 115.
Partner B: You are a shop assistant. Look at your role card on page 121.

2 Swap roles.
Partner A: You are a shop assistant. Look at your role card on page 114.
Partner B: You are shopping. Look at your role card on page 119.

3 Now make your own clothes shopping dialogues.

38 LANGUAGE BANK 13

5 READING

Does stuff make you happy?

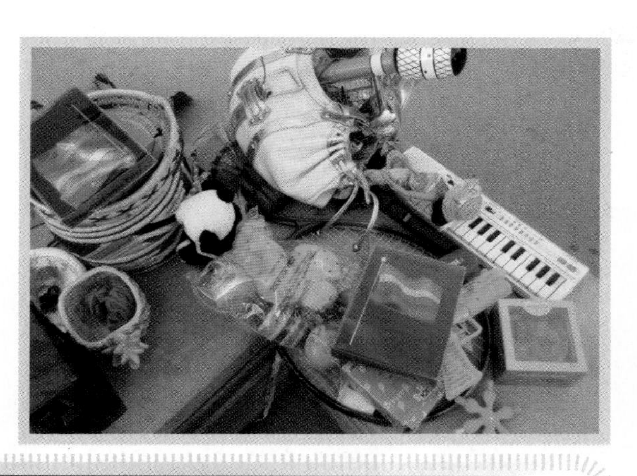

1 Look at the picture and the title of the text. What do you think *stuff* is? Then read *The Story of Stuff* and check.

a clothes and shoes
b gadgets, CDs, DVDs, video games
c bikes and sports equipment
d furniture and other things for your room
e all of the things in **a-d** and lots more things

The Story of Stuff

Do you have too much stuff? We all buy stuff. We throw it away. Then we buy more stuff and throw that away ... But does stuff make us happier? And what happens to all our old stuff? The Story of Stuff Project *is an American project. It's about where things come from and where they go. Read what they say.*

make → buy → throw away

We are using too many of the world's resources: things like trees and water. For example, in the USA, only 4% of the forests are still standing. A lot of factories use chemicals to make stuff. These chemicals pollute the air and some of them stay in our gadgets, furniture and clothes. 5

Companies want people to buy new things. So they change how things look. Then adverts tell us: 'Your stuff is old-fashioned.' So we buy trendier clothes or a more expensive phone. We want to have all the newest gadgets and the most interesting things. Americans buy 50% more stuff today than 50 years ago. 10

The USA makes 30% of the world's garbage. Every person in the USA makes 4.5 pounds of garbage (two kg of rubbish) a day.

make less → buy less → recycle more

Americans today have more stuff than 20 years ago. They're richer than Americans 20 years ago. But are they happier? No. Americans and people in many other countries are actually 5 unhappier today.

We can recycle some things (like glass and paper) and reuse other things. Great! This saves resources and is better for the environment. But it's not 10 enough. The best thing is to make less and buy less.

2 Read the text again. Answer true (**T**) or false (**F**). *The Story of Stuff* says ...

a We're not taking care of our world. ☐
b People buy new stuff because their clothes and gadgets aren't trendy. ☐
c People in the USA throw away too much stuff. ☐
d Americans are happier today. ☐
e We can recycle everything. ☐
f We need to buy more stuff. ☐

3 Find words **a-e** in the text and match them to the correct pictures (**1–5**).

a factory **b** chemicals **c** pollute **d** garbage (US) / rubbish **e** recycle

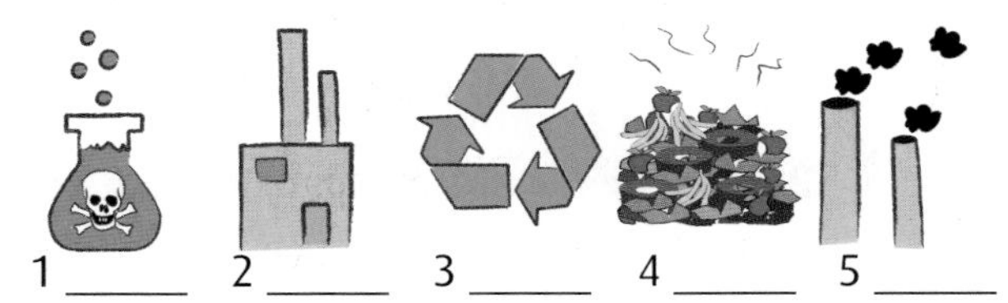

1 ____ 2 ____ 3 ____ 4 ____ 5 ____

4 Does new stuff make you happier? What do you do with the old stuff?

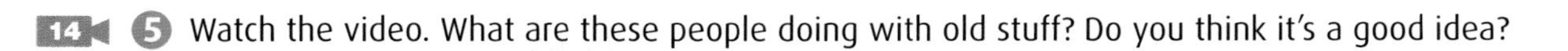

14 **5** Watch the video. What are these people doing with old stuff? Do you think it's a good idea?

6 GRAMMAR

Comparatives and superlatives

1. Look at these sentences from the text. Complete the box below with the words in bold.

   a We buy **trendier** clothes, or a **more expensive** phone.
   b We want to have all **the newest** gadgets and **the most interesting** things.
   c Recycling is **better** for the environment.
   d The **best** thing is to buy less.
   e They're **richer than** Americans 20 years ago.

Adjective	Comparative	Superlative
Short adjectives		
new	newer	
trendy		the trendiest
Long adjectives		
expensive		the most expensive
interesting	more interesting	
Irregular adjectives		
good		
bad	worse	the worst
We use comparative (e.g. richer) +__________ to compare two things or people.		

2. Look at the box in exercise 1. Underline the endings for comparative and superlative forms.

3. Complete the sentences with the correct words.

the most expensive	cooler	the thinnest
more old-fashioned	heavier	smaller

   a Computer 1 is ... than the other two computers.
   b Computer 2 is ... than computer 1.
   c Computer 3 is ... .
   d The red phone is ... than the black phone.
   e The white phone is ... than the red phone.
   f The black phone is ... .

4. Now compare these things. Write sentences like exercise 3. Use words from the box.

long	warm	uncomfortable	dark
tight	cheap	interesting	baggy

7 CONVERSATION

1. Work with a partner. Think of one thing you both have (a bike, a school bag, a mobile phone).
2. Make notes to compare (colour, cost, how old etc).
3. Look at the diagram. With your partner make a diagram like this about your one thing:

   In the centre: Write what is the same for you both.
   In the left circle: Write what is different for **Partner A**.
   In the right circle: Write what is different for **Partner B**.

4. Then tell the class.
   Partner A and B: *We both have black shoes.*
   Partner A: *My shoes are older / cheaper / smarter than Lucy's shoes.*
   Partner B: *Her shoes are more comfortable / more uncomfortable than my shoes.*

39 LANGUAGE BANK 14

8 CLIL: Bank accounts

FACT

31% of people in the UK don't use online banking because they're scared about crime.

1. Do you have a bank account? Can you use it online?

2. Read the text. Answer the questions.
   - a How much interest do banks in the UK pay? How much interest do you get on your account?
   - b At what age can you get a credit card in the UK? What age is it in your country?
   - c Are bank statements on paper, online or both? How do you check your statement?
   - d What do scam emails and websites do? Are you careful with your bank account information?

Account statement

William King *Account number*: 00648730

Date	Description	In	Out	Balance (£)
5 Feb	Debit card *Look Fantastic*		14.99	67.52
1 Feb	Bank credit	60		82.51

About bank accounts in the UK

- Most young people have a **savings account**. You put money in this account and you get **interest** so your money earns more money (1-6%).
- For your account you usually have a **debit card** so you can get money out. For this card you have a secret number: a **PIN number.**
- You can only use a debit card if you have money in your account: it isn't a **credit card**. With a credit card, you can borrow money.
- Your **bank statement** shows you how much money goes in and out of your account. It also shows **your balance**: how much money is in your account now.
- With an online account, you can check your statement online. For online banking you need a safe **password**.
- Careful: **scam emails** or **scam websites** try to get your bank information online.

3. Read the text again and complete the tips below. Use six of the words in **bold** in the text.

Keep your money safe!

1 Keep your ... in a safe place. Tell the bank if you lose it.

2 Remember the ... for your card: don't write it down.

3 Cut old paper bank ... into small pieces.

4 Think of a safe ... with numbers and letters. Don't use your name or your birthday.

5 Always check your bank account on a safe computer. Check that websites aren't ... Look for 🔒.

6 NEVER answer ... NEVER send anybody your bank information.

4. **Your topic**: Choose a topic linked to this unit – something interesting for **you.** For example, you can choose your favourite shop, a famous person you admire because of their style, what makes you happy, recycling at your school etc.
   - Think of **four discussion points** about this topic. Make a **mind map**.
   - Make **notes** about these four points.
   - Think of a **question** about your topic.
   - Talk about your points with a partner. Answer questions and ask your question.

9 WRITING

Ivy's best buy

1 **Read:** Look at Ivy's poster. Read about her best buy. Why was it her best buy?

Your best buy

2 **Prepare:** Think about your best buy. Use the boxes to help you.

What was your best buy?
My best buy was *a T-shirt / a pair of jeans / a video game / some football boots /...*

Where was it from? How much was it?
It was *from a shop / market / an online shop.*
It was *quite cheap / expensive / free.*
It was *in the sale / on special offer / a gift.*
I can't remember the price.

Can you describe it?
They're *dark blue / light green / baggy / really comfortable / long / trendy /...*
It's *small / fast / not very heavy / ...*
The *book / film* is about ...
In the game you need to ...

Why was it your best buy?
It was really cheap.
It looks *great / really trendy.*
They're more comfortable than my other jeans.
It's / they're *better / faster / warmer / trendier / than my old ...*
It's the *newest / fastest / smallest* model.
I *wear / use / play / listen to* it all the time.

3 **Write and share:** Make your poster. Take or draw a picture of your best buy and write about it. Show your poster to your partner.
Do it online! Make an online poster.

My Best Buy
My best buy was a memory box.
The box was from China. It was from a Chinese store. It was very cheap. It was about 20 dollars.
The colour of the box is jade green and its shape is a square. The box is wood and the middle of it is plastic. It is easy to see what is inside of the box. The box is small, but there is enough space in the box for letters and little gifts, notes and cards. It is really useful to me.
I love this box because it helps me keep my important memories. Inside the box are important moments and pictures. And I like to put things in the box. That is why I think it is my best buy.

Ivy, China

10 Your Answer

Do you like shopping?

Do you get an allowance or do you earn money?
Do you spend or save your money?
Do you have a bank account?
Do you spend your money on clothes?
Do you feel happier when you buy stuff?

YOUR SCORE

Can you use all the language below?
Yes ☺, *No* ☹ or *Almost* 😐

Vocabulary:	money ☐ clothes	☐
	adjectives to describe clothes	☐
Communication:	shopping	☐
	making comparisons	☐
Grammar:	comparatives and superlatives	☐
CLIL:	bank accounts	☐

Unit 8

Holidays!

1 The Big Question

Was your last holiday brilliant or boring?

2 VOCABULARY

Home and abroad

8 ❶ Look at the flags in the list in the Fact box. Do you know any of the countries? Write the names. Then listen and check.

8 ❷ **Pronunciation**: Listen again and underline the stress. Then listen and repeat.

❸ Answer the questions.

a Where do people in your country go on holiday? Do they prefer to stay in your country or go abroad?
b Where was your last holiday?

Great places to stay!

9 ❹ Match the photos of the five places (**1–5**) with the correct descriptions (**a–e**). Then listen and check.

a a **hostel** in an old prison in Latvia
b a small **guest house** on a *lake* in Sweden
c a plane at a luxury **hotel** in the *rainforest* of Costa Rica
d a beautiful **campsite** in a *field* in the English countryside
e a train at a **motel** in the *mountains* in Arizona, USA

9 ❺ Listen again. Write the correct place (**1–5**).

a There are beautiful *forests* here. ☐
b You have your own boat to visit the next *island*. ☐
c You can stay in a **tent** or **caravan** and have a bath outside. ☐
d You can also stay in a **holiday apartment** by the *sea* here. ☐
e You have an uncomfortable room. ☐

FACT

Top 10 most popular holiday countries:

1 
2 
3 
4 
5 
6 
7 
8 
9 
10 

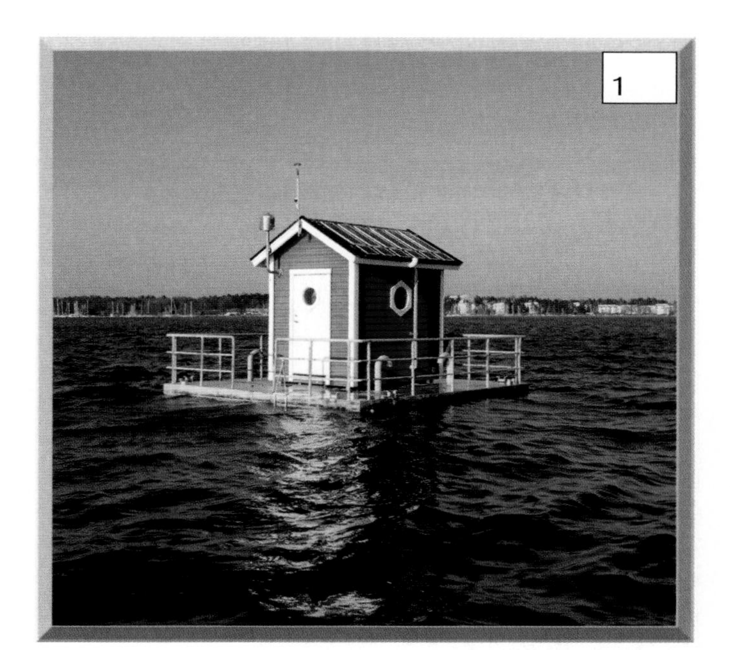

1

2

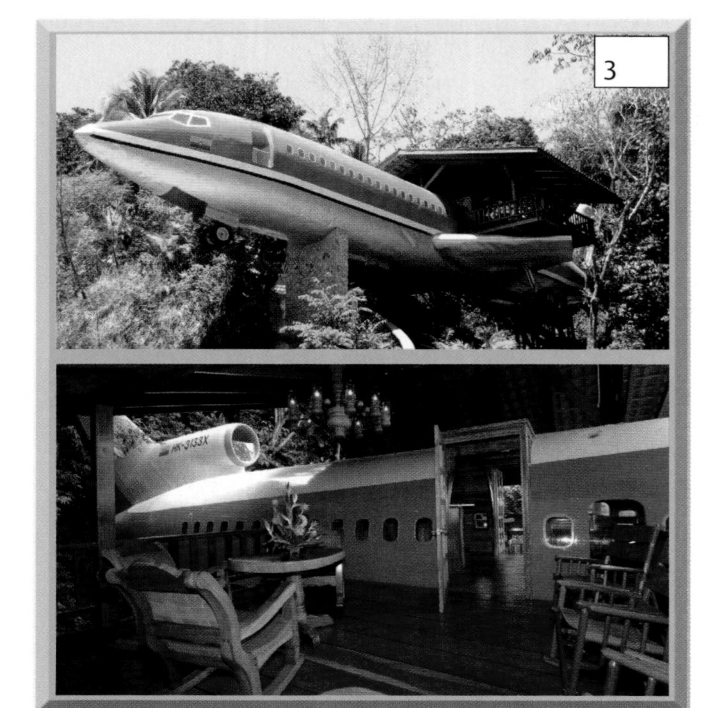

YOUR GOALS

Vocabulary:	holidays and travel, expressions of past time
Communication:	talking about your last school holidays, talking about embarrassing events
Grammar:	the past simple
CLIL:	ecotourism

6 Match the words in **bold** in exercises 4 and 5 with the correct meanings.

a a place to stay on holiday with breakfast and other meals ________
b you can carry this small house and sleep outdoors in it ________
c a cheap hotel, often for young people ________
d you can travel with this home behind a car or horse ________
e a small hotel ________
f a place with a bedroom, bathroom and kitchen ________
g a place to sleep outdoors ________
h a hotel near a road for people in cars ________

7 Write the words for these places (**a–h**). Use the words in *italics* in exercises 4 and 5.

8 Where would you like to stay? Why?

I'd like to stay at ... I wouldn't like to stay in ... .
It looks exciting / uncomfortable / quiet / too small / scary / beautiful / ... .

3 LISTENING

Great days out

1. Look at the website. Do you know any of these places? Which places do you think look most interesting?

2. (10) Listen. A Scottish family is on holiday in London. They're talking about the day trips on the website.
   a Number the places in the order of the conversation.
   b Tick the correct place for the family's trip.

3. (10) Listen again. Why don't they go to the other places? Make notes. Then compare with a partner.

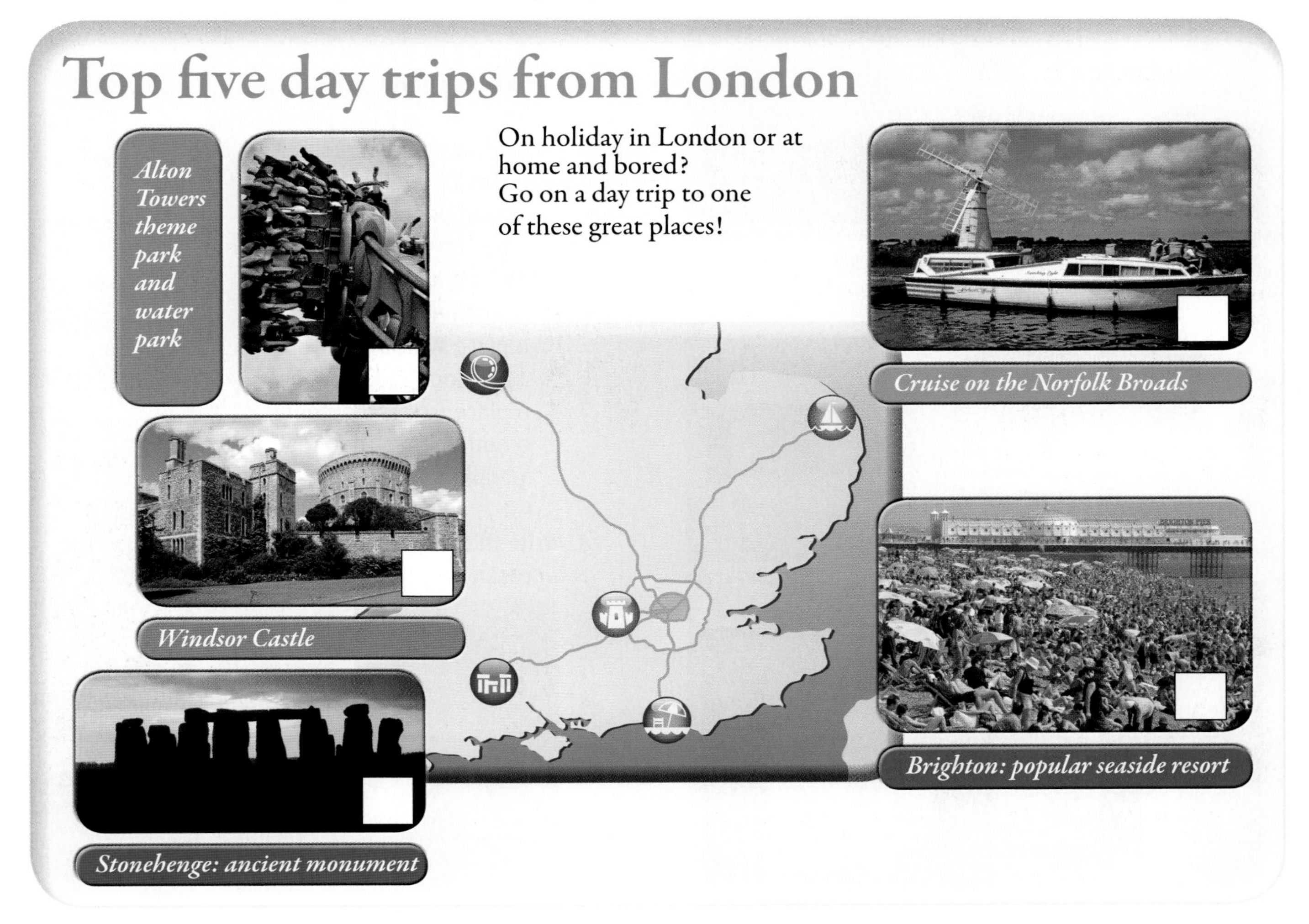

Top five day trips from London
On holiday in London or at home and bored?
Go on a day trip to one of these great places!
Alton Towers theme park and water park
Cruise on the Norfolk Broads
Windsor Castle
Brighton: popular seaside resort
Stonehenge: ancient monument

4. Match the two parts of the sentence.

a	When you go on a day trip	1	there are usually rules for tourists.
b	When you visit an ancient monument	2	you don't stay overnight.
c	When you go to a theme park	3	you travel by boat on a river or lake.
d	When you go to a seaside resort	4	you can go on scary rides.
e	When you go on a cruise	5	you can usually see old furniture and paintings.
f	When you visit a castle	6	you can go to the beach.

5. Work with a partner. Write a website description for a good place for a day trip in your area or country. Tell another pair about your place.

Summer camp

15 **6** Read the advert and watch the video. Answer the questions about Camp Echo.

a What is Camp Echo Lake?
b How long is camp?
c What do campers do?
d Do you have summer camps like this in your country?

11 **7** Listen to Seth. He was at Camp Echo Lake last year. What was the best thing about camp for him?

11 **8** Listen again. Tick the correct pictures and sentences for Seth.

Are you interested in the outdoors?

Why not try summer camp at Camp Echo Lake in the Adirondack Mountains, 3.5 hours north of New York City. All campers stay 51 days and do a full program of activities.

These are some of our facilities:

10 basketball courts
4 soccer fields
16 tennis courts
an indoor fitness center
a dance studio
an art center
a theater
an outdoor center
three pools
three power boats
... and Echo Lake

1 I met some interesting people and made new friends.

2 I had tennis lessons.

3 I swam in the lake every day.

CEL MENU
Breakfast
Muffins & Scrambled Eggs
Juice
Lunch
Sandwich board & Chips
Salad & Pasta
Dinner
Grilled Chicken- Cookout
Corn on Cob
Potato Salad
Pasta w/Oil/Garlic
Watermelon

4 I ate healthy food all summer.

5 I went rock climbing in the mountains.

6 I went water skiing and fell in the water.

7 I saw a black bear on a hiking trip and I took a photo.

8 I told scary stories around the campfire.

9 Complete the report. Use words from exercise 8.

A friend (1) *told* me about Camp Echo Lake. The arts center there was amazing. I (2) __________ lessons in wood work and I (3) __________ a really cool CD shelf for my room. The theater group was good too – we (4) __________ lots of good performances. I (5) __________ on the lake a lot in a power boat but I never (6) __________ in the lake – it was just too cold!

4 ROLE PLAY

1 **Partner A:** Look at page 115. Tell your partner about your school holidays last year. **Partner B:** Listen and make notes for an article about holidays.

2 Swap roles. **Partner B:** Look at page 120.

3 Tell your partner something about your last school holidays.

LANGUAGE BANK 15

5 READING

1 Read these holiday stories. Choose the best title for each story.

a Not the teacher's favourite student
b A big fashion mistake
c Famous for the wrong reason
d How *not* to get a boyfriend
e Embarrassed and hungry

2 How embarrassing is each story? Work with a partner and decide.

 very embarrassing
 quite embarrassing
 not very embarrassing

Embarrassing holiday moments

Zak's story

I was late for breakfast in the hotel restaurant. I saw my sister at the buffet. So I went behind her, put my hands over her eyes and shouted hello right in her ear. But it wasn't my sister, it was another girl. So I didn't have breakfast at all and went out the restaurant fast.

Carla's story

My best friend's family invited me on holiday. On the first day at the beach, lots of people smiled at me. 'Very friendly,' I thought. Then her dad said, 'Erm, did you know about that? There was a big price ticket on the back of my new swimming costume. I went bright red.

Selena's story

On a family campsite holiday, there was a disco one night. Gilles, this really nice French boy, asked me to dance. We danced together, his face was next to mine and … a-a-a-atchoo! I sneezed all over his face. It was horrible. I said sorry and ran to the toilets. He didn't ask me to dance again.

Luke's story

My class went on a school snowboarding trip. I was really nervous and at the top of the hill I dropped my snowboard. It fell down the hill … and hit one of my teachers in the back of her leg. She fell in the snow and everyone in the class laughed. I felt terrible!

Max's story

I was on holiday at a seaside resort near my home town. One evening I sang a song with my dad at a karaoke night. It was so bad! A girl from my school was there and she filmed me on her phone and uploaded the video to YouTube. I told my dad and he phoned the girl's parents.

3 Read the stories again. Write what each person did or how they felt *after* their embarrassing moment.

a *Zak didn't … and …*
b *Selena said …*
c *Carla …*
d *Luke …*
e *Max …*

6 GRAMMAR

The past simple

1. Who did these things? Read the stories again and complete these sentences.

   a __________ danced together.
   b __________ smiled at Carla.
   c __________ shouted in a girl's ear.
   d __________ uploaded a video.
   e __________ phoned a girl's parents.
   f __________ dropped something.

2. Look at the sentences in exercise 1. Underline the ends of the verbs and complete the rule.

> For the past simple form we add _____ to the verb.
> For spelling changes, see Workbook page 38.
> The ending is the same for all people (*I*, *she*, etc).

12 3. **Pronunciation:** The verbs in exercise 1 end in one of the sounds below.

   /d/ /t/ /ɪd/

   a Listen to the verbs and repeat the sounds.
   b Listen again and write the correct sound next to each verb.

4. Complete the text with the correct past simple form of these regular verbs.

> I was at the breakfast buffet with my best friend. I (1 collect) __________ some food and then I (2 want) ________ to get a drink. I (3 walk) __________ over to the drinks, but there was milk on the floor. Suddenly I fell and I (4 drop) __________ my food. My friend (5 try) __________ to help me but I (6 pull) __________ her down too. Everyone in the room (7 laugh) __________. I nearly (8 die) __________ of embarrassment.

5. Irregular simple past forms don't end in *–ed*. Underline ten irregular simple past forms on page 144. What verbs are they from?

6. Work with a partner. Tick (✓) the words you can use with the past simple. Make sentences with them.

   yesterday ☐ last week ☐ now ☐
   two years ago ☐ at the moment ☐
   in 2010 ☐

7. Look at the examples and complete the rule.

   He didn't ask me to dance again.
   Did you know about that?

> In the **present simple** we use *do / does* + verb to make negatives and questions.
> In the **past simple** (regular and irregular verbs) we use __________ + verb.

8. Make questions.

   a what / you / eat / yesterday?
   b you / go / to school yesterday?
   c when / get up / this morning?
   d you / have / homework yesterday?
   e how / you / come to school today?

9. Answer the questions in exercise 8.

7 CONVERSATION

1. Work with a partner. Think about your most embarrassing moment or imagine one. Make notes – use the questions.

   When did it happen? Where were you?
   Who were you with? What did you do then?
   What did you or somebody else do?

2. Ask and answer the questions.

41 LANGUAGE BANK 16

FACT

The largest sea turtle in the world is over two metres long and weighs 900 kilos!

8 CLIL: Ecotourism

1. Look at the pictures. What are the names of these animals in your language?
2. Read about these animals in Mexico. Why were they in danger?

Protected places

In southern Mexico, along the Pacific Ocean, you can see amazing animals in their own habitat. There are sea turtles, iguanas, dolphins and even crocodiles.

There are many types of turtles in the area. Turtles make deep holes in the sand on the beach for their eggs. But turtle eggs are a popular food in Mexico. Hunters often came to the area and took the eggs to sell. People opened the Mexican Turtle Centre in Mazunte to protect the turtles. The centre gives them food, and takes care of them. The turtles can grow and have their babies in a safe place. In the summer, guards protect the eggs from hunters.

Other places in the area protect animals like the iguana. Hunters often took iguanas for their skin and their meat or to sell as pets. Some people were worried about the future of the iguanas, so they started iguana farms to protect them.

Iguana

Turtles

What is ecotourism?

'Take only pictures and leave only footprints'

Ecotourism is 'green travel'. It ...

- ***protects / hurts* the environment of natural areas.**
- **helps *local people / tourists*, especially in poor areas.**
- **is a *simple / luxury* form of travel.**
- **is popular in places like Mexico, South and Central America, *Southeast Europe / Asia*, the Pacific Islands, and Africa.**

3. Read the text *Protected places* again, and answer the questions.
   - a What other animals can you see in Southern Mexico?
   - b Where do turtles lay their eggs?
   - c Why did people open the Mexican Turtle Centre?
   - d What does the centre do for turtles?
   - e Why did people start iguana farms?
4. The Mexican Turtle Centre and the iguana farms are popular ecotourism attractions. Read the text. What is ecotourism? Choose the right words.
5. (16) Watch the video. Would you like to go on an ecotourism holiday? Why/Why not?
6. **Your topic:** Choose a topic linked to this unit – something interesting for **you**. For example, you can choose a country you find interesting, a holiday place in your country, an animal in danger in your area etc.

   Think of **four discussion points** about this topic. Make a **mind map**.

   - Make **notes** about these four points.
   - Think of a **question** about your topic.
   - Talk about your points with a partner. Answer questions and ask your question.

9 WRITING

Marie's best holiday

1. **Read:** Look at Marie's story. Read about her best holiday. Why was it good?

Your holiday

2. **Prepare:** Think about your best or worst holiday. Use the boxes to help you.

When was your best/worst holiday?
Where did you go? Who with?
My best holiday was *last year / two years ago / ...*
My family and I *went to Spain / the mountains / ...*
I went *with my family / with my school /...*

How did you get there?
Where did you stay? How long?
We went *by plane / car / train / ...*
We stayed *in a hotel / caravan / at a campsite / ...*
We stayed there *for two weeks / ...*
It was *only a day / weekend trip.*

What was the weather like?
What did you do?
It was *sunny / cold / ...*
We went *sightseeing / walking / swimming / ...*
We played *tennis / volleyball / ...*

Why was it good or bad?
It was *a fantastic / terrible holiday* because ...
... the people were *friendly/unfriendly.*
... *the campsite / food* was great.

3. **Write and share:** Write a story about your best or worst holiday. Draw or find pictures or use photos, brochures and postcards.
Do it online! Visit an online story site and publish your story.

My Best Holiday

My best holiday was four months ago. All my friends and I went to Turkey with school. Students in every grade came on the trip. We all went by plane. First we flew to another city in Germany and then we flew with another plane to Izmir in Turkey.

1

We stayed in Izmir for one week and in Kusadasi one week. We stayed in a hotel. It was really sunny there. We went to the pool or the beach every day. All of us got really brown. Some days we went to visit a museum or other things.

2

It was a fantastic holiday. We bought a lot of clothes and I bought some souvenirs for my parents. All my friends were with me, the food was good and we all had a great time together.

3

Marie, Germany

YOUR SCORE

Can you use all the language below?

Yes ☺, *No* ☹ or *Almost* 😐

Vocabulary:	holidays and travel	☐
Communication:	expressions of past time	☐
	talking about the last school holidays	☐
	talking about embarrassing events	☐
Grammar:	the past simple	☐
CLIL:	ecotourism	☐

10 Your Answer

Was your last holiday brilliant or boring?

When was your last holiday?
Where did you go?
Where did you stay?
What did you do?
What was brilliant or boring about it?

Unit 9

FACT

A man from the Czech Republic has over 200,000 bus tickets from 36 countries!

Loves and hates

HOBBY FACT CARD

Name ______

Hobby ______

Started ______

Why he / she likes this hobby

______

1 The Big Question

What do you love doing?

2 VOCABULARY

Hobbies

1. Read about the makers and collectors on page 77. Make a hobby fact card for each of them. Which hobby sounds most interesting?

13 2. Listen to Fabrizio, Mel and Oliver. Who has the most hobbies?

13 3. Match the words (**a–h**) with the pictures in the networks. Then listen again and check.

a stamps b key rings c videos d cakes e postcards f clothes g coins h model planes

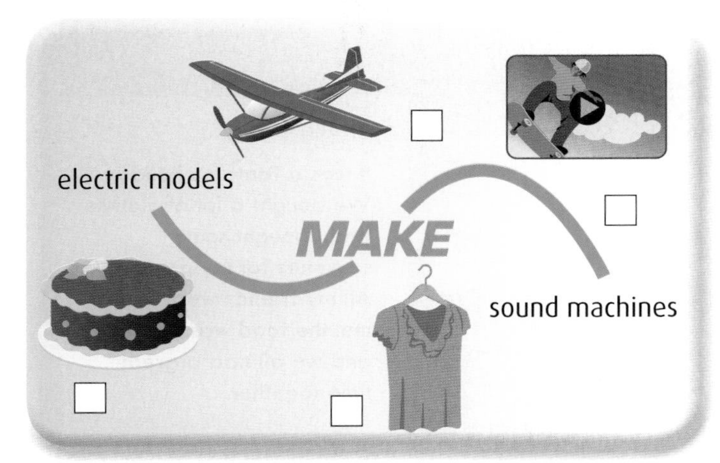

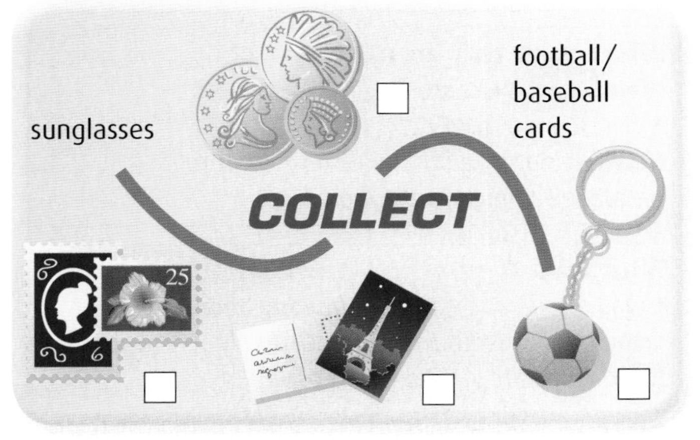

14 4. **Pronunciation:** Listen to the sounds in bold and repeat. Then hold a piece of paper in front of your mouth. Read out the words. When does the paper move most?

foo**t** **b**all **p**ost car**ds**

5. Work with a partner. Say the four words fast, again and again. Who can say the words the most times without a mistake?

17 6. David and Katie are at a Maker Faire. People at these events have all kinds of creative hobbies. Watch the video. Would you like to visit a Maker Faire? Why or why not?

My hobby

7. Do you collect anything? Or make anything? Do any of your family or friends? Tell the class.

8. Make a fact card about your hobby now or when you were younger. Then tell a partner.

My hobby is … . I started it two years ago / when I was …
I like this hobby because …
When I was small / about eight / … my hobby was …
I liked it because …

YOUR GOALS

Vocabulary:	hobbies, sports
Communication:	talking about hobbies and sports, talking about likes and dislikes
Grammar:	*like* + to do / doing link word *but*
CLIL:	phobias

MAKERS

My name's David and this is a flying machine. I'm part of a group of about 50 people. We make things with electronics, wood, metal, all sorts of things. I started this hobby about one and a half years ago. I really like to build things.

I'm Katie. This is a sound machine. My dad is a sound designer and he made it from three different machines. I make machines with my dad. I think it's nice we can do this hobby together.

COLLECTORS

I'm Rommel. I started to collect old baseball and American football cards five years ago. I have over a hundred now. I like this hobby because I can swap things with friends and people on the internet. It's exciting to find or get something new.

My name's Maholy and I collect sunglasses. I collect them because I'm interested in fashion and I like to find different styles and colours. I started to collect them about a year ago.

FACT

In 1978, two table tennis players from the USA, played a game for 132 hours and 31 minutes.

3 LISTENING

Super sports

1. Are you sporty? Do this mini quiz. Check your answers on page 115. Then tell the class.

Are you super sporty?

1 Do you like sport?
- A Yes! I can't live without it!
- B It's OK. I like to keep fit.
- C No, I hate it! TV and computer games are much better.

2 Do you do sport?
- A Yes, all the time – at school and in my free time.
- B Sometimes at the weekend.
- C Only in school sports lessons.

3 Are you in a team or a member of a club?
- A Yes, I'm in a team. It's fantastic to do sport with other people.
- B No, I prefer to do sport on my own.
- C Ugh! I hate sports teams and clubs.

2. Work with a partner. What sports do you know in English? Make a list. Then compare with the class.

15 3. Listen to the sports in 1–10. Match them with the correct pictures (**a–j**).

1	ice-skating	☐	6	gymnastics	☐
2	athletics	☐	7	skateboarding	☐
3	riding	☐	8	baseball	☐
4	table tennis	☐	9	cycling	☐
5	(field) hockey	☐	10	volleyball	☐

16 4. **Pronunciation:** Listen to the sports in exercise 3 and underline the stress. Then listen again and repeat.

17 5. Listen. Write the sports for the speakers (**1–4**). Write if the sport is a school activity (S) or a free time activity (F).

Speaker 1 ____________________
Speaker 2 ____________________
Speaker 3 ____________________
Speaker 4 ____________________

17 6. Write the sports in exercise 3 with the correct verbs. Then listen again and check.

play	**go**	**do**
______	______	______

7. Complete the sentences (**a–c**) about you and add three more. Use phrases from exercise 6.

a I play ...
b I sometimes go ...
c I never do ...

Fight for football

8 Look at the photo of girl football players in Afghanistan. What do you know about this country?

18 9 Listen to a report about girl's football in Afghanistan. Complete the two sentences with the best answers.

For many years, girls ...

a couldn't do sports in Afghanistan.
b could only watch football in Afghanistan.

Today in Afghanistan, girls ...

a can play football but there are still a lot of problems.
b can play football but they don't want to play.

18 10 Listen again. Tick the problems for these girl football players.

a men's opinions ☐
b parents' opinions ☐
c too much homework ☐
d no football pitches ☐
e no money for equipment ☐
f clothes ☐

11 Work with a partner. Talk about the questions.

a Do boys and girls play football in your country? Is it more difficult for girls?
b Does football bring people together? Is this true for all sports?

Sports equipment

12 Complete the sports card.

Sport:	*Football*
Place:	____________
Equipment:	*two goals and a* ________
Clothes:	____________

13 Now look at the equipment below. Which sports do you use these things for?
You use a ... for ...

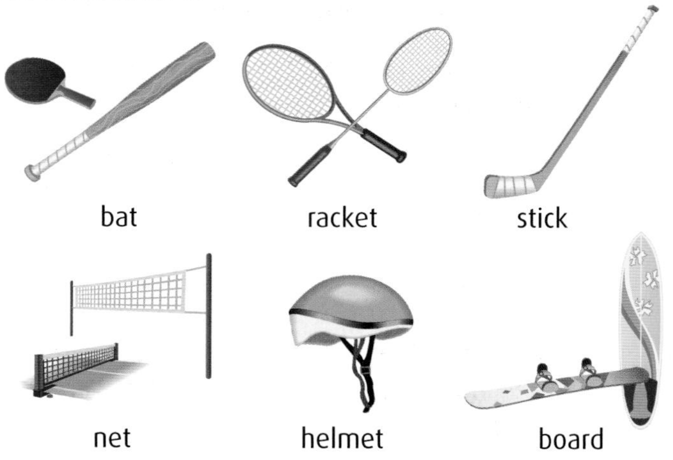

14 Work with a partner. Choose two sports and make cards like the one in exercise 12.

4 ROLE PLAY

1 **Partner A:** Ask Partner B about his / her favourite sport.
Partner B: Look at your role card on page 120. Answer the questions.

2 Swap roles.
Partner B: Ask Partner A about his / her favourite sport.
Partner A: Look at your role card on page 115. Answer the questions.

3 Talk about your favourite sports.

42 LANGUAGE BANK 17

5 READING

1 Look at the photos and the title. What is Shaun White's nickname? Why?

2 Do a reading race: Work with a partner. Look at the photos and read the texts. Find the answers as fast as you can!

a What two sports does Shaun White do?
b How old is he?
c When did he get his first snowboard?
d When did he become a professional sportsperson?
e How many Olympic gold medals does he have?
f What three things is snowboarding about?
g What does Shaun still want to do?
h What musical instrument does he play?

The flying tomato

Biography of Shaun White

Born: San Diego, California, 1986

Family: Mom, Dad, brother, sister

Became professional snowboarder: age 13

Became professional skateboarder: age 17

Medals: Gold medal in snowboarding Winter Olympics 2006 and 2010

16 X Games medals (11 gold) for snowboarding and skateboarding

Shaun White is crazy about sport. When he was very small, he often went skiing in the mountains with his family. He was fast and wild on skis. So when he was only six years old, his mother bought him a snowboard. She wanted him to slow down but Shaun didn't like going slow. The boy with red hair soon became 'the flying tomato'. 5

Today Shaun White has two Olympic gold medals but he still wants to be better. He hates to do the same things again and again. He prefers to learn new things. Music often helps him get ideas for new tricks. He loves listening to rock bands and he also likes playing the guitar.

Snowboarding is ...

"about having fun, with your friends or by yourself. It's about pushing yourself to try new things ... and most importantly, it's about being creative."

3 Complete the sentences with the words.

professional | crazy about something | gold medal | push yourself

a You get a ______ when you are first in a competition.
b You are a ______ when you do a sport as a job.
c You ______ when you want to be better.
d You are ______ when you love it.

4 Do you have a sports hero? What is his / her sport? Why do you like him or her?

6 GRAMMAR

Like + to do / doing

1. Complete the sentences from the text on page 80. Then complete the rule.

Shaun ...

a hates ______________ the same thing.
b prefers ______________ new things.
c loves ______________ to rock bands.
d likes ______________ the guitar.

To talk about likes and dislikes use *like / love / hate / prefer*

and ______ +verb (infinitive)
OR verb +______ (gerund).
For spelling changes, see Workbook page 44.

2. Complete the text about Shaun White. Use the *-ing* form of the verbs.

Shaun loves (1 *travel*) __________, especially to Japan. Shaun also likes (2 *design*) __________ snowboarding clothes and equipment. At home, he likes (3 *hang*) __________ out with family, friends and his dog Rambo. He likes (4 *eat*) __________ Chinese food and (5 *go*) __________ to steakhouses.

and or but

3. Look at the examples. Complete the sentences in the rule box with *and* or *but.*

a She wanted him to slow down **but** Shaun didn't like going slow.
b He loves listening to rock **and** he also likes playing the guitar.

We use __________ to add a similar idea.

We use __________ to add a contrast or a different idea.

4. Read Patricia's poem. Then write your poem. Complete the phrases in **bold** about you. Show your poem to a partner.

I am Patricia.
I love listening to music, playing volleyball and dancing.
But I don't like getting up early, playing football or tidying my room.
This is why I am me.

7 CONVERSATION

1. Look at the questionnaire. Walk round the room and ask questions. Write one name for each like or dislike.

2. Ask one more question. Write the answer.
Do you like going to school? – Yes I do. Why do you like going to school?

3. Share with the class.
Olivia likes going to school. She likes learning new things.

Find out! Who ...

likes		doesn't like	
going to school?	______	tidying their room?	______
getting up early?	______	playing football?	______
doing homework?	______	doing sport?	______
travelling?	______	chatting on the internet?	______
going ice-skating?	______	singing?	______

43 LANGUAGE BANK 18

8 CLIL: Phobias

1 Look at the pictures and words. A lot of people hate these things. Do you (or family members or friends) hate them? Do you hate anything else?

2 Now read the information about phobias. Answer the questions.

a How many kinds of phobias are there? What are they?
b When do you know you have a phobia?
c What can you do when you have a phobia?

Phobias

Lots of people don't like spiders or the dentist. But for some people the problem is so bad it's a 'phobia'.

There are three different kinds of phobias:

1 **Specific phobias**: When you're scared of a specific thing like snakes or flying. Specific phobias are the most common phobias. There are specific phobias for nearly everything. For example:

clouds

beards

clowns

2 **Social phobias**: When you are in a social or public situation: For example, when you give a presentation or go to a party.

3 **Agorophobia**: This is when people are afraid to leave home or a safe area.

A phobia is not the same as hating something. You have a phobia when you …
… are afraid over a long time.
… feel sick or you can't breathe.
… do anything to avoid the situation or thing.
… can't enjoy life because of it.

You can get help. You can …
… learn exercises to relax.
… take medicine if it's really bad.
… learn to face your phobia.

3 Work with a partner. Match the words from the text with the definitions.

a feel sick
b breathe
c avoid
d relax
e medicine
f face

1 it helps you when you're ill
2 keep away from something
3 learn to live with something difficult
4 feel very ill
5 become calmer
6 take in air

18 4 Watch the video. Do you have any of the same phobias?

5 **Your topic:** Choose a topic linked to this unit – something interesting for **you.** For example, you can choose the most popular sport in your country or your school, a hobby you do or you would like to try, a creative event or sports event in your area etc.

- Think of **four discussion points** about this topic. Make a **mind map**.
- Make **notes** about these four points.
- Think of a **question** about your topic.
- Talk about your points with a partner. Answer questions and ask your question.

9 WRITING

Cathy's favourite sport

1. **Read:** Look at Cathy's presentation. Read about her favourite sport. Why does she like it?

Your favourite sport

2. **Prepare:** Think about your favourite sport. Use the boxes to help you.

What's your favourite sport? Do you play or / and watch it?
My favourite sport is ...
I play it *at school / in a club / ...*
I'm in *the ... team*
I play ... on a computer game.
I don't play ... but I watch it on TV.

Why do you like this sport?
I love *playing / watching ...*
because *it's exciting / it keeps me fit / ...*

Do you have a sports hero?
My sports hero is ...
He's / She's *a footballer / plays ...*
He / She won ... *medals at the Olympics / World Championships in ...*
I like *him / her* because ...

What new sport would you like to try?
I'd like to try ... *(because ...)*

3. **Write and share:** Write about your favourite sport. Draw pictures and use photos to make a presentation for the class.
Do it online! Make an online slide presentation and present your work.

MY FAVOURITE SPORT

羽毛球

My favourite sport is badminton. I like it because it's the most popular sport in China. I began to play it when I was 6 years old. I played it at school and in my free time. I enjoyed it and I was in my school badminton team. Our coach always said, 'Just try your best.' I always remember his words when I face difficulties.

My favourite badminton player is Bao Chunlai. He's a really good badminton player and he's also Chinese. He was a member of China's world champion team in 2004, 2006 and 2008. He isn't only a good player, but he's also a funny person on TV shows and he does some charity work.

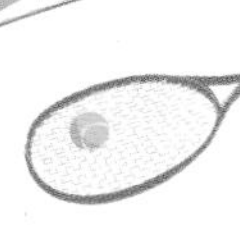

Besides badminton, I also like table tennis, fishing and swimming. But now I would like to try a new sport: tennis. Many of my friends like the sport and I also like to watch tennis matches on TV with my dad. I play tennis on Wii sometimes too.

Cathy, China

YOUR SCORE

Can you use all the language below?
Yes ☺, *No* ☹ or *Almost* 😐

Vocabulary:	hobbies, sports	☐
Communication:	talking about hobbies and sports	☐
	talking about likes and dislikes	☐
Grammar:	like + to do / doing	☐
	link word *but*	☐
CLIL:	phobias	☐

10 Your Answer

What do you love doing?
What hobby do you like doing now?
What did you like doing when you were younger?
What sports do you like doing or watching?
What other things do you love doing?
What things do you hate doing?

Unit 10

FACT

Rice is the most important food for half (50%) of the world's people.

Live to eat?

1 The Big Question

Are you a healthy eater?

2 VOCABULARY

Eight meals from around the world

19 ❶ Look at the eight meals. Match the names to the meals. Then listen and check.

a spaghetti Bolognese
b burger meal
c chow mein
d Mexican soup
e Greek salad
f fruit salad
g sushi
h English breakfast

19 ❷ Listen again. Complete the names of the food in the meals.

20 ❸ **Pronunciation:** Listen to some of the food words in the pictures. Underline the stress. Then listen again and repeat.

❹ Answer the questions.

a Which meal has fish?
b Which meals have vegetables?
c Which meals have meat?
d Which meal doesn't have fish, vegetables or meat?
e Which meal is a dessert?
f Which meals do you think are healthy?
g Which do you think are unhealthy? Why?

1 ___

rice
f_sh
vegetables
l_m_n

2 ___

ch_ _se
tomato
_l_ve
onion
cuc_mber
olive oil

3 ___

b_con (pork)
fried _gg
sausage
_r_nge juice
tea (with milk)

4 ___

p_sta
m_ _t sauce

YOUR GOALS

Vocabulary:	food and drink, adverbs of frequency
Communication:	talking about food and drink, talking about manner and frequency
Grammar:	adverbs of manner and frequency
CLIL:	water and the body

5

ch_cken

noodles

carrot

6

bread

l_ttuce

burger (beef)

Fr_nch fr_es / chips (potatoes)

c_la

7

b_ _ns

p_pper

sour cream

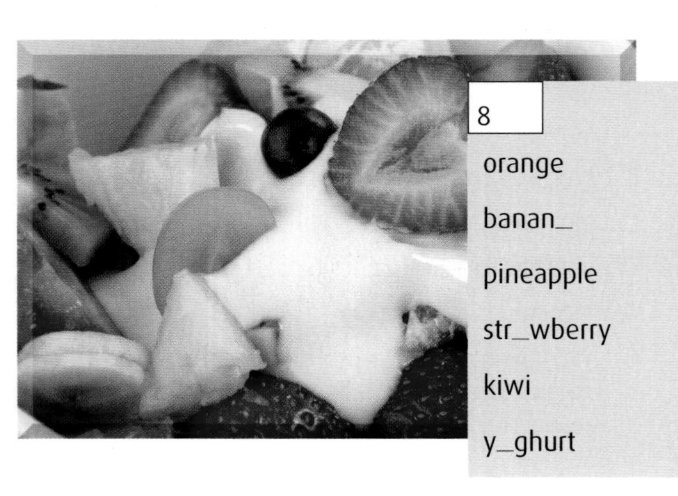

8

orange

banan_

pineapple

str_wberry

kiwi

y_ghurt

5 Find these things in the photos. Write the photo number(s).

____ a **knife** – you cut food with it
____ b **fork** – you eat food with it
____ c **chopsticks** – you eat food with them
____ d **spoon** – you eat soup with it
____ e **plate** – you put food on it
____ f **bowl** – you put food in it
____ g **cup** – you usually drink hot drinks from it
____ h **glass** – you usually drink cold drinks from it

Your meals

6 Work with a partner. Ask and answer the questions. Use the language bank.

a What food do you like or usually eat?
I like / usually eat ...

b What food don't or can't you eat?
I don't like / I never eat ...
I can't eat ... for health reasons.
I don't eat ... because of my religion / because I'm a vegetarian.

c What food is popular in your country?
... is / are popular.

7 Tell the class about your favourite meal.

My favourite meal is red curry. It's chicken with a sauce and some vegetables like peppers and onions. You eat it with rice. My grandma always makes it for me. It's delicious.

19 **8** Watch the video. What do you think of Liliana's dessert?

LANGUAGE BANK 19

3 LISTENING

Where food comes from

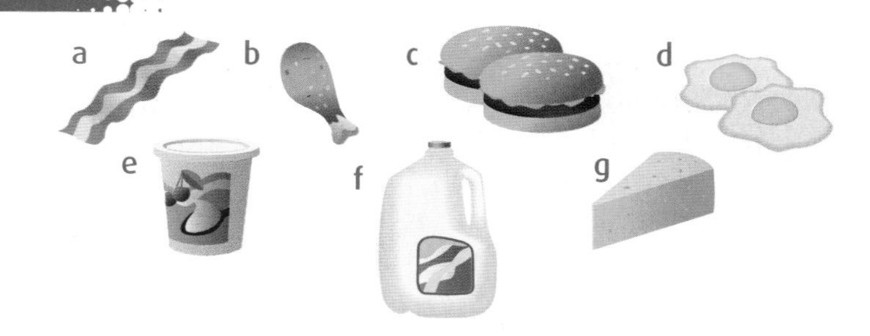

1. What are the names of the food (**a-g**) and the animals (**1–5**) in the pictures?

2. Which animals does the food come from? Match them and tell the class.

   Bacon comes from pigs.

21 3. Listen to a report about children and food in Britain. What don't British kids know?

   a which vegetables grow in Britain
   b which animals produce which foods
   c which animals produce the healthiest foods

21 4. Listen again. Complete the information in the report.

   a More than ________ % (percent) don't know where pork comes from.
   b _____% don't know where yoghurt comes from.
   c __________ have no idea that cheese comes from cows or sheep.
   d 2% of city kids think eggs come from ___________ and that bacon is from ___________.
   e 8% of city kids don't know ____________ come from cows.

21 5. What do the farmers say are the reasons for these results? Choose one or more answers. Listen again and check.

   a Many people today live in towns and cities.
   b Children were cleverer in the past.
   c People don't often cook food.
   d A lot of people buy fast food and ready meals.
   e People aren't interested in food.

6. Read the *Food and your family* questionnaire. Write your answers. Then ask your partner the questions. You can choose more than one answer.

20 7. Watch the video. Where do these teenagers work? What do you think is good about the programme?

Food and your family

1 Where does your family buy food?
   A At a market
   B In a supermarket
   C In small shops
   D We grow our own food / keep chickens / ...

2 Who cooks in your family?
   A My mum / dad / grandma / ...
   B I sometimes cook.
   C We usually eat fast food / ready meals / takeaways / ...

3 Does your family eat together?
   A Yes, all the time.
   B We eat breakfast / dinner together sometimes.
   C Not very often / only at the weekend / ...
   D No, never.

4 Do you eat in restaurants or cafés?
   A No, never.
   B We sometimes eat in a sushi / burger / pizza / steak / Chinese / Italian / ... restaurant.

You are what you eat

8 Look at the cartoon.

a What does it say about the boy and his food?
b Do you eat like him? Or do you just eat three meals and no snacks?

9 Read the information about calories. Answer the questions.

a What are calories?
b How can you burn calories?
c What happens when you eat too many calories?
d Do you think about calories?
e Do you read labels on food?
f Do you choose food because of calories?

Calories

Food gives you energy. We measure this energy in calories.

On average people eat 2798 calories per day. In the USA, it is 3770. In Eritrea, Northeast Africa, it is 1590.

Children and teenagers are still growing, so they can need between 1500 and 3500 calories a day. Boys need more calories than girls.

When you do exercise or sport, you burn calories. Too many calories and not enough sport is not good for your health. You can become overweight.

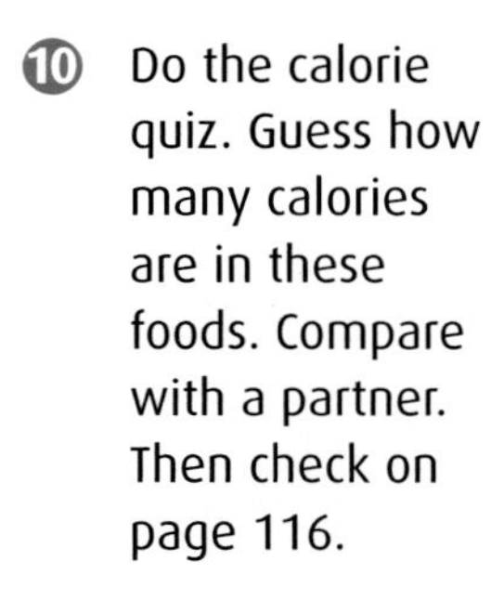

10 Do the calorie quiz. Guess how many calories are in these foods. Compare with a partner. Then check on page 116.

4 ROLE PLAY

1 Work with a partner. Make a restaurant / café menu with 5–10 meals and some drinks. Your meals can be funny: *bacon and egg ice cream, chicken with chocolate sauce .... .*

Then swap menus with another pair.

2 You and your partner are in a restaurant. Use your menus.

Partner A: You are the waiter / waitress.
Partner B: You want to order food and a drink from the menu.

3 Swap roles.

A: *What would you like to drink?*
B: *I'd like ...*
A: *And what would you like to eat?*
B: *I'd like ...*
A: *Anything else?*
B: *Yes, I'd like ... / No, that's it, thank you.*

FACT

13% of the world's people do not have enough food to live.

5 READING

❶ Look at the title, the photos and the records box. What do you think speed eating is? Then read the text and check your answer.

Speed eating champions

What is speed eating?

It's a sport. In the USA, Japan and the UK there are competitions to eat foods like hot dogs, burgers, steak or rice balls. People eat as much as they can in 10 or 15 minutes. They eat quickly, so they usually eat messily with their fingers. And they need to keep the food in their stomach: when people vomit, they go out of the competition. 5

How much do people eat?

Every year there's a famous hot dog eating competition in the USA. Joey Chestnut holds the record: in 2009, he ate 68 hot dogs in ten minutes. Sonya Thomas became the first women's champion in 2011 with 40 hot dogs in ten minutes.

Why do people do it?

People want to be the best. They also want to become famous.

Is it for overweight people?

No. Sonya Thomas only weighs 45 kg. Takeru Kobayashi from Japan weighs 75 kg. 10

How do they do it?

Speed eaters train hard. They go to the gym or run three or four times a week. They always drink a lot of water or milk, so their stomach gets bigger. They never eat much before a competition, so they're very hungry.

Is it really a sport?

Some people say YES. Some say NO: speed eating tells people it is good to eat unhealthily. It's also a waste of food when so many people are hungry. 15

Speed eating records

10 burgers in 3 minutes
29 meatballs in 1 minute
200 worms in 30 seconds
65 eggs in 6 minutes

❷ Read the text again. True (**T**) or false (**F**)?

a Speed eaters usually use knives and forks. ☐
b In speed eating, it's OK to vomit. ☐
c Speed eaters don't need to weigh a lot. ☐
d They don't train for competitions. ☐
e Not everyone thinks speed eating is a sport. ☐

❸ Find words for ...

a where food goes in your body (line 4)
b when food comes back out of your mouth (line 4)
c how you feel when you need food (line 13)
d when you don't use food in the right way (line 15)

❹ Say what you think about speed eating. Is it a sport?

It's gross / disgusting but it's funny.
It's definitely a sport – you need to train hard.
It's horrible. People are hungry.
This isn't a sport. It's stupid and dangerous.

6 GRAMMAR

Manner and frequency

1 Complete the sentences from the text about *how* people do something. Then complete the rule in the box on the right.

a They eat ________, so they eat ________ with their fingers.
b Speed eaters train ________.
c Speed eating tells people it is good to eat ________.

Adverbs of manner

These words usually end in ____.
For spelling changes, see Workbook page 48.

Some adverbs are different:
He trains **hard**. He eats **fast**.

2 Rewrite the eating tips with adverbs of manner. Use the box to help you.

a Eat your food ________ . (slow)
b Use your teeth: chew food ________ . (good)
c Use your knife and fork ________ . (nice)
d Don't eat ________ . (noisy)
e Ask for more food ________ . (polite)

3 Look at the words in bold in the sentences. These words describe how often people do something. Read the rules in the box and circle the correct answers.

a They **always** drink a lot of water.
b They **never** eat much before a competition.
c **Every year** there's a famous hot dog eating competition in the USA.
d They go to the gym **three times a week**.

Adverbs of frequency

Single words usually go *in the middle of the sentence / at the end of the sentence.*

Phrases usually go *in the middle of the sentence / at the end or the beginning of the sentence.*

22 4 **Pronunciation**: Look at the phrases in bold in exercise 3 (**c** and **d**). Now listen. Mark the phrases where the voice goes up (↗) and the phrases where the voice goes down (↘).

5 Put the words or phrases in the right place in the sentence. Then make the sentences true for you and read them to a partner.

a I eat pizza for breakfast. (always)
b I drink cola. (every day)
c I eat unhealthily. (usually)
d I drink water. (never)
e I have a burger. (about three times a week)

7 CONVERSATION

Play the game with a partner. Use the large board game on page 121.

1 You need two coins and dice.
2 Roll the dice.
3 Move round the board with your coin.
4 Go UP ladders and DOWN the snakes.
5 Ask and answer questions with the adverbs.

It's your turn. – OK. One ...
What do you do fast? – I ride my bike fast.
It's your turn. – OK. Two ...
What do you do every day? – I do my homework.

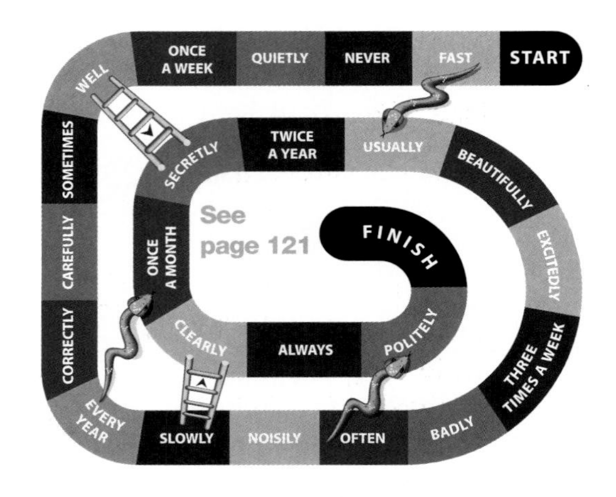

8 CLIL: Water and the body

23 **1** Look at the diagram. Match the percentages (%) of water (**a–e**) with the parts of the body. Then listen and check.

a 75–80% b 20–25% c 70–75% d 80% e 80–85% (x 2)

2 Read the text. Complete the sentences.

a You can live without water for ...
b When your body doesn't get enough water, it ...
c Your kidneys take ...
d You also lose water when you ...
e You need more water when ...
f You put water back into your body through ...

You can live without food for more than a month. You can only live without water for a few days. Water is important for many of the body's jobs. Without water, your body can't work. When you feel thirsty, it means your body doesn't have (5) enough water. You can get headaches, feel tired or feel sick.

Your body loses over two litres of water a day. Your kidneys take 'old water' out of your body and clean your blood. Your skin sweats about half a (10) litre of water a day. When it's hot or you do sport, you sweat much more and need to drink more water. You also breathe out water – about a glass of water a day and more when you do sport.

This is why your body needs about two litres (15) of fresh water every day. All drinks have water in them but water and milk are the healthiest drinks. Remember: water has no calories! Food also contains water – especially fruit and vegetables.

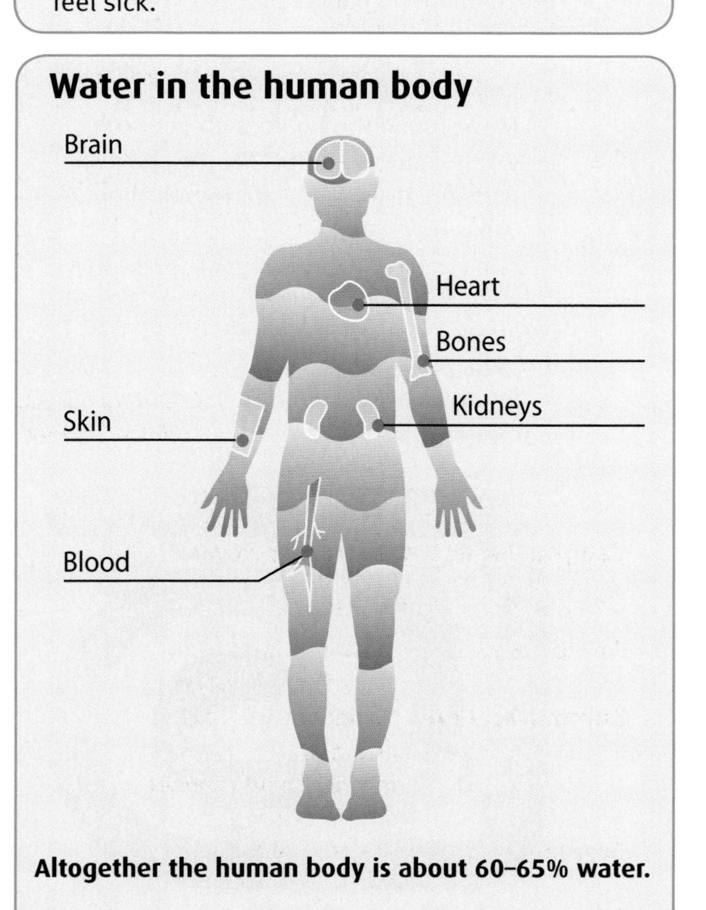

3 How much water do you drink? How much more do you drink when you do sport?

4 **Your topic:**
Choose a topic linked to this unit – something interesting for **you.** For example, you can choose the most popular foods in your country, healthy or unhealthy eating at your school, your favourite restaurant etc.

- Think of **four discussion points** about this topic. Make a **mind map**.
- Make **notes** about these four points.
- Think of a **question** about your topic.
- Talk about your points with a partner. Answer questions and ask your question.

9 WRITING

Liliana's favourite meal

1. **Read:** Look at Liliana's picture of her favourite meal. What does she like to eat?

Your favourite meal

2. **Prepare:** Think about your favourite meal. Use the boxes to help you.

What's your favourite meal?
My favourite meal is ...
There is ... and ... in it.
It's *very healthy / quite unhealthy / ...*
I think it has a lot of calories / ...

Where do you eat this food?
My mum / dad makes this meal at home.
Sometimes I cook this at home.
I eat this when we go to *an Italian / ...* restaurant.

Is this food popular in your country?
It's a traditional food in my country.
It's popular with *young / ...* people.
In my country *we often eat ... / we grow a lot of ... / there are a lot of ... farms.*

What other foods do you love or hate?
I also *like / love ...*
I *don't like / hate ...*
I *don't / can't eat ... for health reasons / ...*

3. **Write and share:** Write about your favourite meal. Add your photo. Swap your work with a partner.
Do it online! Publish your photo and description online.

pictr

Home | Your Photos | Search | Upload

My Favourite Meal

One of my favourite meals is *Enchiladas Salvadoreñas*. It's *tortilla* with cabbage, tomatoes, boiled eggs, radish and cheese. It's fun to make because each *enchilada* comes out different. You can put anything you want on it. It's very healthy and it doesn't have too many calories. It tastes amazing!

My mom and I make *enchiladas* at home for parties or just for fun. We make them for our whole family and everyone likes eating them. It's a very popular dish in El Salvador. Some people eat the *tortilla* with beans and salsa.

I also really like making pies, cookies and cakes. They make people happy and my house always smells delicious! I don't like fish soup or green peppers. And I don't like really spicy food. I try to eat healthy food and I go to my local farmer's market because they always have delicious fruit!

Post Comment | Preview

Liliana, El Salvador

10 Your Answer

Are you a healthy eater?

What are your favourite foods?
What foods don't you like or eat?
What things can you cook?
How often does your family eat together?
How often do you eat in restaurants or eat takeaways?
How much water do you drink?

YOUR SCORE

Can you use all the language below?
Yes ☺, *No* ☹ or *Almost* 😐

Vocabulary:	food and drink	☐
	adverbs of frequency	☐
Communication:	talking about food and drink	☐
	talking about manner and frequency	☐
Grammar:	adverbs of manner and frequency	☐
CLIL:	water and the body	☐

Unit 11

Learning for life

FACT

Children in England have about 70 tests and exams before they're 16.

1 The Big Question

How important are your exams?

2 VOCABULARY

The school system in England

 1 Look at the diagram. Listen. Write the correct ages in the diagram. Then listen again and check.

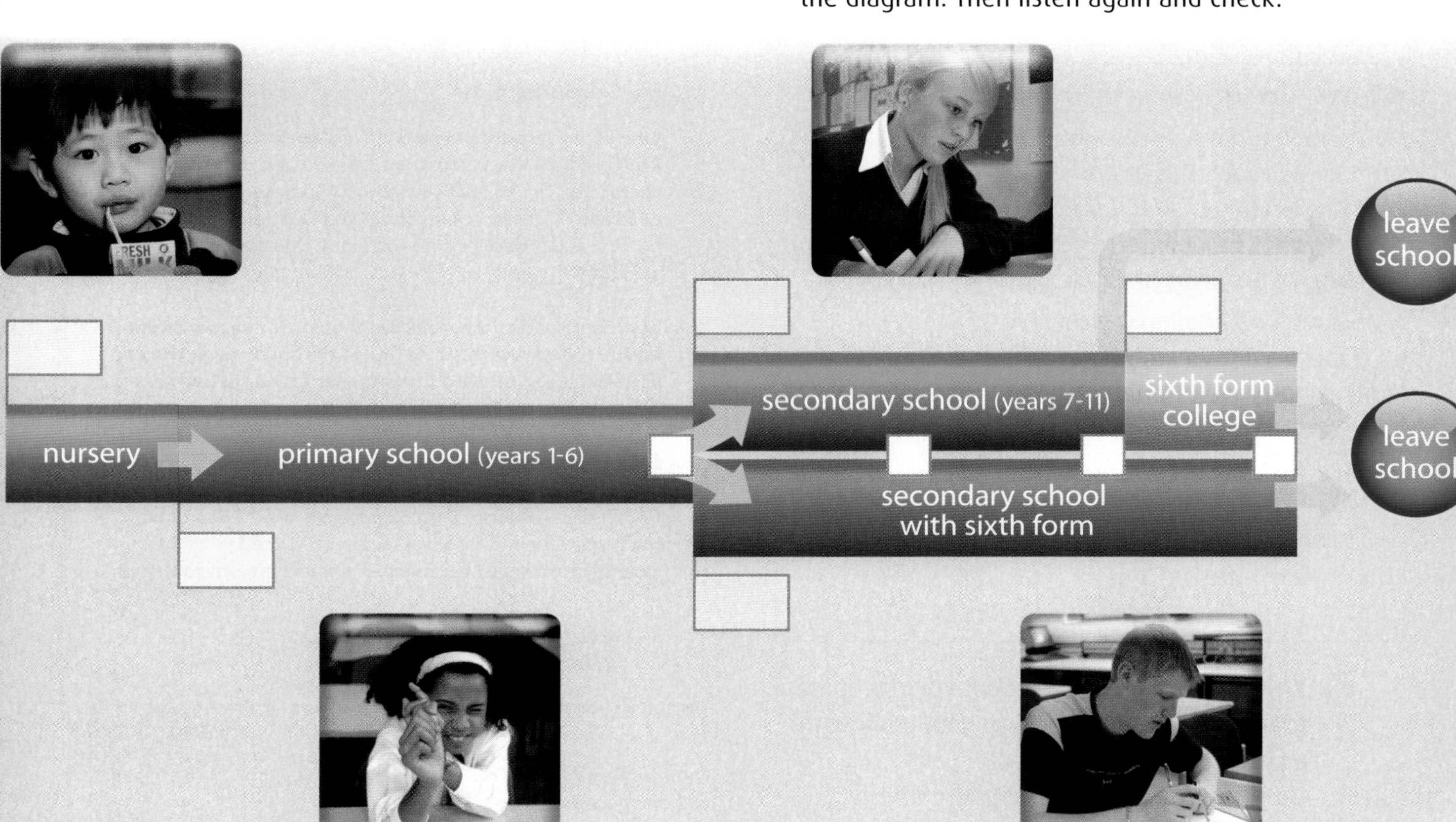

 2 Listen again. When do students take tests and exams? Write the words (**a-d**) in the diagram.

a exams (GCSEs)
b exams (A-levels)
c tests
d coursework

3 Draw a diagram of your school system. Explain it to a partner.

a When do you start school?
b Are there different schools? When do you change schools?
c When do you do tests and take exams?
d Do you do coursework? What do you do for this?
e When can you leave school?

46 LANGUAGE BANK 21

Future careers

25 **4** British students have a class called 'careers'. It's a class about what they can do after their GCSE exams. Listen to a careers teacher. Complete the mind map (**1–7**) with the right phrases (**a–g**).

a apply for a job
b retake exams
c do an apprenticeship
d travel round the world / visit another country
e be a volunteer
f stay on at school
g go to college

YOUR GOALS

Vocabulary:	school systems, future careers, exams and exam stress
Communication:	talking about your school system, talking about future plans
Grammar:	*going to* future
CLIL:	plagiarism

Choices at 16

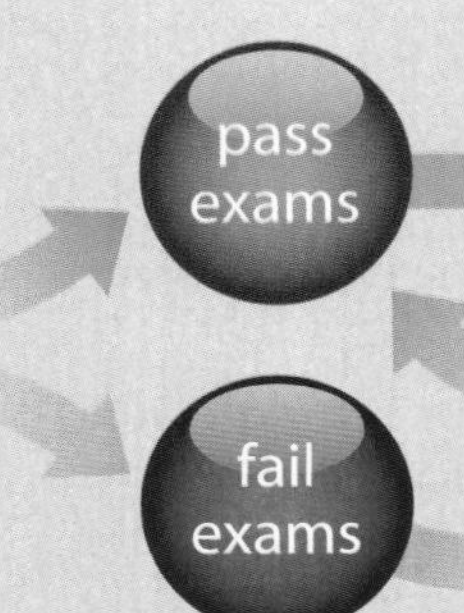

26 **5** **Pronunciation:** Listen to the phrases in exercise 4. Mark the main stress or stresses. Then listen again and repeat.

apply for a job

27 **6** Listen to Lucy. She talks about four of the activities in exercise 4 (**a–g**). Tick them. Which of the four things is she doing now?

27 **7** Listen again. Complete Lucy's tips for students.

Think carefully about all the ______________ .
See some of the ______________ .

8 What you would like to do when you leave school? Tell a partner.

I'd like to ... *I think I want to ...*
I plan to ... *I don't know.*

FACT

In the UK, girls get better results in GCSE exams than boys.

3 LISTENING

Learning at school

1. Look at the two photos. Answer the questions.

   a Who are the people in the pictures?
   b Where are they and what are they doing?
   c How do you think they're feeling?
   d How do you feel in a situation like this?

28 2. Listen and match the opinions (**a-e**) to the correct students (**1–5**). Then listen again and check.

   a My parents think school work and exams are very important. I feel really stressed. ☐
   b Some schools just want good test and exam results. ☐
   c You can't get a good job today without good exam results. ☐
   d Other skills like teamwork are more important than exams. ☐
   e I get worried in exams and get bad marks. ☐

3. Which opinions in exercise 2 do you agree with?

   I agree with a / b / ....
   I don't agree with ...
   I think ... / I don't think ...

4. In the UK, a survey asked students what they do when they are stressed because of tests and exams. What do you think was the top answer with 53%? Decide and then check on page 122.

   do sport
   talk to a teacher
   talk to friends
   talk to family

5. Make other tips for exam and school stress. Use the words below.

   You should ... think positive thoughts.
   You shouldn't ... think positive thoughts.

   ~~think positive thoughts~~
   worry
   relax
   take deep breaths
   sit in your room alone
   play a game or do your favourite activity
   think of something else
   drink a lot of coffee or cola
   think negative thoughts
   write a journal with good things about yourself

6. Work with a partner. Which tips in exercises 4 and 5 do you think are the best? Decide on your top five. Then compare with the class.

21 7. Watch the video. Are the students mostly positive or negative about exams?

Learning online through games

8 Work with a partner. Answer the questions. Then tell the class about your partner.

Are you a gamer?

If yes:

- Do you play online?
- How many hours do you play a week?
- What games do you play?
- What do players do in these games?

use skills / use magic / fight people / travel to different places / drive a car / build a city / shoot things / ...

If no:

- Why don't you play online games?
- What do you think of these games?
- Do you think players learn things from online games?

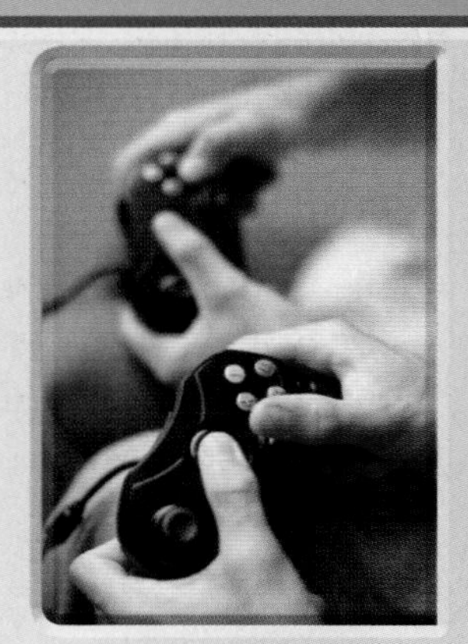

29 9 Listen to a report about online games. Complete the sentences in the box.

According to game designer Jane McGonigal, ...

gamers spend _______ hours every day playing games online until they are 21.

secondary students spend _______ hours in lessons at school.

- are optimistic ☐
- are calm ☐
- are sociable ☐
- are a bit lazy ☐
- work hard ☐

29 10 Listen again. Tick the right answers.

11 Look at the sentences from the listening and the four opinions below. Which opinions do you agree with? Or do you have another opinion?

"I'm not just playing games. I'm learning important life skills. And I'm saving the world."

Rubbish! Gamers don't live in the real world. They only learn to fight and shoot things online.

It's an interesting idea. But I don't think it's true. Online worlds and the real world are very different.

I think you can learn a lot from online games. But school work is still really important.

I think games can change the world because you can learn a lot of important skills.

....

4 ROLE PLAY

1 Work with a partner.

Partner A: Look at page 116. Tell your partner your opinions.
Partner B: Say what you think about Partner A's opinions.

Use these phrases:
I think ... / I don't think ...
I totally agree.
I don't agree (because ...)

2 Swap roles. **Partner B:** Look at page 122.

5 READING

A future designer?

1. Look at Shireen's photo, her art and her jewellery (she makes it). What can you say about her?
   She seems ...

2. Read the interview with Shireen. Does she plan to make jewellery design her career?

photography

self-portrait

Shireen, *student artist*

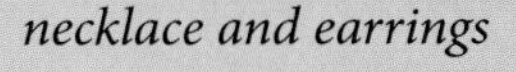

necklace and earrings

bracelet

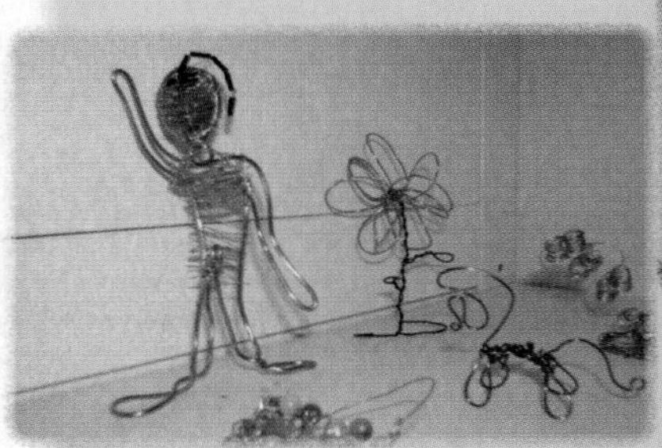

sculpture

scrapbooking

When did you start making jewellery?

I love all kinds of art – photography, sewing, knitting and scrapbooking. When I was little, I made dresses out of plastic bags. And I built things from garbage. When I was about ten, I started to make sculptures and jewellery.

Why do you enjoy working with metal? And where do you get your ideas for your designs?

I like metal because you can do different things with it. I like making all kinds of shapes and I love trying new ideas. Other artists give me ideas too.

You do technical arts at your school. What classes are you going to take next year?

I plan to take a lot of different classes. For the first semester, I'm going to do an architecture class and a class in glass. In the architecture class we're going to learn about design in general. During the next three years, I'm going to take two jewellery classes.

You did work experience with a designer. How was it?

A couple of years ago, I worked for a few days with a local jewellery designer in her studio. I learnt a lot about jewellery-making as a job. I'd like more experiences like this, so I can get ideas for my future.

What are you going to do after school?

I plan to go to college. But I have no idea what I'm going to study. And I don't know what I'm going to do later. I'd like to have a creative job. In the meantime, I plan to work with jewellers, teach classes, or even sell some of my pieces.

3. Read the interview again. What does Shireen plan to do in the next three years at school and after school?
   In the next three years, she plans to ...
   After school, she plans to ...

4. What types of jewellery does Shireen make? What type of art does she like?

JEWELLERY b ______ n ______ e ______

ART p ______ s ______ s ______ s ______

5. Watch the video. Would you like to go to a school like Shireen's?

6 GRAMMAR

going to future

1 Complete the sentences about Shireen's plans from the interview. Then complete the rule.

What classes are you going to take?

a For the first semester next year, I'm ...
b In the architecture class, we're ...
c During the next three years, I'm ...

To talk about future plans, we use the *going to* future:

________ + *(not) going to* + verb

30 **2** **Pronunciation:** Listen to the sentences in exercise 1 and repeat. Notice we usually use the short form of *be*.

Listen again. How do we say the word *to* in these sentences? Circle the right sound. Then listen and repeat.

/tu:/ /tə/

3 Complete the sentences about Shireen with the correct form of *be*. Use the short form if possible.

Shireen sometimes teaches art classes to children.

a This week she ________ going to teach them about sculptures.
b They ________ going to learn to make animal sculptures.
c "We ________ going to use different colours," says Shireen.
d "I ________ going to teach them to make shapes."
e Her students ________ going to make their favourite animals.
f The student in this photo ________ going to make a horse.

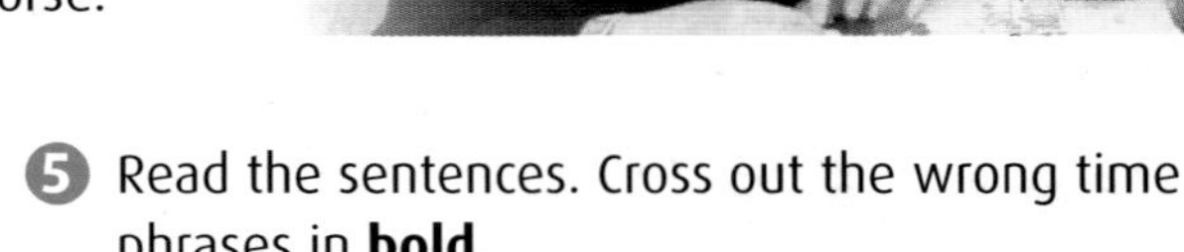

4 Complete the conversation with the correct form of *going to*.

Carlos (1 *we / perform*) ________ a new play.
Shireen (2 *you / act*) ________ in it?
Carlos No, (3 *I / not / act*) ________ this time. (4 *I / be*) ________ the director.
Shireen Congratulations. (5 *when / it / be*) ________ on?
Carlos At the end of the semester. I hope (6 *you / come*) ________.

5 Read the sentences. Cross out the wrong time phrases in **bold**.

a I'm going to play tennis **tomorrow**.
b We're going to watch a film **this evening**.
c My sister is going to cook dinner **yesterday**.
d We're going to go on a school trip **next week**.
e He's going to buy a new bike **last month**.
f I'm going to get a job **in the school holidays**.

7 CONVERSATION

1 Work with a partner. Ask and answer about your future plans. Make notes about your partner's answers.

What are you going to do ...?
tomorrow / at the weekend / in the next summer holidays / when you leave school

2 Tell the class one interesting thing about your partner.

8 CLIL: Plagiarism

1 You need to write an essay for school but you don't know a lot about the topic. Answer the questions.

a How do you find information?
b Where do you look?
c How do you get ideas?

Plagiarism /ˈpleɪʤərɪzəm/ is when you use somebody's work and don't give the author's, artist's or website's name.

2 Read the definition of plagiarism above. Then tick the examples of plagiarism.

a You copy some ideas from a friend. ☐
b You copy an essay from an essay-writing website. ☐
c You find information on a website. You change some words so it sounds a bit different. ☐
d You find information on a website. You use the facts and write where you found the information. ☐
e You find information on a website. You cut and paste the text into your essay. ☐
f You quote information from a website. You write the address of the website and when you used it. ☐

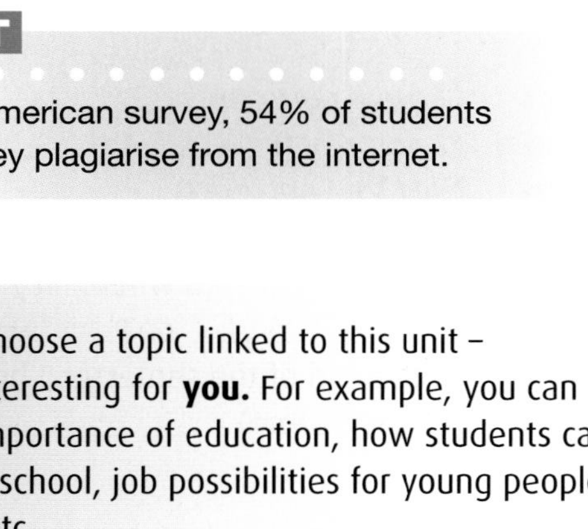

3 Match the words with the correct explanations.

a	copy	1	repeat what somebody said or wrote
b	cut and paste	2	where something comes from (an author, a book or a website)
c	quote	3	write down something from somewhere else
d	source	4	electronically take out and put in

31 **4** Listen to a teacher talk about plagiarism. Do most students plan to plagiarise?

31 **5** Listen again. Complete the rules for students. Do you follow these rules?

FACT

In an American survey, 54% of students said they plagiarise from the internet.

Are you going to use the internet for school work?

When you use websites ...

Write down the ________________.

Write down the ________________ of the article and the ________________.

Write down the ________________ when you use the website.

No ________________ – no mark!

6 **Your topic:** Choose a topic linked to this unit – something interesting for **you.** For example, you can choose the importance of education, how students can learn outside school, job possibilities for young people in your area etc.

- Think of **four discussion points** about this topic. Make a **mind map**.
- Make **notes** about these four points.
- Think of a **question** about your topic.
- Talk about your points with a partner. Answer questions and ask your question.

9 WRITING

Tessa's future plans

1. **Read:** Look at Tessa's poster. Read about her future plans and goals. Which plan or goal do you think is most interesting?

Your future plans and goals

2. **Prepare:** Think about your future plans. Use the boxes to help you.

When are you going to take important exams?
I'm going to take ...
These exams are important because ...

What are you going to do when you leave school?
I'm going *to go to college / apply for a job as a ...*
I'd like to *travel / work in another country / be a volunteer with ...*

What job would you like to do?
I'm going to be *a designer / ...*
I think I'd like to be ...
I don't know what job I want to do.
I want to *enjoy my work / earn a lot of money / help people / be successful / ...*

What other plans do you have?
I'd like to travel *to / around ...*
I plan to live in ...
I hope to have *a family / an exciting life / ...*

3. **Write and share:** Make your poster. Add photos and drawings.
Do it online! Make an online poster.

My Future Plans
I'm going to take my exams in two years. I'm frightened of the exams. They're so important. When I leave school, I want to go to the sixth form. I need good marks for the sixth form. I hope I get them.
I want to be a psychologist for kids with cancer. I want the kids to have a good time when they're ill. I want to take away the fear of death. I need to pass the leaving exam for that job.
My other plans for the future are to travel around the world. I want to live in America for a time. And I want to have a family.

Tessa, Germany

10 Your Answer

How important are your exams?

When do you do tests and exams in your country?
Do you find exams easy or stressful?
Do you think learning other skills is important?
What are you going to do when you leave school?
Do you need good exam results for your job?

YOUR SCORE

Can you use all the language below?
Yes ☺, *No* ☹ or *Almost* 😐

Vocabulary:	school system, future careers	☐
	exams and exam stress	☐
Communication:	talking about your school system	☐
	talking about future plans	☐
Grammar:	*going to* future for plans	☐
CLIL:	plagiarism	☐

Unit 12

FACT

In a website survey of US teenagers, 40% aged 13–15 said they're bored in the summer holidays. 10% say they're too busy.

Events and experiences

1 The Big Question

What great experiences have you had?

2 VOCABULARY

Weekend and seasonal activities

1 Look at the photos and read the ideas about activities during school holidays. Write the correct activities or places in **bold** under the photos.

32 2 Listen to a conversation between two friends. Which activity in exercise 1 do they decide to do?

Don't know what to do in the school holidays? Try some of these ideas!

GO
- **bowling**
- **hiking**
- to a **festival** or a **cultural event**
- to an **art exhibition**
- to a **sports event** (a football or baseball match, a car race)

VOLUNTEER
- in a **charity shop**
- in a **homeless shelter**
- in a **soup kitchen**

HAVE
- a **barbecue** (BBQ) or a **picnic** with your family, friends or neighbours
- a **garage sale** (use the money for a trip or give it to charity)
- a **water fight** in the garden or at a pool

32 3 Listen again. Why doesn't Ben want to do the other activities? Complete the reasons.

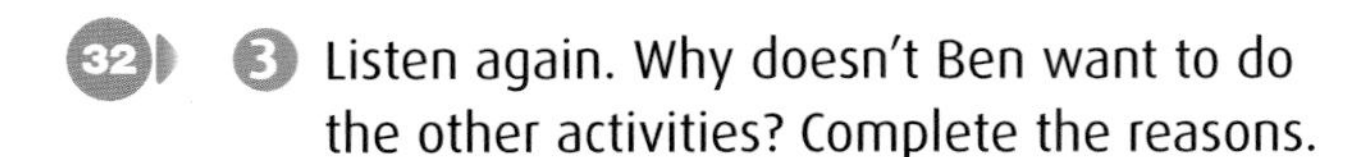

Activity	Reason why not
go to an exhibition	...
have a water fight	...
see a football match	...
have a barbecue	...

1 ______

2 ______

3 ______

4 ______

5 ______________________________

YOUR GOALS

Vocabulary:	weekend and seasonal activities, space
Communication:	talking about past events, talking about experiences
Grammar:	past simple (revision and more irregular forms), present perfect with *ever* and *never*
CLIL:	gravity

6 ______________________________

7 ______________________________

8 ______________________________

32 4 Listen again. Complete each phrase with **two** different ideas.

Idea 1	Idea 2

a We could ...
b Let's ...
c What about ...?

33 5 **Pronunciation:** Listen to the sentences in exercise 4 and repeat. How do we say the words *an* and *a*? Then listen and repeat again.

Your activities

6 Which activities on these pages would you like to do? Tick them. Then work with a partner. Decide on three activities together. (Use the phrases in exercise 4.)

We could go bowling? – Mmm, I don't like bowling. / Yes, good idea.

7 Do you have ideas for other holiday activities? Make a list with your partner. Then share your ideas with the class.

8 Work with a partner. Ask about what he / she did last summer / last weekend.

48 LANGUAGE BANK 23

3 LISTENING

Great events

1. Look at the photos of four events. Explain what you see.

34 2. Listen to four speakers. They're talking about the events in the photos. Which speaker (**1–4**) had the best experience?

34 3. Read the sentences below. Listen again. Write the correct event 1, 2, 3 or 4 for each sentence.

1 La tomatina *tomato throwing festival, Spain*

- ☐ a There were lots of accidents.
- ☐ b The guests got free food.
- ☐ c It started with a gun shot.
- ☐ d It was good for your health.
- e It took one hour exactly. ☐
- f It was to say thank you. ☐
- g There was a strange prize. ☐
- h There was a special pool. ☐

2 Mud festival, Korea

3 Monkey banquet, Thailand

35 4. Listen carefully and complete the irregular past verbs from the listening with *a, e,* or *o*. Then check on page 144.

a The fight beg_n with a loud gun shot.
b And then everybody thr_w tomatoes.
c The monkeys dr_nk cola from cans.
d The runners r_n down a really steep hill.
e One br_ke his arm.
f He only g_t the cheese.

5. Which event would you like to go to? Tell a partner. Explain why.

I'd like to go to ... because I like ... / it looks ...
I wouldn't like to go to ... because ...

4 Cheese rolling competition, England

Great experiences

6 Read the information about the Duke of Edinburgh's Award. Answer the questions.

a What three levels are there? b What four things do you do at each level?

The Duke of Edinburgh's Award (DofE) is a programme for young people between 14 and 24. There are three levels:

BRONZE is the easiest level. You can start when you're 14 and it takes about 6 months.

SILVER is the next level and you need to be 15. It takes 6–12 months.

GOLD is the hardest level. You can start at 16 and it takes 12–18 months.

At each level you do:

An expedition: A trip of 2-4 days on foot or by bike, by canoe or kayak or on horseback; students camp overnight and cook their own food.

A skills activity: For example, playing a musical instrument, filmmaking or hairdressing.

A physical activity or sport: For example, mountain biking, aerobics, cricket or football.

A volunteer activity: Working with people, animals or the environment.

23 7 Watch the video. Would you like to do the DofE programme?

36 8 Listen to Lewis. He's talking about his experiences on the programme. Complete the sentence.

"It made me feel ________ about myself, more __________ ."

At gold level you also do **a 'residential' away from home:** For example, you can volunteer at a camp for children in wheelchairs, or learn to cook at a cooking school.

36 9 Listen again. Circle the correct answers.

1 **Expedition**: 30 km *on foot / in a kayak*
2 **Skills**: *filmmaking / computers*
3 **Physical**: *tennis / table tennis*
4 **Volunteer**: at *an old people's home / an animal shelter*

36 10 Listen again. Add two more details about Lewis's experiences in exercise 9. Then compare with a partner.

11 You're going to do a Duke of Edinburgh's Award. Decide on your four activities. Describe them to a partner.

4 ROLE PLAY

1 Work with a partner.

Partner A: Tell Partner B about a great event. Look at page 116.
Partner B: Listen and make notes.

2 Swap roles.

Partner B: Tell Partner A about a great experience. Look at page 122.
Partner A: Listen and make notes.

5 READING

1. Look at the photos. What can you do at Space Academy?

   You can ...
   a have lessons about astronauts.
   b talk to astronauts.
   c do training like an astronaut.

2. Read Kesha's report about her experience at space camp. What was the best part of the programme for her? What was the worst part?

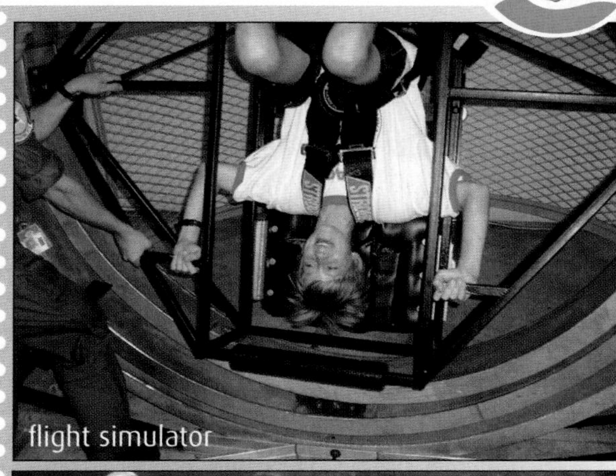
flight simulator

underwater simulator

moonwalk simulator

My Space Academy experience

Have you ever wanted to be an astronaut? Last year I went to Space Academy in Alabama, USA, with my class and did astronaut training. It was a great experience! We had six days there. You could choose to learn about space and the planet Mars, being a pilot or robotics. I chose space and Mars, so I learnt a lot about the space shuttle and its history.

We trained for space on flight simulators. One flight simulator was like a ride at an amusement park. It moved round and round and upside down – first slow and then quite fast. I felt a bit sick at first, but then it was fun. There was a moon walk simulator too – you could walk like astronauts on the moon. That was so cool!

We also trained underwater in the underwater astronaut trainer. We did activities with scuba diving equipment. When you're underwater, you're weightless – like in space. I've tried scuba diving before and I've never been scared underwater, but some of the other students didn't like it.

I liked the practical training at Space Academy best. We didn't just learn about space – we did training like real astronauts. The worst part was when we left. I didn't want to go home.

3. Answer the questions.

   a What did the flight simulator do?
   b Did Kesha like the flight simulator?
   c What could you do on the moon walk simulator?
   d What did Kesha's group do in the underwater astronaut trainer?
   e Why did the group train underwater?

4. Watch the video. Would you like to try the simulators at Space Academy? Are you interested in space? Why or why not?

6 GRAMMAR

Present perfect

1 Look at the sentences from the text and the meanings in brackets. Circle the correct explanation (a *or* b) in the box.

Have you ever wanted to be an astronaut?
(= in all your life until now.)

I've tried scuba diving before.
(= This wasn't a new experience in my life.)

I've never been scared underwater.
(= I wasn't scared in the past and I'm not scared now.)

You use the present perfect + *ever / never / before* to talk about experiences in your life ...

a) from the past to the present

past present

b) in the past

past present

2 Complete the rule.

We make the present perfect with ________ + past participle.
We make the past participle of regular verbs with ________ .
Learn the form for irregular verbs: see page 144.

37 3 **Pronunciation:** In everyday English, we usually shorten the verb *have* in the present perfect. Listen to the pairs of sentences and repeat. Pay attention to the pronunciation of *have* and *has.*

I *have* never been scared underwater.
→ I*'ve* never been scared underwater.

He *has* tried the moon walk too.
→ He*'s* tried the moon walk too.

They *have* never visited the USA.
→ They*'ve* never visited the USA.

4 Look at the pictures. Complete the speech bubbles with the past participle of one of these verbs.

be design fly wear

a I've never ________ a robot before.
b I've never ________ clothes like this.
c I've never ________ weightless before.
d I've never ________ a space shuttle.

5 Write the questions. Then ask and answer with a partner.

1 (you / ever / spend) ____________ a week away from home?
2 (you / ever / visit) ________ the USA?
3 (you / ever / try) ____________ scuba diving?
4 (you / ever / see) ________ a space shuttle?

7 CONVERSATION

1 Write five questions for a partner about his or her experiences. Use *Have you ever ...?*

2 Ask and answer your questions. Give as much information as you can.

Yes, I have. (I tried it last summer. It was ...)
No, I haven't. (But I'd like to try it. / I'm not interested in ...)

3 Tell the class one thing about your partner.

LANGUAGE BANK 24

8 CLIL: Gravity

1. Read the information and look at the diagrams **a** and **b**. Which diagram shows *pull*?

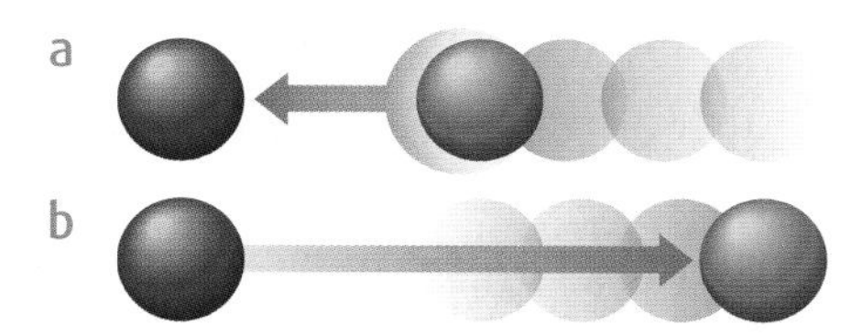

THE PULL OF GRAVITY

Gravity is when an object (a thing) pulls another object.
Have you heard the story of Isaac Newton? Isaac Newton (1641-1727) was a professor of Maths.

One day he was in his garden and he saw an apple fall from a tree.

Facts

Bigger objects have more pull than smaller objects.

Objects nearby pull more than objects far away.

The Earth's gravity pulls things to its centre.

The Earth pulls the Moon towards it because the Moon is smaller and lighter. ☐ 1

The Sun is much bigger and heavier than the Earth. ☐ 2

In space gravity isn't very strong. ☐ 3

On the Moon, gravity is 1/6 of the gravity on the Earth. ☐ 4

2. Read the facts again. Put sentences **a–d** in the correct places (**1–4**).

   a So astronauts don't fall, they float.
   b So the Earth moves around the Sun.
   c So the Moon moves around the Earth.
   d So it's hard for astronauts to walk on the Moon.

3. Have you learnt about this topic in other lessons? If yes, is it easier to understand now? If no, do you understand this topic?

4. **Your topic:** Choose a topic linked to this unit – something interesting for **you**. For example, you can choose a summer volunteer job, festivals in your country, space travel, an interesting planet etc.

   - Think of **four discussion points** about this topic. Make a **mind map**.
   - Make **notes** about these four points.
   - Think of a **question** about your topic.
   - Talk about your points with a partner. Answer questions and ask your question.

9 WRITING

Alena's experience of a lifetime

1. **Read:** Look at Alena's story. Read about the best experience of her life. Why was it a great experience?

Your experience of a lifetime

2. **Prepare:** Think about your experience of a lifetime. Use the boxes to help you.

When and where was it?
My experience of a lifetime happened *in 2009 / last summer / when I was 10 / two months ago / ...*
I was *at an amusement park / on a school trip / on holiday in Spain / at a football stadium /...*

What happened?
I went *to New York / snowboarding / ...*
I saw *the best football match ever / ...*
I did *a 20 km hike for charity / a dance performance for 500 people ...*

Can you give some more details?
I was with ...
The match was between ... and ...
I *walked / wore / saw ....*
I was really *excited / surprised / ...*

Why was it the experience of a lifetime?
I've never done anything like it before.
My team scored six goals!
I saw a lot of fantastic things.
I made new friends. / I helped somebody.

My Best Experience

The best experience of my life happened two years ago during the summer holidays. My friend Mary and I went to her grand-father's place. His old house is at the bottom of a hill near a forest and two rivers.

◀ 1 ▶

That day it was very windy and we decided to go windsurfing. But the wind was too strong. I went very fast and I didn't know how to turn back. A few minutes later, I was on a small island. It was too far to swim back. It was nearly dark and I was cold.

◀ 2 ▶

I made a fire with sticks. I got warm but I was hungry. Suddenly, I heard the noise of a boat and voices. I was so happy! It was Mary and her grandfather. They said I was lucky because there were so many islands and it was easy to get lost. On that day, I learned a lot of things.

◀ 3 ▶

Alena, Russia

3. **Write and share:** Draw or find pictures about your experience. Use your notes and write about it. Then swap your story with a partner. **Do it online!** Visit an online story website and publish your story.

10 Your Answer

What great experiences have you had?

What summer activities have you done?
What great events have you been to?
What have you never done but would like to try? Why?
What was the best experience of your life?

YOUR SCORE

Can you use all the language below?
Yes ☺, *No* ☹ or *Almost* 😐

Vocabulary:	weekend and seasonal activities	☐
	space	☐
Communication:	talking about past events	☐
	talking about experiences	☐
Grammar:	past simple	☐
	present perfect with *ever* and *never*	☐
CLIL:	gravity	☐

The Big Read 3

1 Read the first page of a book called *Holes* below. Write the names of the things in the three pictures.

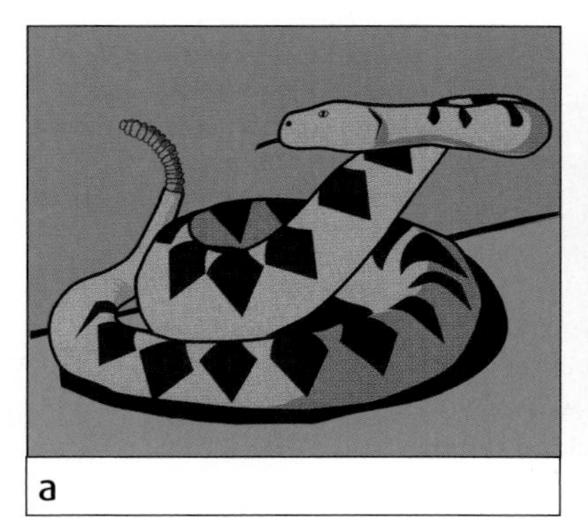
a

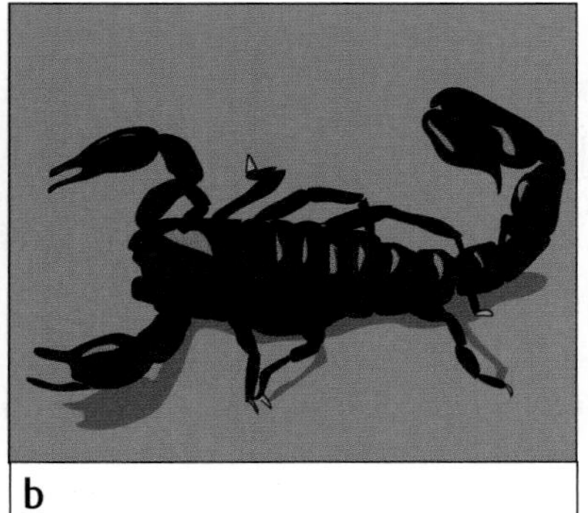
b

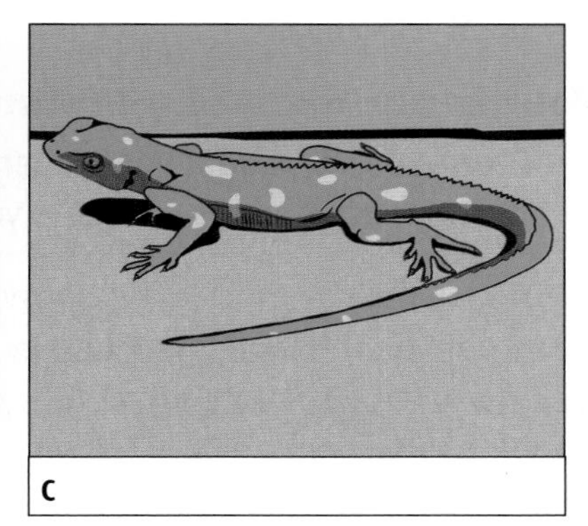
c

There is no lake at Camp Green Lake. There was once a very large lake, the largest lake in Texas. That was over a hundred years ago. Now it is just a dry, flat wasteland.

During the summer the daytime temperature is around thirty-five degrees Celsius in the shade – if you can find any shade. There's not much shade in a big dry lake.

Out on the lake, rattlesnakes and scorpions find shade under rocks and in the holes dug by the campers.

Here's a good rule to remember about rattlesnakes and scorpions: If you don't bother them, they don't bother you.

Usually.

A bite from a scorpion or a rattlesnake is not the worst thing that can happen to you. You don't die.

Usually.

But you don't want a bite from a yellow-spotted lizard. That's the worst thing that can happen to you. You die a slow and painful death.

Always.

2 Answer the questions.

- a Where's Camp Green Lake?
- b What does the place look like?
- c What's the weather like?
- d What happens when a scorpion or a snake bites you? A yellow-spotted lizard?

3 Read the story on page 109. Why was Stanley scared?

4 Find the words for these definitions in the story. Underline them.

- a a kind of bag for clothes when you travel
- b to move slowly with your body near the ground
- c a home for birds, insects or small animals
- d the sharp bits on animals' feet
- e to make a regular sound

5 Read the story again. Put the events in the right order (**1–6**).

- ___ a There were now eight lizards in the hole.
- ___ b The warden saw a lizard.
- ___ c A lizard ate a tarantula.
- ___ d Stanley saw that he was in a lizard's nest with six lizards.
- ___ e Mr Pendanski, Mr Sir and the warden came to get the suitcase.
- ___ f Another lizard crawled up Zero's arm.

6 What do you think happened? Did the lizards bite Stanley and Zero? Work with a partner. Write an ending for the story.

Holes

Stanley Yelnats is at Camp Green Lake. The police think he stole something. Camp Green Lake isn't a summer camp but a place for bad boys – instead of prison. The boys at the camp dig holes all day because the warden is looking for something. Stanley and his friend Zero run away from the camp, but then one night, they come back. They dig a hole and find a suitcase but then the warden (Mr Pendanski) and Mr Sir arrive ...

The flashlight was on Zero. The suitcase was on his lap.

Mr Pendanski held the flashlight. Mr Sir stood next to him with a gun.

The warden moved toward Zero. In the distance Stanley could see two more flashlights in the darkness. He felt helpless in the hole.

"You boys just arrived –" The warden stopped talking and she stopped walking. Then she slowly moved back.

A lizard was on top of the suitcase.

Its big red eyes glowed. Its mouth was open and its white tongue moved in and out between its black teeth.

Zero sat as still as a statue.

A second lizard crawled up and over the side of the suitcase and stopped near Zero's little finger.

Stanley was afraid to look and afraid not to look. The second lizard crawled across Zero's fingers and half way up his arm.

Stanley looked down and nearly screamed. He was in a lizard nest. He could see six lizards. There were three on the ground, two on his left leg and one on his right sneaker.

He tried to stay very still. Something was on the back of his neck.

Stanley felt tiny claws dig into the side of his neck and up past his chin. He could hear his heart beat. Each beat told him he was still alive, at least for one more second.

The sun was up and Stanley's heart was still beating. There were eight lizards in the hole with him. Each had exactly eleven yellow spots.

"Why don't you take the suitcase from Zero?" the warden suggested.

"Yeah, right," said Mr Sir.

"The lizards obviously aren't hungry," said the warden.

"Then you get the suitcase," said Mr Sir.

They waited.

***

Sometime later Stanley saw a tarantula crawl across the dirt, not too far from his hole. He was fascinated by it. Its big hairy body moved slowly along.

"Look, a tarantula," said Mr Sir, also fascinated.

Stanley felt something sharp on the side of his neck. But it wasn't a bite. The lizard jumped off Stanley's neck onto the tarantula. One hairy leg stuck out of the lizard's mouth.

"Not hungry, huh?" said Mr Sir.

The Big Read 4

1 Look at the picture of the book *Girl, Missing*. What can you see?

2 Read the definitions below. What do you think happened in the story?

missing /'mɪsɪŋ/ **adj** lost, or not in the right or usual place: *a missing person*

adopt **verb** to take a child into your own family by law
adopted **adj** *an adopted child*

3 Now read the story. Complete the summary with a, b or c.

Lauren was adopted when she was three. She had an essay for homework about herself. ...

a Her friend Jam came to help her. He used a website to change a photo of Lauren. She looked older in the photo.
b When she was small Lauren was missing for a few days. But her parents found her again and took her back home to the USA.
c Lauren looked on a website for missing children. She found a girl and thought maybe it was her. Jam tried to help her and made the girl look older.

4 Find the words in the text. Match them with the correct letters (**a–d**) in the picture.

1 search engine (line 13)
2 homepage (line 17)
3 to click on (line 17)
4 link (line 55)

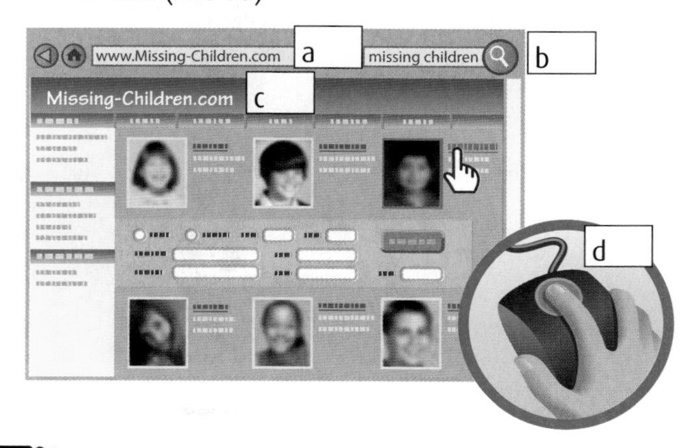

5 Read the story again. Write the correct names for the sentences below: *L* for *Lauren*, *M* for *Martha* or *L+M* for both.

a ______ She is 14.
b ______ She is adopted.
c ______ She doesn't know where she comes from.
d ______ She is missing.
e ______ She has brown hair and blue eyes.
f ______ She is British.
g ______ She is American.
h ______ She doesn't know what to do.

6 Were your ideas in exercise 2 right? Discuss with the class.

7 Answer the questions.

a How did Lauren find the missing children website?
b How did Lauren find Martha's information?
c How did Jam make Martha older in her photo?

8 Write Lauren's essay: *Who am I?* Start like this:

My name is Lauren Matthews. ...

GIRL MISSING

Who am I?
I sat at the computer in Mum's office and stared at the essay heading. New teachers always give you homework like that.
When I was younger, it was easy. I wrote stuff like: *I am Lauren Matthews. I have brown hair and blue eyes.* 5
But now it was likes and dislikes. Who we are 'inside'.
How can anyone know who they are when they don't know where they come from?
And I have no idea where I come from. 10
I was adopted when I was three.

Who am I?
Adopted. Lost. I typed the words into the search engine box.
Nearly a million hits. 15
And then I saw it: *Missing-Children.com*. An international site for lost or missing children. I clicked on the homepage and typed in my name. *Lauren.*
There were one hundred and seventy-two. I added my birth month. Three Laurens appeared on the screen. I stared at the third child. 20
Martha Lauren Purditt
Date of birth: March 12
Age now: 14
Birth place: Evanport, Connecticut, USA
Hair: brown Eyes: blue
I looked at the date she went missing: September 8. Two months before I was adopted. 25
My heart seemed to stop beating.
The birth date was a couple of days later than mine. And I was British, not from America.
So it wasn't possible. Was it? 30
Could I be her?

***

'Lauren, Jam's here,' Mum shouted. I ran to the door.
'Hi Lauren,' my friend Jam smiled. 'Finished your homework?'
'Yeah. Er … no, actually.' 35
Jam followed me to the living room. Mum was on the sofa.
'Mum, where are our photo albums?'
She stared at me. 'In the cupboard. Why?'
'It's for this "Who am I?" essay,' I said. 'I want to put in a picture of me when I was younger.' 40
Mum's face relaxed. 'That's a good idea. Try the green album.'
I opened it at the first page. There I was. 'When was this?' I asked.
'Just after we got you,' she said. 45

***

I went back to mum's office and looked at the *Missing-Children.com* site. I held the photo of me next to the picture of Martha Lauren Purditt.
It could be me.
'What are you doing?' Jam walked over to the computer. 50
'Why are you looking at a missing children site?'
Jam looked from the photo of Martha Lauren Purditt to the photo of me. 'What? Do you think that's you?'
'I don't know,' I whispered.
Jam clicked on a link. A new picture came on the screen. 55
It showed how Martha Lauren Purditt might look today. It was me. But at the same time it wasn't. The face was too long and the nose was different.
'Mm,' said Jam. 'It's hard to say. But … there's a phone number. Maybe you should call and … 60
'No. No way. … I need time to think,' I said.
'Don't you want to find out if that is really you?' Jam said.
'Maybe.'
I didn't know. I didn't know anything any more.

Units 1–3 Partner exercises for A

Unit 1

Page 11, Role play

Partner A

A day in the life of a pop star

You get up **at 11.30.**
You **have breakfast** at 12.30.
You don't **have lunch.**
In the afternoon you **sing and listen to music**.
At 6 pm you have a dance class.
At 8 pm you **have dinner** with friends.
At 10 pm you go to a club with friends.
At 2 am you go to bed.

Unit 2

Page 19, Role play

Partner A

(A new student at the school)

Name:	*Paul / Paula*
From:	*Brazil*
Lives:	*about 2 km from the school*
Transport to school:	*bus*
Likes school:	*not really*
Favourite subject:	*chemistry*

Unit 3

Page 29, Exercise 6

Partner A

Unit 4

Page 35, Role play

Partner A

Unit 5

Page 41, Exercise 7

Partner A

Place	Temperature	Weather
Yakutsk, Russia	-50° C	
Timbuktu, Mali, Africa	54°C	
Auckland, New Zealand	7°C to 23°C	
Singapore	23°C to 32°C	(171 thunderstorm days a year)

Page 43, Role play

Partner A

When? summer 2010, 2 August
Where? swimming pool in park
Weather? was really hot and the temperature was 36°C
What? an old lady was on the grass, was dead, it was too hot for her
Feeling? very sad

Unit 6

Page 51, Role play

Partner A

music school / practise at home, not very good!

in my room, good at cartoons

everywhere; know lots of songs

Page 53, Conversation

Partner A

Unit 7

Page 63, Role play

Partner A

Shopper

You see a white jacket.
Ask the price.
Ask if they have the jacket in blue.
Thank the shop assistant.

Shop Assistant

Shorts: €25
Changing room: next to the coats.

Unit 8

Page 71, Role play

Partner A

(go) on holiday to France
(be) on a campsite for two weeks
(make) some new friends
(take) lots of photos
(eat) some good food

Unit 9

Page 78, Mini quiz

Partner A and Partner B

Mostly A's:	You're super sporty! Just make sure you do other things too.
Mostly B's:	You're quite sporty. You know it's fun and also good for your health.
Mostly C's:	You're not sporty at all. Get off the sofa and get fit!

Page 79, Role play

Partner A

Favourite sport	
Team or club?	gymnastics club
Support?	my local gymnastics club
Watch?	gymnastic performances at competitions
Why like this sport?	keeps you fit and healthy

Unit 10

Page 87, Exercise 10

Partner A and Partner B

can of cola	155	small apple	77
glass of orange juice	112	small banana	90
bottle of water	0	slice of cheese pizza	192
cheeseburger	319	piece of fish	165

Unit 11

Page 95, Role play

Partner A

I think students should have exams in life skills
– things like managing stress or teamwork.

I think school is great – we learn lots of new and interesting things.

I think the school days are too long – I'm always tired in class.

I think an interesting job is more important than money.

I think it's too early now to decide on a job.

Unit 12

Page 103, Role play

Partner A

Event	El Colacho, the baby jumping festival
Where	In a village in the north of Spain
What happened	A man in strange clothes jumped over babies in the street. People said it gives the babies good health.
What you thought	Dangerous; didn't want to watch it.

Unit 1

Page 11, Role play

Partner B

A day in the life of a football player

You get up **at 6.30** and go running.
You have breakfast at **7.30**.
In the morning you **play football**.
At 1pm you **have lunch**.
At 4 pm you go to the gym.
At 7 pm you **have dinner** at home.
After dinner you watch TV or play computer games.
At 10 pm you **go to bed**.

Notes for Partner B

(A day in the life of a pop star)

I get up ________. I ________ at 12.30.
I don't ________.
________ I sing and listen to music.
________ I have dance classes. At 8 pm
I ________ with friends. ________
I go to a club. ________ I go to bed.

Page 13, Exercise 4

Partner B (Melody)

(eye)	films
(phone)	friends
(book)	a lot

Unit 2

Page 19, Role play

Partner B

(A new student at the school)

Name:	*Angelo / Angelina*
From:	*Italy*
Lives:	*near the school / in the town centre*
Transport to school:	*bike*
Likes school:	*yes, a lot*
Favourite subject:	*History*

Unit 3

Page 29, Exercise 6

Partner B

Unit 4

Page 35, Role play

Partner B

Unit 5

Page 41, Exercise 7

Partner B

Place	Temperature	Weather
Cherrapunji, India	8°C to 29°C	(11,777 mm of rain a year)
Newfoundland, Canada	−10°C to +20°C	
Mawson Station, Antarctica	2°C to −21°C	(300 kph winds)
Faro, Portugal	9°C to 28°C	(3,000 hours of sun a year)

Unit 5

Page 43, Role play

Partner B

When?	autumn 2009, 4 November, about 7.30 pm
Where?	my room, home
Weather?	was quite cold and the temperature was 2°C
What?	was stormy, with thunder and lightning and really big hailstones my parents' car was outside and there was a big hole in the window
Feeling?	really surprised

Unit 6

Page 51, Role play

Partner B

school, in school team, good player

and at home;
very good at some games

at school, on the bus,
at home; very fast reader

Page 53, Conversation

Partner B

Unit 7

Page 63, Role play

Partner B

Shop assistant

Jacket: €40
Colours: white, black

Shopper

You see some shorts.
Ask the price.
Ask if you can try them on.
Thank the shop assistant.

Unit 8

Page 71, Role play

Partner B

(be) at home
(go) on some day trips with my family
(see) lots of interesting places
(meet) my friends on the other days
(have) a good time

Unit 9

Page 78, Mini quiz

Partner A and Partner B

Mostly A's:	You're super sporty! Just make sure you do other things too.
Mostly B's:	You're quite sporty. You know it's fun and also good for your health.
Mostly C's:	You're not sporty at all. Get off the sofa and get fit!

Page 79, Role play

Partner B

Favourite sport?	
Team or club?	in school under 15's team
Support?	New York Knicks, school team
Watch?	basketball on TV with my dad, NBA games
Why like this sport?	fast and exciting

Unit 10

Page 89, Conversation

Partner A & Partner B

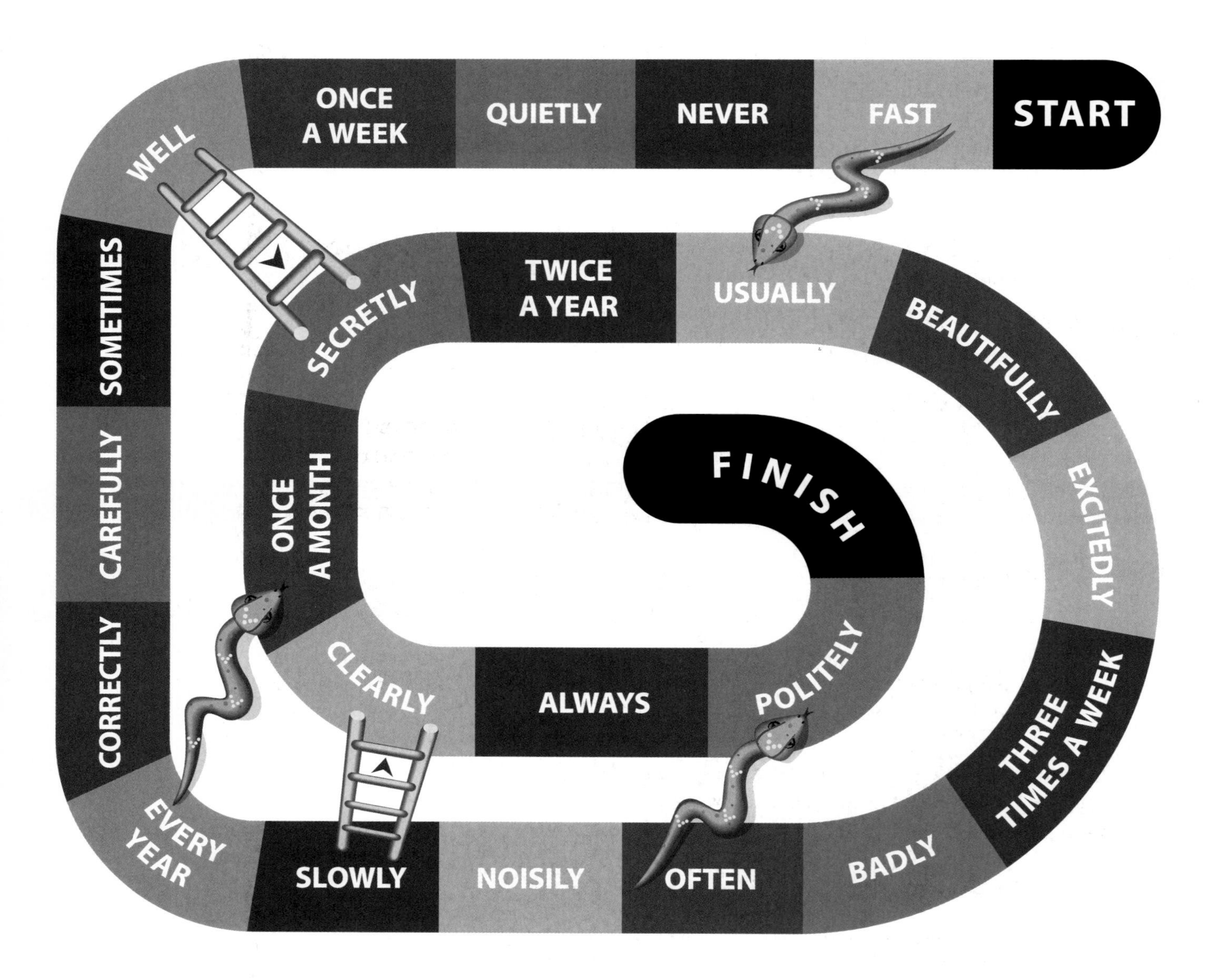

Unit 11

Page 95, Role play

Partner B

I think computer games should be a school subject.

I think friends are the best thing about school.

I don't think school teaches us the most important things for jobs.

I think a good education is really important for a good job.

I think every student should spend a year after school as a volunteer.

Page 95, Exercise 4

Answer: talk to friends (53%)

Unit 12

Page 103, Role play

Partner B

Experience	Manchester United football camp
Where	Staffordshire, England
What you did	We trained for football every day for six days. On the last day we went to Old Trafford, Manchester United's football ground.
What you thought	Fantastic; didn't want to go home.

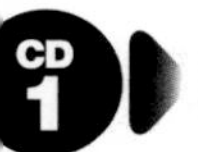

Unit 1 Home life

2 VOCABULARY

2 Exercise 1

(Laura) I live with my mum, my grandma and my cat. We live in an apartment on the seventh floor. It has a big balcony. My uncle, that's my mum's brother, lives next door.

(Daniel) I live with my mom and my stepfather. My stepbrother Ryan lives with us and I have two little half-sisters. We live in a new house by the beach.

3 Exercises 2, 3

mother (mum)	father (dad)
stepmother	stepfather
grandmother (grandma)	grandfather (granddad)
daughter	son
sister	brother
half-sister	half-brother
stepsister	stepbrother
cousin	cousin
girlfriend	boyfriend
aunt	uncle
wife	husband
grandparents	parents

4 Exercises 6, 7

(Daniel)
Our house is really big. Downstairs there's a living room, a dining room and a kitchen. There's a big family room too with a TV and computer and video games – I love it! There's a bathroom downstairs too. We have a big backyard and – we're lucky – and there's a swimming pool on the roof!

Upstairs there are three bedrooms. I share a room with Ryan, then there's my sisters' bedroom – they share a room too. My mom and stepfather's bedroom has a big balcony. And there are two bathrooms upstairs.

3 LISTENING

5 Exercises 2, 3

(Aiko) I don't have any brothers or sisters, I'm an only child. My parents start work early and they get up at six o'clock. I have breakfast alone on weekdays before I go to school. And when I come home from school in the afternoon, there's nobody there. Sometimes I feel lonely. ... But there are some good things. It's always nice and quiet at home. I have my own room ... it's tidy. And on Saturdays and Sundays, at the weekend, my parents and I hang out together.

(Josh) I don't live with my dad. I live in a children's home with 11 other boys. I'm never lonely because there's always somebody there. We finish school at 4 o'clock and then we play football together. In the evening we hang out and talk, have dinner together and listen to music or watch TV before we go to bed. That's great but I miss my dad sometimes. ... It's never quiet here. I share a room with two other boys. They always talk when I want to go to sleep. And our room is so messy! The other boys' things are everywhere.

6 Exercise 6

(Aiko) On weekdays I get up at seven o'clock. School starts at half past eight so I go to school at 8 o'clock. I usually come home at five o'clock. I go to bed early – about 9 o'clock or half past nine.

At the weekend, I sleep late. I get up about 10 o'clock. I have lunch with my parents at half past 12. Then I hang out with my parents or friends in the afternoon. At the weekend I go to bed late – about 11 o'clock.

7 Exercise 8

Get up, get up, get up
It's late, late, late It's half past eight,
You're late for school

Oh, mum, stay cool
I have half an hour
Time to take a shower
No problem, mum, stay cool

6 GRAMMAR

9 Exercise 3

Pronunciation: lives, learns, puts, works, watches, practices

10 Exercises 6, 7

Interviewer: What do you do in the circus?
Jessinta: I do lassos and whips.
Interviewer: Do you like the circus?
Jessinta: Yeah, I love it.
Interviewer: And where do you live?
Jessinta: We live in the caravans.
Interviewer: Do you miss school or school friends?
Jessinta: No.

Unit 2 Cool schools

2 VOCABULARY

12 Exercises 2, 3

Rune: Hi, my name is Rune.

Ida: Hi, my name is Ida.
Rune and **Ida:** Welcome to Henriette Hørlücks School in Odense.
Ida: Our school is quite small, there are only 475 students.
Rune: It's a private school – everyone can go there but parents pay some money for lessons and books. It's for students from six to 16.
Head teacher: Well, this is our school and it's a very old school.
Rune: It's the head teacher's school. He lives in the school too. There are four buildings.
Ida: In each class there are about 23 students. In our class there are 24 students.
Rune: The teachers are not very strict. And there are not many rules at our school.
Ida: We call our teachers by their first names. Our English teacher's name is Johanne.
Rune: We don't wear uniforms at our school, we wear our normal clothes.

13 2 Exercise 5

Rune: Our school has a beautiful main hall. There are lots of old things and art everywhere.
Ida: There isn't a cafeteria. The school has a little shop and some students buy lunch there. We eat lunch in our classroom. The school has a gym where we do sport, but it doesn't have a swimming pool.
Rune: Our school doesn't have a football pitch or tennis courts. But there's a school playground where students hang out or play games. The school has a cinema. The chairs are from an old plane.
Ida: There is a small library. The sofas are great!

14 2 Exercise 6

Pronunciation: main hall, cafeteria, shop, classroom, gym, swimming pool, football pitch, tennis courts, school playground, cinema, library

3 LISTENING

15 3 Exercise 1

English, biology, music, IT, art, chemistry, maths, history, sport, physics

16 3 Exercises 2, 3

I have a lot of different subjects. Monday is a good day. I have chemistry, I like that, and biology – I like that too. Then I have music – that's OK. Then maths – I love maths. Next is English, I love that too. English is my favourite subject because it's fun and the teacher is nice. The last lesson is geography – that's OK.
Tuesday is not a good day. We have IT first – that's OK. But then we have physics, art and history. I don't like physics, I don't like art and I don't like history. Then we have sport in the afternoon. Luckily, I like sport.

17 3 Exercises 9, 10

Girl: Hi, you're Philip, right? I'm Helena.
Boy: Hi.
Girl: Where are you from?
Boy: England. My mum has a job in Denmark.
Girl: Oh, right ... Where do you live here?
Boy: In the town centre, near the school.
Girl: So how do you go to school? By bike?
Boy: No, I walk. It's only two streets.
Girl: That's lucky! So ... do you like school?
Boy: Mmm, yes, sometimes!
Girl: What's your favourite subject?
Boy: Maths.
Girl: Really? That's my favourite subject too ...

6 GRAMMAR

19 6 Exercises 5, 6

Pronunciation:
a Do you like to visit new countries?
b Do you learn to cook at school?
c When do you have lunch at school?
d What sports do you do at your school?
e Do you do sports after school?
f Where do you do your homework?

Unit 3 Hangouts

2 VOCABULARY

20 2 Exercises 1, 2

a the café
b the shopping centre / the shopping mall
c the street
d online
e the library
f the skate park
g the swimming pool
h the beach
i my friend's house
j the park

21 2 Exercise 3

1 We live near the beach so my friends and I often hang out there. We love the beach.
2 There's not much to do here. We usually hang out in the street or ride bikes.
3 We often go to the library. There are magazines

and books and the internet. The library's great.

4 I often meet my friends in a café near here. We hang out there for hours and chat.

5 Sometimes we go to the shopping mall and meet some other friends there. I like to shop.

6 We usually go to the park. We play basketball and hang out and talk. Or we go to the sports centre and play basketball there.

7 Well, sometimes I hang out at home with a friend and talk.

8 I like the skate park. It's near here. I meet lots of my friends there.

9 My favourite place is the swimming pool. I always go there with my friends in the summer.

10 I live in a very small town so most of my friends are online. We play games, chat and do homework together.

22 2 Exercise 6

a bank **b** museum **c** cinema **d** train station **e** restaurant **f** police station **g** hospital **h** theatre

3 LISTENING

23 3 Exercise 1

Turn right. Turn left. Go straight on.
Turn right. Turn left. Go straight on.

24 3 Exercises 2, 3

Conversation 1

Woman: Hello! ... Excuse me, is there a store here?
Boy: A store. No.
Woman: Well, is there a store *near* here?
Boy: Yeah, er ... go straight on.
Woman: To where?
Boy: To the next town. Go straight on along the road for about 20 minutes.
Woman: And then?
Boy: Just go straight on. It's on the left. You can't miss it. There's only one road ... and only one store!

Conversation 2

Man: Excuse me, how do I get from here to the cinema?
Girl: Which cinema? There are lots of cinemas here.
Man: Er ... Apollo. It's near here.
Girl: Ah, OK. Turn left here, then right, then left. Then go across the road. The cinema's between a clothes shop and a restaurant. It's opposite a bank. You can't miss it.
Man: Left, right, left. Opposite a bank. Thanks.

6 GRAMMAR

26 6 Exercise 5

Pronunciation:

a There aren't many shops.
b There isn't much graffiti.
c There's some traffic.
d There are some hotels.
e There isn't any grass.
f There aren't any trees.
g There are a lot of buildings.
h There's a lot of litter.

Unit 4 Not just a job

2 VOCABULARY

28 2 Exercise 1

1 My mum works in a hospital. She's a doctor.
My big brother's a police officer. He loves his job – but he doesn't like the hat!
My cousin has a Saturday job as shop assistant. She works in a clothes shop.

2 My parents have a small ice cream café. My sister is a waitress at weekends and my brother works there as a waiter.
My cousin works with old people. He's a nurse.
My grandfather's an actor in the theatre. He wears lots of different costumes.

3 My mum's a driver. She drives a taxi. She's really happy with her job.
My stepbrother's a cleaner. He cleans offices in the evening.
My cousin travels to different countries and writes books about them. She's sort of an explorer.

4 My dad's a farmer. He gets up very early in the morning and works really hard.
My stepsister's an engineer. She fixes the machines in a car factory.
We think my uncle is a spy. Really! He doesn't talk about his work and he travels a lot.

29 2 Exercise 2

Pronunciation: actor, cleaner, doctor, driver, engineer, explorer, farmer, nurse, police officer, shop assistant, spy, waiter / waitress

3 LISTENING

30 3 Exercises 2, 3

Interview, part 1

Interviewer: ... so what are your favourite books?

Boy: I like the Alex Rider books by Antony Horowitz. There are films of the books too. ... Alex Rider is 14 years old and he lives with his uncle. His uncle is a spy ...
Int: A spy?
Boy: Yes, he works for the British government. ... But Alex doesn't know about his uncle's job. He thinks his uncle works in a bank.
Int: In a bank, right ...
Boy: Then the people who work with his uncle say his uncle is dead. So Alex becomes a spy too. He doesn't want to be a spy. But he doesn't think his uncle is dead and he wants to find him.

31 3 Exercise 5

clever, creative, brave, friendly, confident, calm

32 3 Exercise 8

Interview, part 2
Int: So Alex Rider becomes a spy. But he's only 14.
Boy: Yes, but he's very clever. He can do a lot of things.
Int: Like what?
Boy: Well, he can do martial arts and climb mountains.
Int: Really? Mmm.
Boy: And he can speak French, German and Japanese!
Int: Three languages, eh? Not bad.
Boy: He can ride quad bikes and mountain bikes ... and he can ride a horse – but isn't a very good horse rider. ... Oh yes, and he can drive ...
Int: Drive a car? You can't drive when you're 14 ...
Boy: Well Alex Rider can! ... He's a great driver. What else? Oh, he can scuba dive – he's a really good scuba diver.
Int: Mmm. But what about school? Does he go to school?

6 GRAMMAR

34 6 Exercise 2

Pronunciation:
- **a** Fire fighters can't work alone.
- **b** I can save your life!
- **c** The answer is never 'No, I can't.' It's always 'Yes, I can.'
- **d** Some people think girls can't be fire fighters.
- **e** Can I do it?

8 CLIL: The music industry

35 8 Exercise 2

Jobs you can do in the music industry. ... Well, first of all there's the artist – you know a singer, musician or band. The artist performs and records music. The artist has a manager. The manager organises the artist's career. Then there's a tour manager. The tour manager organises concerts in different places. People like roadies work for the tour manager. A roadie prepares the sound and light equipment for concerts. What else? Oh yes, A&R. The A&R person finds new bands for record companies. Then there's a producer. The producer produces recordings with the artist. And the sound engineer. The sound engineer does the sound recording.

Unit 5 Scary stories

2 VOCABULARY

36 2 Exercise 1

1. It's cold ... where's the sun?
   It's the clouds, look it's really cloudy... just wait a minute ...
2. Wow ... all white and snowy ... bit scary.
   Yeah, everything looks different in the snow ...
3. Aarrrgh, it's cold ... Owww! Stupid ice!
4. This fog is terrible ... I can't see anything. ... Where are we?
5. It's OK, it's OK, boy. I know, you hate thunder and lightning. I hate storms too ...
6. Oh, it's nice here in the sun ...
7. Rain, rain and rain again.
8. Oh, that wind – close the door!

37 2 Exercises 2, 3

Pronunciation:
- **a** Snow. It's snowy.
- **b** Sun. It's sunny.
- **c** Ice. It's icy.
- **d** Wind. It's windy.
- **e** Rain. It's rainy.
- **f** Fog. It's foggy.
- **g** Storm. It's stormy.
- **h** Cloud. It's cloudy.

38 2 Exercise 5

1. It's 40 degrees Celsius. It's hot.
2. It's 25 degrees. It's quite warm.
3. It's 4 degrees. It's cold.
4. It's minus 10 degrees. It's really cold.

3 LISTENING

39 3 Exercise 3

Thirty days has September,
April, June and November;
February has twenty-eight alone.
All the rest have thirty-one,
But in Leap Year that's the time,
When February's days are twenty-nine.

40 3 Exercise 4

The first of January
The second of January
The third of January
The tenth of January
The twelfth of January
The thirty-first of January

41 3 Exercise 5

Pronunciation:
The tenth of January.
The things that these things think,
they're the things that these things think.

42 3 Exercise 6

1939, 1977, 1986, 2010, 1974, 2004

43 3 Exercises 8, 9

Story 1: 'Lightning strikes man seven times' sounds like a story in a film. But for American park ranger Roy C. Sullivan it was a true story. The lightning strikes were all on different dates and in different places – in the park, in his garden, in a car – even in a building! After the fourth strike he was very scared of lightning. The seventh and last strike was on June 5th 1977 – on the top of his head. After this he was in hospital – but still alive!

Story 2: On the 16th of June 1939, there was frog rain in Trowbridge, England. Yes, frog rain! There was a bad storm with thunder and lightning. Mr Ettles, manager of the town swimming pool, was very surprised. After the storm there were hundreds of small frogs near the pool.

Story 3: On the 28th of February 2010 there were small fish everywhere after a rain storm in the small Australian town of Lajamanu. But this wasn't the first time: in 1974 and in 2004 there was fish rain in the same town! One man said: 'I'm just happy it wasn't crocodile rain!'

Story 4: The 14th of April 1986 was a sad day in Bangladesh. After a bad storm in Gopalganj, 92 people were dead. The reason? Huge hailstones. Hailstones are usually small balls of ice. But these were very big balls of ice – each one was over a kilogram! That's right – 1kg. The hail storm was very scary!

44 3 Exercise 11

1 I was so excited about my trip to the USA. It was hard to sleep the night before.
2 I don't like to speak in front of the class. My face was really red after my talk.
3 It was a terrible film. It was too slow.
4 The book was great at the beginning. But the ending was bad.

6 GRAMMAR

46 6 Exercise 3

Pronunciation:
a The next king *was* Edward. But his uncle *wasn't* happy.
b The princes *were* prisoners. But they *weren't* alive for long.

Unit 6 Tech time

2 VOCABULARY

47 2 Exercise 3

Pronunciation:
gadget, game

48 2 Exercise 4

Pronunciation:
play, favourite, camera, email, take, chat

49 2 Exercises 6, 7

1 My friends and I hang out at my house most days after school. This was a birthday present. It's great but the games are quite expensive. ... We play together and see who gets the most points.
2 This is my mum's, she works at home and she uses it for her work. But I can use it in the evening. I go on Facebook or I watch music videos on YouTube.
3 A lot of my friends have one but my dad says they're too expensive. Well, sometimes they're free but then you pay a lot of money every month.
4 We only have one in our house. Some people have three or four – one in every room. My friends and I watch films at weekends, and I watch my favourite series every night in the week.
5 I take it everywhere and I listen to music all the time. I can't live without it! I have about 2,000 songs so far. I add more every week.

3 LISTENING

50 3 Exercise 2

Boy: Show me your phone... Nice!
Girl: Mmm. The battery on my old phone was no good. I can use this one for 12 hours.
Boy: Twelve hours? Without a charger?
Girl: Yes. And I can go on the internet and download lots of apps on this.
Boy: Apps? Where?
Girl: Here. Can you see the screen? Just here.
Boy: Where's the keyboard? How do you write text messages?

Girl: On the screen here. You just type messages on the screen.
Boy: Cool.

51 3 Exercises 3, 4

And the winners are ... Mok-Min Ha and Yeong-Ho Bae from South Korea! Mok-Min Ha and Yeong-Ho Bae are fast, very fast and they don't make mistakes! The two students were the winners of an international text message competition. Mok-Min sends about 150 to 200 messages a day. She says that's normal: some of her friends send 500 messages! She texts when she walks, eats and watches TV. She even texts in school under the desk. Yeong-Ho can type eight letters or numbers *a second* on a keyboard. He usually sends 200–300 messages a day. He prefers text messages to phone calls because text messages are fast. The prize for the competition was 100,000 American dollars. Both winners want to use the money for their studies. Yeong-Ho wants to be an opera singer and Mok-Min would like to be an engineer.

6 GRAMMAR

52 6 Exercise 2

Pronunciation:

- **a** I'm working on a song.
- **b** We're mixing the music.
- **c** He's helping me with the sound.
- **d** Sean isn't singing with us.
- **e** We aren't performing together.

CD 2 Unit 7 Spend or save?

2 VOCABULARY

2 2 Exercises 5, 6

(Chloe) I have a babysitting job. I look after our neighbour's little boy every Friday evening and I earn £15 each week, so that's £60 a month. I save half and I spend the rest. I usually buy clothes and makeup but sometimes I go to the cinema, so I spend money on tickets.

(Jack) I get an allowance of £40 a month. I spend all of it. I don't spend much money on clothes ... But I buy DVDs and music downloads. And I spend a lot of money on food .... I'm good at computers so I design websites for people. I get about £200 a month. I save that money.

(Andy) My mum and dad have a clothes shop and I work there on Saturdays. They give me £80 a month. I don't save any money, I spend it all on video games and credit and apps for my phone. I can save later, when I get a real job.

3 LISTENING

3 3 Exercises 2, 3

Boy 1 Hey, nice T-shirt. I like this ...
Boy 2 Mmm, it's OK ...
Boy 1 Oh man, look at these sneakers. They're cool!
Boy 2 I don't need sneakers ...
Boy 1 Not for you, for me!
Boy 2 You already have, like about ten pairs of sneakers. Do you need another pair?
Boy 1 Need? No. Want? Yes. ... How much are they?
Boy 2 A hundred and ninety-nine dollars.
Boy 1 No way! ... OK, I don't need new sneakers. ...
Boy 2 Hey, come on, I need to get some nice pants for a family party next week.
Boy 1 Can't you just wear jeans?
Boy 2 No. Nice pants and a white shirt, my mom says.
Boy 1 Oh, man. Really?. ... hey, what about these? They're OK.

4 3 Exercise 4

Boy 2 Mmmm ... no price. ...Excuse me, how much are these pants?
Shop assistant They're 25 dollars.
Boy 2 OK. Do you have them in a bigger size?
Shop assistant Umm, yes. ... Here you are.
Boy 2 Can I try them on?
Shop assistant Sure, the changing room is over there.

5 3 Exercise 5

1. In this photo I'm wearing sunglasses and a baseball cap. I always wear sunglasses and not because sunglasses are trendy. I just don't like the sun in my eyes.
2. It was quite warm on this day so I'm wearing sandals with jeans. I really like this pink and white top – it's my favourite.
3. I'm wearing jeans and a white scarf. I wear scarves a lot. I love these grey boots, they're really comfortable.
4. In this photo, I'm wearing my blue and white hoodie. And I have my glasses on, of course. I can't see anything without my glasses.

6 3 Exercise 7

Pronunciation:

shorts
sweater
shirt
scarf
skirt
shoes

7 3 Exercise 10

Cristina Aranda lives and works in London. She's a fashion stylist. Fashion stylists make people look good. They give people a strong style or look. They are very creative and have lots of ideas about clothes and colours.

Cristina works on lots of different fashion projects. She does work for fashion pages in magazines and for adverts. For a fashion project, Cristina first finds out about different clothes, shoes, bags and scarves. She gets ideas for a style. Then she chooses the clothes. She takes the clothes to the fashion shoot. Sometimes it is in a studio. Sometimes it is in a different place – on the street, in an office or on a beach. Cristina dresses the models and makes sure they look good.

Sometimes Cristina works for private customers. They want help to find a style. Cristina talks to them and decides which clothes are best for them – comfortable clothes or trendy clothes? Jeans and trainers or smart dresses and jackets? She shows them some examples. Cristina knows a lot about clothes and she can give people new ideas. Her customers are always happy with their new style!

Unit 8 Holidays!

2 VOCABULARY

8 2 Exercises 1, 2

1	France	**6**	United Kingdom
2	United States	**7**	Turkey
3	Spain	**8**	Germany
4	China	**9**	Malaysia
5	Italy	**10**	Mexico

9 2 Exercises 4, 5

Are you looking for a special place to stay on holiday? We have five great tips!

(Place 1) In this little guest house on Lake Malaren in Sweden, you don't stay by a lake, you stay on it. The bedroom is downstairs, under the water so you can watch the fish. You also get a small boat so you can visit the next island.

(Place 2) This motel in the mountains of Arizona in the USA is near the famous road, Route 66. You can stay in an old train from 1929, with two bedrooms and a bathroom. Around the motel, there are beautiful forests.

(Place 3) This plane in the rainforest of Costa Rica is part of a luxury hotel. It has two bedrooms and bathrooms, a dining room, a small kitchen and a TV room. You can also stay in a holiday apartment by the sea here.

(Place 4) You can live prison life in this hostel in Latvia and find out about its history. The rooms in the old prison are cold and uncomfortable. People shout at you and dinner is old bread with tea!

(Place 5) This great campsite is in a field in the English countryside. You can stay in a beautiful old caravan or in a tent. There's no electricity, but there are showers and an outside bath.

3 LISTENING

10 3 Exercises 2, 3

Dad OK, so where can we go?

Boy Well, there are five day trips on this website. ... The first one is Alton Towers – you know, the theme park and water park.

Dad Oh no!

Boy It sounds great. Listen to this. Lots of amazing rides ... fly up to the sky, then fall to the ground. ...

Dad OK, OK. Sorry, no. You know I hate theme parks. What else?

Girl Stonehenge. Wow, it's five thousand years old. I'd like to go there. You can go on a trip in the evening and go inside the circle.

Dad Mmm, yes, but it's a long trip, about three hours by train and bus there and then three hours back. ... What's that with the boat?

Girl Erm... The Norfolk Broads ... 300 km of rivers and lakes. You can go on a cruise on a big boat or hire a boat. It says it's quiet and relaxing ... that means boring!

Dad I think that sounds nice. A nice quiet day on the river ...

Boy Mmm, boring. ... The next one is Brighton. Hey, what about Brighton? Great weather for the beach.

Girl Yeah, and there are all those great shops, you know in those little streets.

Dad Mmm, yes, I like Brighton too. OK, that sounds good. What's the last one?

Boy Windsor Castle. Windsor is the oldest castle in the world, one of the homes of the royal family ... beautiful rooms and famous paintings ...

Girl The weather's too nice to be inside in a castle.

Dad Yes, you're right. Perhaps we can go there on a rainy day. Brighton then?

11 3 Exercises 7, 8

I went to Camp Echo Lake for the first time last year. I wasn't sure about it at first because summer camp is usually for younger kids. And seven weeks is a long time! But there were about 25 kids my age. I met some great people and I made a lot of new friends. The time went really fast too, there were just so many things to do!

There were also art and music activities, but I didn't want to be inside. I live in New York City, so the best thing about the camp for me was all the outdoor stuff. I went rock climbing in the Adirondack Mountains and water skiing on Lake George – I fell in the water lots of times but it was really fun. There was one scary moment – we saw a black bear on a hiking trip. Luckily, it went away. I like photography so I took lots of photos of the lakes and mountains and even one of the bear. In the evening the other kids told scary stories around the campfire. But I was usually so tired I just went to bed.

6 GRAMMAR

12 6 Exercise 3

Pronunciation:

- **a** danced
- **b** smiled
- **c** shouted
- **d** uploaded
- **e** phoned
- **f** dropped

Unit 9 Loves and hates

2 VOCABULARY

13 2 Exercises 2, 3

(Fabrizio) I collect stamps – on letters and postcards, and also new stamps. Some people think it's strange to be interested in bits of paper. But I love learning things about different countries. I also collect foreign coins. I have a really big collection.

(Mel) My sister makes all sorts of things. She's really creative. She makes her own clothes, really cool stuff, different to the clothes in the shops. She makes videos too. She films us all the time at home and on holiday, it's really embarrassing. ...Oh, and she makes amazing cakes. I help her to eat them!

(Oliver) I make model planes. I started when I was small ... when I was six ... and I still enjoy it. I also collect key rings from football clubs. I buy them on the internet with my allowance. I have 63 at the moment.

14 2 Exercise 4

Pronunciation:

foo**t**
ball
post
car**d**s

3 LISTENING

15 3 Exercise 3

1. **(ice-skating)** Erm, I can't do this. Yes, you can, it gets easier. Just hold my hand, I have you. You can't fall. ... Oh, are you Ok?
2. **(athletics)** And it's Veronica Powell of Jamaica in the lead, just in front of Shelly Carter. But Shelly is running faster and they're nearly at the line. ... Yes, Shelly is the winner of the women's 100 metres!
3. **(riding)** Good boy, Brownie. Let's go a bit faster, come on.
4. **(table tennis)** Wang hits it back, that was a high one. ... And another high one ... but Wang gets it back again ... just look how fast the ball is moving ...
5. **(hockey)** Hey! Over here. ... Got it. ... Ow, my leg ...
6. **(gymnastics)** Now Nikolai Aleksandrov from Russia is on the rings. Good control. And you can see how strong his arms are ... a fantastic gymnast ...
7. **(skateboarding)** Wow. Cool new board! ...Yeah, birthday present. Not bad, huh? ...Yeah, nice.
8. **(baseball)** And Jim Campbell for Atlanta. A high ball ... and he hits it hard. He's running to second base ... yep, he's there.
9. **(cycling)** Hey, get out the way! This is a cycle path – it's for bikes not dogs!
10. **(volleyball)** Nice play there by Brad Hamilton for Sydney. ... And the score now is seven all ... good teamwork on both sides.

16 3 Exercise 4

Pronunciation:

1. ice-skating
2. athletics
3. riding
4. table tennis
5. hockey
6. gymnastics
7. skateboarding
8. baseball
9. cycling
10. volleyball

17 3 Exercises 5, 6

(Speaker 1) What sports do I do? Well, we play football at school but I'm not that interested in it. In my free time, I go skateboarding with my friends at the skate park and I go cycling on my mountain bike.
(Speaker 2) At school I do gymnastics. And I go ice-skating in the winter – I go to classes at a stadium near where I live. The training is really hard.
(Speaker 3) I love baseball. I play on the school team and we train two days after school. I watch a lot of baseball on TV too. And sometimes I play ping pong or table tennis at home with my dad.
(Speaker 4) I often go riding at the weekends. At school, we do athletics in the summer. I like athletics. We play hockey in the winter, but I really hate that!

18 3 Exercises 9, 10

Girls' football, or soccer in the US, is popular in a lot of countries. But for girls in Afghanistan, it was an impossible dream for many years. Until 2001, the government (the Taliban) made life very hard for girls and women. They couldn't go to school or university, and they couldn't have paid jobs. Girls could only go outside with their father or brother. They also couldn't ride bikes, do sports or go to sports clubs. They couldn't even watch sports games.

That changed in 2001 when the Taliban lost a lot of their power. Today in Kabul, the capital of Afghanistan, there are 15 girls football teams with players from ages 13 to 20. There is also a national women's team, Kabul United.

But it's still not easy for girls to play football. Many men still think girls shouldn't play football and some parents don't want their daughters to be football players. Often the girls have nowhere to play because girls can't use the boys' football pitches.

Another problem is clothes. The girls wear long trousers to play football so they don't show their legs. Some girls wear baseball caps and others wear head scarves so they don't show their hair. It's difficult to play football when you are worrying about your clothes.

For the girls in the Kabul United team, these problems are real. But they try to see beyond them because they love the game. Football brings them closer together. And as a team, they are ready to fight for football.

Unit 10 Live to eat?

2 VOCABULARY

19 2 Exercises 1, 2

1 My grandma taught me to make sushi. It's important that the food looks nice but the most important thing, though, is that the food is fresh, especially the fish. You don't always cook the fish, so it has to be fresh. You also need special rice and small pieces of vegetables. We sometimes serve it with lemon.
2 I just love Greek salad. I often make this, it's so easy – and it's really healthy. First you need cheese – feta cheese. Then some tomatoes, olives and an onion. We always put cucumber in our salad but some people make it without. Then you just pour olive oil over the salad.
3 My favourite meal is English breakfast. My dad usually cooks this on Sunday. We have bacon, fried eggs, sausage and tomatoes. We always drink orange juice with it, and tea – with milk of course.
4 This is my favourite meal. You see it everywhere now but my mother makes the best spaghetti Bolognese ever! She makes the pasta herself and the meat sauce is my grandmother's recipe.
5 I often make chow mein because it's quick and easy and I love noodles. I make it with chicken and carrots and any other vegetables we have.
6 My favourite meal is a burger and French fries, or 'chips' as the British call them. I love a burger with that special burger bread and everything on it – lettuce, onion and tomato. And cola to drink, of course. Mmmm, tastes great.
7 We eat this soup a lot at home. It's a Mexican bean soup – beans are one of my favourite foods. It also has onions, tomatoes and peppers in it. Sometimes we eat it with sour cream on top.
8 I eat lots of fruit, so one of my favourite things is fruit salad. I usually use bananas, oranges, grapes, strawberries and kiwis – but you can use anything really. You just cut it up and put it all in a bowl. You can eat it with yoghurt – or you can just eat the fruit.

20 2 Exercise 3

Pronunciation:

1 vegetables
2 lemon
3 tomato
4 olive
5 onion
6 cucumber
7 bacon
8 sausage
9 noodles
10 carrot
11 lettuce
12 pepper
13 pineapple
14 strawberry
15 yoghurt

3 LISTENING

21 3 Exercises 3, 4, 5

A survey by Dairy Farmers of Britain asked young people in Britain aged 8 to 15 years old about food. And the results were surprising. More than 11% don't know where pork comes from. Eighteen per cent don't know where yoghurt comes from. And 11% have no idea that cheese comes from cows, sheep or goats.

Kids in the city have more problems with which animals produce which foods. Two per cent of city kids think that eggs come from cows and that bacon is from sheep. Eight per cent of city kids don't even know that burgers are beef and come from cows. Luckily, all the children knew that cows produce milk.

Farmers say children need more information about where food comes from. Many children today live in towns and cities. They don't see animals or learn about life in the countryside. And today a lot of people buy fast food or ready meals and don't cook for themselves.

6 GRAMMAR

22 6 Exercise 4

Pronunciation:

a Every year there's a famous hot dog eating competition in the USA.
b They go to the gym three times a week.

8 CLIL: Water and the body

23 8 Exercise 1

The human body is 60–65% water. Babies and children have more water than adults. Your brain is actually 80–85% water. And your kidneys contain the same amount of water: 80–85%. You might be surprised to know that your blood is 80% water. And your heart contains 75–80%. And did you know your skin is 70–75% water? Your bones have the smallest amount of water: only 20–25%.

Unit 11 Learning for life

2 VOCABULARY

24 2 Exercises 1, 2

Hi, I'm Ben, I'm 15 and I go to a secondary school in Nottingham in England.

In England, kids start school at five. Some kids go to nursery before school, when they're three or four. But primary school starts at age five and lasts six years. Students start secondary school when they're 11 – and do an important test then. Every child in England does the same test. You start studying for GCSEs when you're 14. You do coursework – that's usually essays about the subject – from 14 to 16. Then you take GCSE exams at the end of secondary school, when you're 16. You can leave school at 16 after GCSEs. Or you can stay on at school and study in the sixth form. Some schools don't have a sixth form, so students go to sixth form college. Sixth form lasts two years from 16 to 18 and at the end students do A-level exams. You need A-levels for university.

25 2 Exercise 4

So as you all know, your GCSE exams are next year. So today we're going to look at life after GCSEs. Right, so what can you do? Well, first you need good exam results. But don't worry: if you fail your exams, you can retake them. You can always try again.

Now, some of you want to stay on at school, in the sixth form. But some of you want to leave school after your GCSEs. What can you do? Well, you can go to college and study a practical subject like art. Or you can apply for a job, of course. But that's not easy without work experience. So maybe it's a good idea to do some work experience first. Some of you want to do an apprenticeship – like when you work in a garage and learn about cars. You can also be a volunteer – perhaps work with children or old people or do something for the environment. The last choice, of course, is to travel. Some students like to travel round the world for a year or just visit another country and see something new.

Right, let's look first at sixth form ...

26 2 Exercise 5

Pronunciation:

a apply for a job
b retake exams
c do an apprenticeship
d travel round the world / visit another country
e be a volunteer
f stay on at school
g go to college

27 2 Exercises 6, 7

Interviewer: So you failed your exams?
Lucy: Yes, it was horrible, my parents were very disappointed. We talked a lot about my future and I decided to travel around the USA. My parents paid for my ticket to Chicago ...
Interviewer: Why Chicago?
Lucy: My mum's sister lives there. So I stayed with my aunt and uncle in Chicago first. I worked for a month as a waitress and saved some money. And then I travelled around the USA with my cousin. We had to do lots of jobs to pay for everything, but we had a great time.
Interviewer: Where did you work?
Lucy: Mostly in restaurants and hotels. And I found I really liked working in the hotel business. So when I went back home, I decided to retake my exams. I took my exams again in the summer.
Interviewer: And you passed ...
Lucy: Yes, this time I passed. So then I went to college and did a tourism course. Now I'm applying for a job.
Interviewer: Do you have any tips for students in school?
Lucy: Think really carefully about all the choices. Then go and see some of the world if you can. Different people want different things – only you can decide.

3 LISTENING

28 3 Exercise 2

1 I spend a lot of time working for tests and exams. I think exams are really important for your future – you can't get a good job today or go to university without

good exam results. I want to go to university and study physics, so I can be a scientist. It's important I get good marks for that.

2 I don't worry about exams. I want to do well in school but I think skills like teamwork and thinking for yourself are more important. I'm very creative and...er, I think I can be a good artist without top marks in exams.

3 My parents always check my homework and ask about tests and exams. They think school work is really important. So they think I should always have top marks. I feel really stressed. I work hard and I do well in school but I don't have much time with my friends.

4 I always try to learn for tests and exams, but I find it really hard. I sit down with my books and I really want to learn. But after about, you know, half an hour, I feel bored. I watch TV or listen to music and I don't finish learning the stuff. Then I get worried in exams and get bad marks.

5 In this country, it's important for schools to have good test and exam results. So a lot of the time we just learn stuff for tests. I think it's more important to learn useful things ... you know, important things for the real world.

29 3 Exercises 9, 10

Are you a gamer? Do you play online games a lot? And do your parents give you a hard time about this? Well, next time they say 'Do your homework, stop playing games!' or 'School work is more important than games', tell them this...

American games designer Jane McGonigal says games are very important. Gamers in the USA spend *10,000 hours* playing online games before they are 21. Kids in the USA also have 10,000 hours of lessons at secondary school. So American gamers spend the same time on games as they do at school! That's right, the same time on online games as school work.

And these gamers are learning lots of useful skills. For example, gamers are optimistic because they always believe they can win. They are sociable because they work together with other people. Gamers work hard and they spend a lot of time online. They're also learning life skills online. And they're using these skills to save the world – online. But Jane McGonigal says games can help the real world. For example, an online game about energy can help you save energy in real life.

So the next time your parents say 'Stop playing games', say: 'I'm not just playing games. I'm learning important life skills. And I'm saving the world.'

30 6 Exercise 2

Pronunciation:

a For the first semester I'm ...

b In the architecture class, we're ...

c During the next three years, I'm ...

8 CLIL: Plagiarism

31 8 Exercises 4, 5

Today there's a lot of pressure on students to do well in school. They often feel stressed about exams and marks. Our world is all about success. And when there's a lot of pressure, students often try and find answers on the internet. The internet makes it easy for students to take other people's ideas. But I think a lot of students don't actually plan to plagiarise other people's work. It's easy to read something on the internet and then copy it. A lot of students don't know that it isn't right to do this, or they forget to write down where their information came from. That's why we do a course on essays and the internet at our school. We tell students they need to write down the <u>website</u>; they need to write down the <u>title</u> of the article and the <u>author</u>; and they need to write the <u>date</u> when they used the website. Students must give this information in their work. And if they don't give their sources, we don't give them a mark.

Unit 12 Events and experiences

2 VOCABULARY

32 2 Exercises 2, 3, 4

Luke: Hey Ben, what do you want to do today?
Ben: I don't know really.
Luke: My sister went to this great photo exhibition last week. We could go to an exhibition.
Ben: Nah. It's too hot.
Luke: Let's have a water fight then.
Ben: No, I washed my hair this morning.
Luke: Oh no, your hair. ... What about bowling? Or maybe we could see a football match?
Ben: Too expensive. And I need food. I'm really hungry.
Luke: Yeah, me too. ... What about a barbecue?
Ben: A barbecue takes too long. And we need meat. I don't want to go shopping. ... I know, let's have a picnic. On the beach.
Luke: Yeah, right. I can call a few people and then everyone can bring something from home. We can cycle there.
Ben: OK. ... erm, what about your sister? We can ask her...
Luke: Sorry mate, she's working in an animal shelter this week. If you want her attention, you need four legs.
Ben: Very funny.

33 2 Exercise 5

Pronunciation:

a We could go to an exhibition.
We could see a football match.

b Let's have a water fight.
Let's have a picnic.

c What about bowling?
What about a barbecue?

3 LISTENING

34 3 Exercise 2, 3

(Speaker 1) I went to *La Tomatina* last August. It's a big tomato fight in Buñol. The fight began with a loud gun shot and then everybody threw tomatoes. You had to squash the tomatoes first, so nobody got hurt. After an hour there was a second shot and everybody stopped. Everything and everybody was red. I had bits of tomato and tomato juice in my eyes, my hair, everywhere! But it was really great fun. I loved it!

(Speaker 2) Every September in South Korea, in Boryeong, there's a mud festival. I went with my family last year. The mud is good for your skin. There was a big mud pool and we all went in with our clothes on. I didn't like it that much because the mud was very heavy and cold. But my skin was nice and soft later when I washed the mud off.

(Speaker 3) In Lop Buri here in Thailand there are a lot of monkeys. Every year in November there's a banquet for the monkeys – a big meal with lots of food. It's to say thank you to the monkeys because they bring good luck and lots of tourists. I was at the banquet two years ago on a school trip. There were tables with fruit and vegetables and drinks. The monkeys drank cola from cans! That was funny, but I was actually a bit scared of the monkeys.

(Speaker 4) I was on holiday with my family in Gloucestershire last summer. We went to see a competition where people run after a cheese. The runners ran down a really steep hill and a lot of them fell down. Some had bad accidents – one broke his arm and another broke his leg. And the winner didn't get any prize money – he only got the cheese! It was an interesting experience but it wasn't very exciting.

35 3 Exercise 4

a The fight began with a loud gun shot.
b And then everybody threw tomatoes.
c The monkeys drank cola from cans.
d The runners ran down a really steep hill.
e One broke his arm.
f He only got the cheese.

36 3 Exercises 8, 9, 10

Interviewer: Why did you do the Duke of Edinburgh's Award?
Lewis: Erm, well, it's a long story but I had a lot of problems at school. I had problems with reading and so I hated lessons. My teacher suggested I start the Duke of Edinburgh bronze award because it's about more practical skills.
Interviewer: What did you like best?
Lewis: The expedition was fantastic! We went hiking and did a 30 km expedition on foot. I learned to read a map, put up a tent and cook food outside. When we finished the expedition, it was the best feeling ever!
Interviewer: And the skills activity?
Lewis: Choosing that was easy. I'm really interested in computers. So I did a course about the different parts of a computer. I even built my own computer! That was cool.
Interviewer: What about the physical activity? What did you do for that?
Lewis: Table tennis. I started a table tennis club at my school. Lots of students play now.
Interviewer: What about the volunteer part?
Lewis: Well, I worked in an old people's home. I talked to people or just listened to them. They had a lot of good stories. They were really interesting.
Interviewer: Did you enjoy the Award?
Lewis: Yeah. It made me feel better about myself, more confident. It showed me I'm good at a lot of things.

6 GRAMMAR

37 6 Exercise 3

Pronunciation:
I have never been scared underwater.
I've never been scared underwater.

He has tried the moon walk too.
He's tried the moon walk too.

They have never visited the USA.
They've never visited the USA.

Glossary

Unit 1 Home life

act	part of a show or performance	*12, 1C*
alone	not with anyone else	*10, 1B*
apartment	a home all on the same floor, in a big building	*8, 1A*
autograph	a person's name on paper	*15, 1D*
backyard [US]	garden	*9, 1A*
balcony	a small outside area on the side of a building	*9, 1A*
beach	this is by the sea	*9, 1A*
boat	you travel on water in this	*15, 1D*
boring	not interesting or fun	*12, 1C*
boyfriend	a special friend (boy / man)	*8, 1A*
breakfast	the morning meal	*10, 1B*
caravan	you can travel with this small home	*12, 1C*
cells	these are a part of all plants and animals	*14, 1D*
children's home	a special home for children with no parents	*10, 1B*
chromosome	your genes are in this	*14, 1D*
circus	a kind of show, with clowns, jugglers etc.	*12, 1C*
clown	a funny circus performer with a big red nose	*12, 1C*
contain, to	to have inside	*14, 1D*
cook, to	to make a meal	*10, 1B*
costume	special clothes	*12, 1C*
cousin	the son or daughter of your aunt or uncle	*8, 1A*
curry	a kind of Indian food	*13, 1C*
dinner	the evening meal	*10, 1B*
easy	not hard	*12, 1C*
enchilada	[Spanish] a kind of Mexican food	*15, 1D*
family member	a person in a family	*8, 1A*
family tree	a diagram of all your family	*8, 1A*
floor	a level in a building	*8, 1A*
fruit	apples, bananas, oranges etc.	*15, 1D*
furniture	tables, chairs, beds etc.	*9, 1A*
garden	the area outside a house with grass and plants	*9, 1A*
genes	they decide who you are	*14, 1D*
genetics	the science of genes	*14, 1D*
girlfriend	a special friend (girl or woman)	*8, 1A*
grandparents	your mum's or your dad's mother and father	*8, 1A*
gym	where you can go to get fit or do sport	*11, 1B*
half	½ , 50%	*8, 1A*
half-brother	your brother from another mother or father	*8, 1A*
half-sister	your sister from another mother or father	*8, 1A*
hang out, to	to be with someone or in a certain place in your free time	*10, 1B*
hard	not easy	*12, 1C*
healthy	not ill	*14, 1D*
home	you live here	*8, 1A*
husband	a married man	*8, 1A*
identical twins	twins with the same face, eyes, hair etc.	*14, 1D*
interview, to	to ask someone questions	*11, 1B*
juggler	he / she throws things in the air in the circus	*12, 1C*
lake	a large area of water, but not the sea	*15, 1D*
lasso	a long rope (you catch horses with it)	*13, 1C*
live on the streets, to	to have no home	*10, 1B*
lonely	sad because you are alone	*10, 1B*
messy	not tidy	*10, 1B*
miss, to	to feel sad because you are not with someone or don't have something	*13, 1C*
next door	the home next to another one	*8, 1A*
online	on the internet	*15, 1D*
pair	two of something	*14, 1D*
parents	your mother and father	*8, 1A*
perfect	great	*15, 1D*
performance	a show	*12, 1C*
performer	a person in a show (e.g. a singer or clown)	*12, 1C*
personality	what you are like as a person	*14, 1D*
plan	a diagram of where things are	*9, 1A*
rent, to	to pay money to use a home, car etc.	*15, 1D*
routine	things you do every day or often	*10, 1B*
skill	you are good at this	*14, 1D*
star	a very famous person	*11, 1B*
stepfather	your mother's husband (not your father)	*8, 1A*
stepmother	your father's wife (not your mother)	*8, 1A*
tall [how tall you are]	your height (e.g. 1m 60cm)	*14, 1D*
take a shower, to	to stand under water and wash	*11, 1B*
ticket	a bit of paper to see a show	*12, 1C*
tidy	everything in the right place	*10, 1A*
tongue	the long pink thing in your mouth	*14, 1D*
travel, to	to go	*12, 1C*
twins	a brother and sister, two brothers, or two sisters with the same birthday	*14, 1D*
weekdays	Monday–Friday	*10, 1B*
weekend	Saturday and Sunday	*10, 1B*
whip	a long piece of leather or rope in the circus	*13, 1C*
wife	a married woman	*8, 1A*

Unit 2 Cool schools

art	drawing and painting pictures	*18, 2B*
bike	you sit and travel on it	*19, 2B*
biology	the study of living things	*18, 2B*

building	a house, school etc.	*16, 2A*
cafeteria	you buy your lunch here	*17, 2A*
chart	a diagram, a graph	*18, 2B*
chemistry	the study of H_2O, CO_2 etc.	*18, 2B*
cinema	you watch films here	*17, 2A*
classroom	you have your classes here	*17 LB3*
clothes	jeans, T-shirts etc.	*16, 2A*
cool	good, fun, modern	*16, 2A*
country, in the	not in a town or city	*23, 2D*
desk	a table in a classroom or office	*21, 2C*
expensive	you pay a lot of money for it	*23, 2D*
fantasy school	your dream school, a very good school	*23, 2D*
favourite	you like this most	*18, 2B*
football pitch	you play football here	*17, 2A*
free	when you don't pay money	*22, 2D*
free time	time when you can do what you want	*20, 2C*
geography	the study of the world	*18, 2B*
history	the study of the past	*18, 2B*
homework	you do this work for school at home	*20, 2C*
IT [= information technology]	how to use computers	*18, 2B*
inside	in a building	*20, 2C*
international	for or from a lot of countries	*22, 2D*
kayaking	a sport in a small boat	*20, 2C*
library	there are a lot of books here	*17, 2A*
main hall	a big meeting room in a school etc.	*17, 2A*
mini	small	*23, 2D*
modern	not old	*16, 2A*
move around, to	to go from one place to another	*20, 2C*
outside	not in a building	*20, 2C*
physics	the study of things like light and sound etc.	*18, 2B*
plane	you travel through the air in this	*17, 2A*
playground	the area around a school; students use it for sports and breaks	*17, 2A*
poor	without a lot of money	*22, 2D*
prefer, to	to like something more than something else	*19, 2C*
presentation	a talk about a subject	*23, 2D*
primary school	school for children from about 5–11	*22, 2D*
private school	you pay for this kind of school	*20, 2C*
public school	[= not private] you don't pay for this kind of school	*20, 2C*
right	the law says you can have or do this	*22, 2D*
rule	something you need to do	*16, 2A*
school uniform	everyone wears these clothes for school	*16, 2A*
secondary school	school for children from about 11–18	*22, 2D*
sleep, to	to close your eyes and rest	*20, 2C*
sponsor	this person pays for something for somebody else (e.g. their education)	*22, 2D*
strict	with lots of rules	*16, 2A*
study, to	to learn	*20, 2C*
subjects	you study these things at school (e.g. maths, English, history etc.)	*18, 2B*
swimming pool	you do sport in water (swim) here	*17, 2A*
tennis court	you play the sport tennis here	*17, 2A*
traditional	not modern, in old ways	*16, 2A*
train	people (and things) travel on this to places near and far	*19, 2B*
tram	a small electric train in cities	*19, 2B*
transport	buses, cars, trains etc. are all kinds of transport	*19, 2B*
university	you can study here when you leave school	*22, 2D*

Unit 3 Hangouts

across	from one side to the other side (e.g. of a street)	*26, 3B*
along	from one end to the other end (e.g. of a street)	*26, 3B*
bank	you keep your money in this building	*25, 3A*
behind	at the back of	*27, 3B*
between	with something on both sides, in the middle of	*27, 3B*
boxing	in this sport you fight people with your hands and arms	*28, 3C*
bright	not dark	*30, 3D*
bored	not interested	*28, 3C*
café	you have a drink here	*24, 3A*
century	100 years	*31, 3D*
communicate, to	to give information	*30, 3D*
crime	something against the law	*28, 3C*
dangerous	not safe (you can get hurt)	*28, 3C*
die, to	to stop living; to lose your life	*28, 3C*
directions	how to get somewhere	*27, 3B*
down	from a high to a low level, like this ↘	*26. 3B*
extreme cycling	riding a bike in dangerous places	*31, 3D*
gang	a group of dangerous people	*28, 3C*
get fit, to	to get strong and healthy through sport	*28, 3C*
get hurt, to	this happens to you when you fall, or when someone uses a knife or gun	*28, 3C*
graffiti	writing on walls	*29, 3C*
grass	a green plant on the ground in gardens and parks	*29, 3C*
gun	you can kill with this	*28, 3C*
hospital	you go here when you are very ill	*25, 3A*
hotel	you pay to sleep here	*29, 3C*
in front of	not behind; before	*27, 3B*
knife	you cut things with this (e.g. food)	*28, 3C*
left	(directions) this way: ←	*26, 3B*
litter	old paper in the street	*29, 3C*
map	a diagram of streets	*27, 3B*
martial arts	sports like karate and judo	*28, 3C*
member	a person in a club etc.	*24, 3A*

message	information for another person	*30, 3D*
monastery	a kind of old church; men live here	*31, 3D*
museum	a big building with lots of old things	*25, 3A*
neighbourhood	you live in this area	*31, 3D*
next to	to the side of something	*27, 3B*
offer, to	to give to someone	*28, 3C*
opposite	on the other side of something	*27, 3B*
organisation	this group of people works together to help others	*28, 3C*
park	an area in a town with trees and grass	*25, 3A*
past	from one side to another of a building or area	*26, 3B*
peace	no violence	*28, 3C*
picnic	you take this food with you and eat it outside	*31, 3D*
police station	the police work here	*25, 3A*
prepare for, to	to get ready for something	*28, 3C*
restaurant	you eat meals here	*25, 3A*
right	(directions) this way: →	*26, 3B*
route	the way from A to B	*27, 3B*
safe	not dangerous	*28, 3C*
shopping centre	a big building with lots of shops	*24, 3A*
shopping mall [US]	a big building with lots of shops	*24, 3A*
skate park	you go skateboarding here	*25, 3A*
sports centre	you do sports here	*27, 3B*
spray paint	paint in a can	*30, 3D*
stencil	you make a picture with this	*30, 3D*
sticker	paper with a picture on it	*30, 3D*
straight on	not right or left	*26, 3B*
style	how you do something	*30, 3D*
tag	a street artist's name as graffiti	*30, 3D*
theatre	you see a show here	*25, 3A*
traffic	cars, buses etc.	*29, 3A*
train station	you go here to take a train	*25, 3A*
train, to	to get strong and practise a sport	*28, 3C*
tree	a tall plant	*29, 3C*
ugly	not beautiful, not nice to look at	*30, 3D*
up	from a low to a high level, like this: ↗	*26, 3B*
violence	when people get hurt in fights with knives, guns etc.	*28, 3C*

Unit 4 Not just a job

accident	something bad (e.g. when a car drives into another car)	*36, 4C*
actor	a performer in a film or at the theatre	*32, 4A*
artist	he / she paints pictures	*33, 4A*
artist	[here] singer	*38, 4D*
band	a group of musicians	*38, 4D*
brave	not scared of dangerous things	*34, 4B*
break	a short rest from work or school	*37, 4C*
calm	not nervous when there is a problem	*34, 4B*
character	a person in a book, film etc.	*34, 4B*
check, to	to make sure something is ok	*36, 4C*
cleaner	he / she makes offices etc. clean and tidy	*32, 4A*
clever	learns and understands things fast	*34, 4B*
climb, to	to go up (e.g. a mountain)	*35, 4B*
company	a business	*33, 4A*
composer	he / she writes music	*38, 4D*
concert	a music performance	*38, 4D*
confident	sure about your skills	*34, 4B*
creative	has new ideas or makes new things	*34, 4B*
doctor	he / she helps people when they are ill	*32, 4A*
download	you take this from the Internet and put it on your computer, music player etc.	*38, 4D*
dead	when you die, you are dead	*34, 4B*
driver	he / she drives a taxi, a bus etc.	*32, 4A*
emergency	when somebody needs help fast	*36, 4C*
engineer	he / she designs and makes roads, machines etc.	*32, 4A*
equipment	you need these things to do a job	*36, 4C*
exciting	really fun	*34, 4B*
explorer	he / she goes to places to learn more about them	*32, 4A*
factory	people work and make things here	*32, 4A*
farm	farmers grow food and have animals here	*32, 4A*
fire fighter	he / she puts out fires and helps in accidents	*36, 4C*
farmer	he / she grows food and has animals like cows and sheep	*32, 4A*
fly, to	[here] to drive a plane	*35, 4B*
government	these important people make the laws in a country	*34, 4B*
heavy	not light, hard to carry	*36, 4C*
in training	when you learn a job	*36, 4C*
instructions	what you have to do	*36, 4C*
lyrics	the words of a song	*38, 4D*
manager	he / she organises a singer's or band's career	*38, 4D*
music industry	all the people with jobs in music	*38, 4D*
nurse	he / she cares for sick people	*32, 4A*
office	a room with desks where people work	*32, 4A*
patient	can wait for something and stay calm	*39, 4D*
police officer	he / she fights crime	*32, 4A*
politician	he / she works in politics or for the government	*33, 4A*
producer	he / she produces recordings with a singer or band	*38, 4D*
put out a fire, to	to stop a fire	*36, 4C*
quad bike	a motorbike with four big wheels	*35, 4B*
roadie	he / she prepares the sound and light equipment for concerts	*38, 4D*

safety	how to be safe	*36, 4C*
save someone's life, to	to keep someone from death	*36, 4C*
scared	how you feel when you are in a dangerous situation	*36, 4C*
shop assistant	he / she works in a shop	*32, 4A*
songwriter	he / she writes songs	*38, 4D*
sound engineer	he / she records the sound	*38, 4D*
spy	he / she finds out secret information about a country	*32, 4A*
studio	musicians make recordings here	*39, 4D*
team [work]	these people work together in a group	*36, 4C*
tour manager	he / she organises concerts in different places	*38, 4D*
waiter	he gives people their drinks and food in a café or restaurant	*32, 4A*
waitress	she gives people their drinks and food in a café or restaurant	*32, 4A*

Unit 5 Scary stories

alive	not dead	*44, 5C*
autumn	the season between summer and winter	*42, 5B*
calendar	a chart with the months, days and dates	*42, 5B*
cloud	grey or white areas in the sky	*40, 5A*
cloudy	with lots of clouds	*40, 5A*
cold	not warm	*40, 5A*
cry, to	when water comes out of your eyes	*46, 5D*
dark	black, with no light	*47, 5D*
date	a day, month and year	*42, 5D*
death	when someone dies	*44, 5C*
degree	you use this for temperature (e.g. it's 5°)	*40, 5A*
depressed	very sad for a long time	*46, 5C*
depression	a very sad feeling for a long time	*46, 5C*
disappointed	sad when something doesn't happen, e.g. when you don't win something	*43, 5B*
dry	without water or rain	*42, 5B*
embarrassed	how you feel when you do something wrong	*43, 5B*
equator	the line around the middle of the Earth	*42, 5B*
fall, to	to go down to the ground	*43. 5B*
FAQs [= Frequently Asked Questions]	questions and answers on the internet about a subject	*46, 5D*
fish	this animal lives in water	*43, 5B*
fog	in this weather, it is hard to see things	*40, 5A*
foggy	when there is a lot of fog	*40, 5A*
footsteps	the sound when someone walks	*47, 5D*
frog	this small animal is often green and likes water	*43, 5B*
ghost	an image of a dead person	*44, 5C*
hailstone	a ball of ice from the sky	*43, 5B*
have energy, to	to feel very active	*46, 5D*
hot	very warm	*41, 5A*
huge	very big	*43, 5B*
ice	water below 0°C	*40, 5A*
icy	when there is a lot of ice	*40, 5A*
ill	not healthy	*44, 5C*
leap year	a year with 366 days	*42, 5B*
lightning	light in the sky when there is a storm	*40, 5A*
lucky	good things happen to lucky people	*43, 5B*
minus	less than 0°C (e.g. −13°C)	*41, 5A*
month	January, February etc.	*42, 5B*
mood	how you feel (happy, sad etc.)	*46, 5D*
murder	when a person kills someone	*44, 5C*
order	someone tells you to do this	*45, 5C*
power	control over other people	*44, 5C*
prince	the son of a king	*44, 5C*
prison	you go here when you do something against the law	*44, 5C*
prisoner	a person in a prison	*44, 5C*
queen	the wife of a king	*45, 5C*
rain	water from the sky	*40, 5A*
rainy	with lots of rain	*40, 5A*
scary	makes you feel scared	*40, 5A*
season	part of a year (e.g. spring)	*42, 5B*
skeleton	all the bones in a body	*44, 5C*
sky	you see this when you look up outside	*43, 5B*
snow	in this weather everything is white	*40, 5A*
snowy	with lots of snow	*40, 5A*
spring	the season between winter and summer	*42, 5B*
storm	bad weather with rain and strong winds, and sometimes thunder and lightning	*40, 5A*
stormy	when there is a storm	*40, 5A*
suddenly	from one moment to the next	*47, 5D*
summer	the season between spring and autumn	*42, 5B*
sun	the bright thing in the sky; it keeps us warm	*40, 5A*
sunny	when there is a lot of sun	*40, 5A*
temperature	how hot or cold something is	*41, 5A*
tired	how you feel when you want to sleep	*41, 5A*
thermometer	this shows you how hot or cold it is	*41, 5A*
thunder	a very noisy sound in a storm	*40, 5A*
warm	not cold	*41, 5A*
wild	not calm	*41, 5A*
wind	this weather can move things	*40, 5A*
windy	when there is a lot of wind	*40, 5A*
winter	the season between autumn and spring	*42, 5B*

Unit 6 Tech time

album	you put photos in here (a book or online)	*54, 6D*
animated film	a film with drawings or models	*54, 6D*
animation	making a film from drawings or models	*54, 6D*
app	(application) software for a mobile phone, tablet or computer	*50, 6B*
battery	a small thing with electricity for small gadgets	*50, 6B*
best friend	your favourite friend	*55, 6D*
cartoon	a drawing or drawings with a story	*51, 6B*
celebrate, to	to do something special, e.g. have a party	*55, 6D*
cell phone [US]	you can carry this telephone with you	*48, 6A*
championship	a big sports competition	*55, 6D*
charger	you use this to put electricity into a battery	*50, 6B*
chat, to	to talk to someone	*48, 6A*
college	you can study here when you leave school	*54, 6D*
compete, to	to be in a sports event (e.g. a race)	*55, 6D*
course	a programme of study (e.g. an English course)	*54, 6D*
download, to	to take something from the Internet and put it on your computer, music player or other gadget	*50, 6B*
DVD player	you watch DVDs on your television with this	*48, 6A*
excursion	a trip	*55, 6D*
face to face	when you are with someone and can look at them	*50, 6B*
forest	a big area with lots of trees	*55, 6D*
fresh	new and interesting	*52, 6C*
gadget	a small machine	*48, 6A*
games console	you use this to play computer games	*48, 6A*
habit	you do this often	*54, 6D*
hair	this grows on your head	*51, 6B*
hip hop	a kind of modern music	*52, 6C*
IM [= Instant Message]	a message on the internet	*50, 6B*
journal	you write what you are doing and thinking in this book	*51, 6B*
keyboard	you use this to type letters (A, B, C) on a computer	*50, 6B*
magazine	a kind of book with articles and photos	*51, 6B*
mix music, to	to put different music together to make a new recording	*52, 6C*
mobile phone	you can carry this telephone with you	*48, 6A*
model	a small copy of a person or thing	*54, 6D*
moment	a short time	*55, 6D*
music player	you can use this to listen to music	*48, 6A*
nails	these are at the ends of your fingers	*51, 6B*
negative	bad, not good	*52, 6C*
nervous	a bit scared	*52, 6C*
positive	good	*52, 6C*
practise, to	to do something again and again to become good	*53, 6C*
proud	a really good feeling (e.g. when you win a competition)	*55, 6D*
remember, to	to think about something in the past	*55, 6D*
remix, to	to mix again	*52, 6C*
screen	you see pictures and writing on this part of a computer, phone, TV etc.	*50, 6B*
series	programmes on television with the same title	*48, 6A*
sling	you put your arm in this when you break it	*53, 6C*
social network page	an online page on something like Facebook	*53, 6C*
sound level	how loud something is	*52, 6C*
squash, to	to make something flat	*54, 6D*
stage	people perform here	*52, 6D*
storyboard	pictures with the story of a film	*54, 6D*
stretch, to	to make something long and thin	*54, 6D*
tablet	a small computer with a touch screen (you do things on the screen with your fingers)	*48, 6A*
text message	a message on a mobile phone	*50, 6B*
text, to	to write and send text messages	*50, 6B*
trip	a short holiday or stay	*53, 6C*
type, to	to write with a keyboard	*50, 6B*
unity	when people work together and help others	*52, 6C*
upload, to	to put something on the internet	*52, 6C*
video clip	a short video film	*54, 6D*
visual effects	when you use computers to change things or add things in films	*54, 6D*

The Big Read 1 *Waves*

amazing	fantastic	*56, BR1*
angry	a very strong feeling when you really don't like something	*57, BR1*
as clear as day	very clearly	*57, BR1*
breathe, to	to take air in and out	*57, BR1*
cliff	high rocks by the sea	*57, BR1*
empty	with nothing or nobody in it	*57, BR1*
exactly the same	with nothing different	*57, BR1*
high	tall	*57, BR1*
key	you use this to open a door	*57, BR1*
memory	something you remember	*57, BR1*
postcard	a card with a picture and a message	*56, BR1*
sand	you walk on this on the beach; often soft	*56, BR1*
sheets	you put these on beds; often white	*57, BR1*
shoulder	part of the body, at the top of your arm	*57, BR1*
surfboard	surfers use this on the waves	*57, BR1*
surfer	he / she rides on waves with a surfboard	*56, BR1*
tin	you put things in it	*57, BR1*
wave	the moving water on the sea	*56, BR1*
whisper, to	to speak very quietly	*57, BR1*

The Big Read 2 *I am number four*

action story	a story with a lot of exciting and dangerous things	*58, BR2*
alien	a person or thing from space	*59, BR2*
backpack	a bag for your back	*58, BR2*
big deal	important	*58, BR2*
drive, to	to take someone by car	*58, BR2*

fever	a high body temperature	*59, BR2*
follow, to	to walk behind someone	*58, BR2*
glasses	you wear these to help you see better	*58, BR2*
guardian	he / she looks after young people	*59, BR2*
hang around, to	to wait for something; to hang out	*59, BR2*
hide, to	to go somewhere where people can't see you or find you	*58, BR2*
hurt, to	to be violent with someone and injure them	*59, BR2*
kid	a child, a young person	*58, BR2*
real estate agent [US]	he / she sells houses and other buildings	*59, BR2*
register, to	to put your name on the list for a class or course	*59, BR2*
science fiction	a story with events in the future or in space	*58, BR2*
sheriff [US]	a police officer	*59, BR2*
soft	kind	*58, BR2*
telescope	you can use this to look at the stars	*58, BR2*
violent	when you fight or hurt someone	*59, BR2*
walk away, to	to leave	*58, BR2*

Unit 7 Spend or save?

admire, to	to like a lot	*66, 7D*
advert	words and pictures to sell something	*64, 7C*
allowance	an amount of money (often once a week or month)	*60, 7A*
baggy	not tight, comfortable	*62, 7B*
balance	the amount of money in your bank account	*66, 7D*
bank account	you keep your money in this at a bank	*60, 7A*
bank statement	this shows you all the money going into and out of your account	*66, 7D*
best	superlative of *good*	*65, 7C*
best buy	something for a good price of good quality and not expensive	*67, 7D*
better	comparative of *good*	*65, 7C*
bottle	a container for drinks	*60, 7A*
brand	the name of a product by a fashion designer or company	*63, 7B*
business	a company	*60, 7A*
cash card	a card to get money from your bank account	*66, 7D*
changing room	you try clothes on here in a shop	*62, 7B*
charity	this organisation helps people with problems	*60, 7A*
cheap	not expensive	*62, 7B*
chemical	something from chemistry, often dangerous	*64, 7C*
comfortable	nice to wear	*62, 7B*
comic	a kind of magazine with drawings	*60, 7A*
compare, to	to look at two things at the same time	*60, 7A*
credit [phone]	money on a card (for your mobile phone)	*60, 7A*
credit card	a card to pay for things; you pay later	*66, 7D*
currency	the money of a country or region (e.g. Euro, US dollar)	*60, 7A*
dark [colour]	not light	*62, 7B*
debit card	a card to pay for things; you pay now	*66, 7D*
earn, to	to get money for a job	*60, 7A*
extra	more	*60, 7A*
fashion	trendy clothes	*63, 7B*
fashion stylist	he / she works with fashion	*63, 7B*
fast	quick	*67, 7D*
follow fashion, to	to wear trendy clothes	*63, 7B*
garbage [US]	rubbish; everything you throw away	*64, 7C*
gift	a present	*60, 7A*
haircut	a hair style	*60, 7A*
interest	extra money (from the bank)	*66, 7D*
jewellery	you wear this on your fingers or around your neck etc.	*60, 7A*
light [colour]	not dark	*62, 7B*
local	in your area	*60, 7A*
long	not short	*62, 7B*
market	a building or street with lots of small shops for clothes, fruit and vegetables etc.	*67, 7D*
mp3 player	you use this for listening to music	*60, 7A*
old-fashioned	not trendy or fashionable	*62, 7B*
on special offer	for sale at a low price	*67, 7D*
pair of jeans	blue trousers	*60, 7A*
pants [US]	trousers	*62, 7B*
password	a secret word	*66, 7D*
PIN number	a secret number	*66, 7D*
point	an idea, a fact	*66, 7D*
pollute, to	to make dirty	*64, 7C*
price	the cost of something	*60, 7A*
recycle, to	to make something old into something new	*64, 7C*
recycling	using things again	*66, 7D*
resources	natural things from the Earth (water, oil, trees etc.)	*64, 7C*
reuse, to	to use again	*64, 7C*
rubbish	everything you throw away; garbage [US]	*64, 7C*
sale	when clothes etc. cost less	*67, 7D*
save, to	to keep money	*60, 7A*
savings account	the bank gives you extra money with this type of account	*66, 7D*
scam	a trick to get money from you	*66, 7D*
short	not long	*62, 7B*
size	how big something is	*62, 7B*
sneakers [US]	trainers, shoes for sport	*62, 7B*
stuff	things (clothes, gadgets, CDs ...)	*64, 7C*
style	how someone looks in clothes	*63, 7B*
take care of, to	to look after	*64, 7C*
take-away	food from a shop or restaurant to eat at home	*60, 7A*
the environment	the natural world (land, sea, air, plants and animals)	*64, 7C*
thin	not fat, not thick	*65, 7C*
throw away, to	to put in a bin (e.g. rubbish)	*64, 7C*
tight	small, not baggy	*62, 7B*
trainers	shoes for sport, sneakers [US]	*60, 7A*
trendy	fashionable	*62, 7B*
try on, to	to put clothes on, to check the size	*62, 7B*
uncomfortable	not comfortable, not nice to wear	*62, 7B*

worse	comparative of *bad*	*65, 7C*
worst	superlative of *bad*	*65, 7C*

Unit 8 Holidays!

abroad	in foreign countries	*68, 8A*
ancient monument	a very, very old building	*70, 8B*
attraction	an interesting place for tourists	*74, 8D*
basketball court	you play basketball here	*71, 8B*
bear	a big, dangerous animal	*71, 8B*
bright [colour]	strong	*72, 8C*
brilliant	fantastic, great	*68, 8A*
brochure	a little book with information	*75, 8D*
buffet	a meal (usually at a hotel) with lots of different things to eat	*72, 8C*
camper	a young person at camp	*71, 8B*
campfire	a small fire outdoors	*71, 8B*
campsite	a place for tents	*68, 8A*
castle	a big house for a king or queen	*70, 8B*
collect, to	to get, to take	*73, 8C*
countryside	an area not in a town or city	*68, 8A*
crocodile	a dangerous river animal with big teeth	*74, 8D*
cruise	a trip or holiday on a boat	*70, 8B*
dance studio	you learn how to dance here	*71, 8B*
day out	a day away from home	*70, 8B*
day trip	a day journey away from home	*70, 8B*
disco	a place to dance	*72, 8C*
dolphin	a kind of clever sea animal	*74, 8D*
ecotourism	this kind of tourism doesn't hurt the environment	*74, 8D*
egg	female animals produce eggs	*74, 8D*
embarrassing	makes you feel stupid and unhappy	*72, 8C*
facilities	buildings, equipment etc.	*71, 8B*
field	an area with plants or animals, often on a farm	*68, 8A*
fitness center [US]	a gym	*71, 8B*
flag	a symbol of a country	*68, 8A*
floor	you walk on this in a room	*73, 8C*
footprints	you make these when you walk in the sand	*74, 8D*
future	the time after the present	*74, 8D*
green [environment]	not bad for the environment	*74, 8D*
grow, to	to get bigger	*74, 8D*
guard	he / she looks after things, people or animals	*74, 8D*
guest house	a small hotel	*68, 8A*
habitat	where an animal lives (e.g. rainforest, river etc.)	*74, 8D*
healthy	good for you	*71, 8B*
hiking	walking in the countryside or mountains	*71, 8B*
holidays	time away from work or school; vacation [US]	*68, 8A*
hostel	a cheap hotel, often for young people	*68, 8A*
hungry	how you feel when you need to eat	*72, 8C*
hunter	this person kills wild animals for sport	*74, 8D*
iguana	a kind of big lizard	*74, 8D*
in danger	not safe	*74, 8D*
indoor	in a building; inside	*71, 8B*
invite, to	to ask	*72, 8C*
island	an area of land in a lake or the sea	*68, 8A*
karaoke	a machine plays a song tune and you sing the words	*72, 8C*
luxury	very comfortable and expensive	*68, 8A*
meat	food from an animal	*74, 8D*
milk	a white drink from cows	*73, 8C*
mistake	something wrong or bad	*72, 8C*
motel	a hotel near a road for people in cars	*68, 8A*
outdoors	not in a building; outside	*68, 8A*
overnight	until the next day	*70, 8B*
painting	a picture	*70, 8B*
popular	lots of people like it	*68, 8A*
power boat	a kind of very fast boat	*71, 8B*
pretty	fairly	*72, 8C*
protect, to	to look after, to keep out of danger	*74, 8D*
rainforest	a very rainy area with lots of trees	*68, 8A*
ride	a fun activity at a theme park	*70, 8B*
seaside resort	a town for holidays by the sea	*70, 8B*
shout, to	to say very loud	*72, 8C*
sightseeing	visiting tourist attractions	*75, 8D*
skin	this covers your body	*74, 8D*
sneeze, to	to blow air out strongly through your nose	*72, 8C*
snowboarding	like skiing but with a board	*72, 8C*
soccer field	you play soccer here	*71, 8B*
summer camp [US]	a camp for young people, with lots of activities	*71, 8B*
swimming costume	you wear this in the pool, sea etc.	*72, 8C*
tent	you sleep in this outside	*68, 8A*
theme park	a fun place with rides	*70, 8B*
title	the name of a story, film etc.	*72, 8C*
top	favourite, most popular	*70, 8B*
tourist	a person on holiday or on a day trip	*70, 8B*
turtle	a kind of sea animal	*74, 8D*
type	a kind, a sort	*74, 8D*
woodwork	making things with wood	*71, 8B*
worried	a bit scared	*74, 8D*

Unit 9 Loves and hates

athletics	sports like running and jumping	*78, 9B*
avoid, to	to not do something	*82, 9D*
baseball	an American sport with a bat and ball	*78, 9B*
beard	hair on a man's face, below his mouth	*82, 9D*
build, to	to make	*77, 9A*
club	an organisation for a sport, hobby etc.	*78, 9B*
coin	money made of metal (e.g. £1 or 50p)	*76, 9A*
crazy [about something]	when you love something a lot	*80, 9C*
dentist	he / she looks after your teeth	*82, 9D*
face, to	to do something about a problem	*82, 9D*
gymnastics	physical exercises	*78, 9B*
hate	you do not like this at all	*76, 9A*
hero	you admire this person a lot	*83, 9D*

hobby	a free-time activity	*76, 9A*
hockey	you play this sport with a stick and a small ball	*78, 9B*
ice-skating	a sport on ice using special shoes	*78, 9B*
key ring	you keep your keys on this	*76, 9A*
musical instrument	for example, a guitar, a piano	*80, 9C*
phobia	you have this when you are very scared of something	*82, 9D*
professional	a professional sportsperson who earns money doing their sport	*80, 9C*
push yourself, to	to make yourself do something difficult	*80, 9C*
relax, to	to become calm	*82, 9D*
skateboarding	a sport on a board with wheels	*78, 9B*
snake	a kind of long, thin animal with no legs	*82, 9D*
sound machine	you make noises with this machine	*76, 9A*
spider	a kind of small animal with eight legs	*82, 9D*
sportsperson	this person does a lot of sport	*80, 9C*
sporty	good at sports or active	*78, 9B*
stamp	you put this on a letter before you send it	*76, 9A*
steakhouse	a kind of restaurant; you can eat steaks here	*81, 9C*
table tennis	you play this sport on a table with a small ball	*78, 9B*
team [sport]	a group of sports players (e.g. a football team)	*78, 9B*
trick	a special move	*80, 9C*
volleyball	a sport with a high net and a large ball	*78, 9B*
wild	not careful; looking for fun	*80, 9C*

Unit 10 Live to eat?

blood	the red liquid in your body	*90, 10D*
bones	the long, hard, white things in your body	*90, 10D*
brain	this is inside your head; you think with it	*90, 10D*
calorie	the energy in food	*87, 10B*
chew, to	to use your teeth to break food into small pieces	*88, 10C*
chow mein	a kind of Chinese food	*84, 10A*
dish	food; a meal	*84, 10A*
fast food	often unhealthy food such as burgers and chips	*86, 10B*
feel sick, to	to feel ill in your stomach	*90, 10D*
for health reasons	for the good of your body	*85, 10A*
heart	this makes your blood move in your body	*90, 10D*
hot dog	a kind of sandwich with a sausage	*88, 10C*
kidneys	these take water out of your body	*90, 10D*
label	a bit of paper with information	*87, 10B*
liver	this helps to clean your blood	*90, 10D*
lungs	you use these to breathe	*90, 10D*
muscles	you need these to move and be strong	*90, 10D*
order, to	to ask for	*87, 10B*
overweight	too heavy	*87, 10B*
ready meal	a prepared dish	*86, 10B*
slice	a piece	*87, 10B*
snack	something small to eat between meals	*87, 10B*
soup	you can drink this kind of food	*84, 10A*
spaghetti Bolognese	pasta with meat sauce	*84, 10A*
speed	how fast something goes	*88, 10C*
stomach	where your food goes in your body when you eat	*88, 10C*
sushi	a kind of Japanese food	*84, 10A*
sweat, to	to lose water through your skin	*90, 10D*
vomit, to	when food comes back out of your mouth	*88, 10C*
waste	using something in a bad way	*88, 10C*
worm	a long, thin, pink animal; it lives in the ground	*88, 10C*

Unit 11 Learning for life

A-level	an exam in England for students aged about 18	*92, 11A*
apply for a job, to	to try and get a job	*93, 11A*
apprenticeship	training for a technical job	*93, 11A*
architecture	the study of buildings	*96, 11C*
career	all the jobs during your life	*93, 11A*
coursework	school work (e.g. essays, projects)	*92, 11A*
director	he / she tells the actors in a play what to do	*97, 11C*
gamer	he / she plays online games	*95, 11B*
GCSE	an exam in England for students aged about 16	*92, 11A*
high school [US]	a secondary school for students aged 14–18	*92, 11A*
inspire, to	to give you good ideas	*96, 11C*
jeweller	he / she makes jewellery	*96, 11C*
knitting	making things like scarves	*96, 11C*
lazy	not active or energetic	*95, 11B*
magic	tricks (e.g. making things disappear)	*95, 11B*
nursery	a place for small children before school	*92, 11A*
optimistic	positive, not worried	*95, 11B*
photography	taking photographs	*96, 11C*
piece	something made by an artist or jeweller	*96, 11C*
plagiarism	using someone else's work without giving their name	*98, 11D*
retake an exam, to	to do an exam again	*93, 11A*
rubbish!	you can say this when you don't agree	*95, 11B*
school system	all the schools in a country	*92, 11A*
scrapbooking	when you make a kind of journal with pictures and words	*96, 11C*
sculpture	a work of art (e.g. of wood or stone)	*96, 11C*
semester	half of the school year	*96, 11C*
sewing	making things like clothes	*96, 11C*
sixth form college	the last level of secondary school in England	*92, 11A*
sociable	friendly	*95, 11B*
stressed	very worried	*94, 11B*
studio	where an artist works	*96, 11C*
take deep breaths, to	to breathe slowly, taking in a lot of air	*94, 11B*
test	a small exam	*92, 11A*
volunteer	this person works but doesn't get any money	*93, 11A*

Glossary

Unit 12 Events and experiences

academy	a place for special training	*104, 12C*
aerobics	a kind of exercise at a gym	*103, 12B*
amusement park	a theme park	*104, 12C*
astronaut	he / she travels in space	*104, 12C*
banquet	a big, special meal	*102, 12B*
barbecue	you cook and eat this meal outside	*100, 12A*
bowling	an indoor game with a heavy ball	*100, 12A*
cricket	a mostly UK sport with a ball and a bat	*103, 12B*
cultural event	an event with music, art etc.	*100, 12A*
exhibition	a show of art or interesting things	*100, 12A*
expedition	a trip with activities	*103, 12B*
experience	an event in your life	*100, 12A*
festival	an event with shows, concerts etc.	*100, 12A*
flight simulator	a machine like a real plane or shuttle for training	*104, 12C*
float, to	to move around in the air or on the top of water	*106, 12D*
gravity	this makes things fall to the ground	*106, 12D*
guest	a person invited to a meal or home	*102, 12B*
gun shot	the loud noise from a gun	*102, 12B*
hairdressing	cutting and styling hair	*103, 12B*
monkey	a kind of animal with a long tail	*102, 12B*
moon	the big white planet in the sky at night	*104, 12C*
mountain biking	riding a bike in the countryside	*103, 12B*
mud	water and earth mixed together (e.g. by a river)	*102, 12B*
pilot	he / she flies a plane or a space shuttle	*104, 12C*
practical	using real equipment	*104, 12C*
robot	an electronic machine	*103, 12B*
robotics	designing and making robots	*104, 12C*
roll, to	to make something like a ball move along the ground	*102, 12B*
score a goal, to	to win a point (e.g. in a football match)	*107, 12D*
seasonal	relating to part of the year (winter, summer etc.)	*100, 12A*
soup kitchen	a place with free meals for people without food	*100, 12A*
space	where the stars and planets are	*104, 12C*
space shuttle	a kind of plane for travelling in space	*104, 12C*
upside down	with your head where your feet usually are	*104, 12C*
weightless	with no weight	*104, 12C*
wheelchair	a special chair for people with walking problems	*103, 12B*

The Big Read 3 *Holes*

be up, to [of the sun]	to be in the sky	*109, BR3*
beat	the noise of your heart	*109, BR3*
beat, to	to make a regular sound	*108, BR3*
bite	an injury from an animal's teeth	*108, BR3*
bother, to	to annoy someone, to make someone angry	*108, BR3*
chin	the part of your face below your mouth	*109, BR3*
claws	the sharp bits on animals' feet	*108, BR3*
crawl, to	to move slowly with your body near the ground	*108, BR3*
daytime	not at night; during the day	*108, BR3*
dig into, to	to push into	*109, BR3*
dirt	soil, earth	*109, BR3*
fascinated	really interested	*109, BR3*
flashlight [US]	a small light	*109, BR3*
flat	smooth, without hills or mountains	*108, BR3*
glow, to	to be light, like the moon	*109, BR3*
helpless	not able to do anything	*109, BR3*
in the distance	a long way away	*109, BR3*
lap	the top part of your legs when you are sitting down	*109, BR3*
lizard	a kind of small animal, like a snake with legs	*108, BR3*
nest	a home for birds, insects or small animals	*109, BR3*
obviously	clearly	*109, BR3*
painful	hurting a lot	*108, BR3*
rattlesnake	a kind of snake; it can make a noise with its tail	*108, BR3*
scorpion	a small, dangerous animal	*108, BR3*
scream, to	to shout because you are frightened	*109, BR3*
shade	not in the sun	*108, BR3*
sharp	can cut like a knife	*109, BR3*
spot	a small mark	*109, BR3*
statue	a sculpture of a person	*109, BR3*
still	not moving	*109, BR3*
suitcase	a kind of bag for clothes when you travel	*108, BR3*
tarantula	a kind of large spider	*108, BR3*
tiny	very small	*109, BR3*
warden	he / she looks after prisoners	*108, BR3*
wasteland	an empty place without plants	*108, BR3*

The Big Read 4 Girl, *Missing*

adopt, to	to take a child into your family	*110, BR4*
birth month	the month when you were born	*111, BR4*
click, to	you do this with a computer mouse	*110, BR4*
heading	title	*111, BR4*
hit	when your search engine finds something on the internet	*111, BR4*
homepage	the first page of a website	*110, BR4*
inside [of a person]	what someone is really like	*111, BR4*
link	this takes you to another website	*110, BR4*
maybe	perhaps	*110, BR4*
missing	lost	*110, BR4*
no way	you can say this when you don't want to do something	*111, BR4*
office	a room for work	*111, BR4*
search engine	you use this to find things on the internet	*110, BR4*
stare, to	to look at something very hard	*111, BR4*

Infinitive	Past simple	Past participle
be	was / were	been
become	became	become
begin	began	begun
break	broke	broken
bring	brought	brought
build	built	built
buy	bought	bought
can	could	been able to
choose	chose	chosen
come	came	come
cost	cost	cost
do	did	done
dig	dug	dug
drink	drank	drunk
drive	drove	driven
eat	ate	eaten
fall	fell	fallen
feel	felt	felt
fight	fought	fought
find	found	found
fly	flew	flown
forget	forgot	forgotten
get	got	got / gotten [US]
give	gave	given
go	went	gone
have	had	had
hear	heard	heard
hit	hit	hit
hurt	[illegible]	hurt
keep	[illegible]	[illegible]
know	[illegible]	[illegible]

Infinitive	Past simple	Past participle
learn	learnt	learnt
leave	left	left
lose	lost	lost
make	made	made
meet	met	met
pay	paid	paid
put	put	put
read	read [rɛd]	read [rɛd]
run	ran	run
say	said	said
see	saw	seen
sell	sold	sold
send	sent	sent
sing	sang	sung
sit	sat	sat
sleep	slept	slept
speak	spoke	spoken
stand	stood	stood
steal	stole	stolen
stick	stuck	stuck
swim	swam	swum
take	took	taken
teach	taught	taught
tell	told	told
think	thought	thought
throw	threw	thrown
understand	understood	understood
wake	woke	woken
wear	wore	worn
win	won	won
write	wrote	written